LEARNING

RE-ABLED

LEARNING

RE-ABLED

The Learning Disability Controversy and Composition Studies

Patricia A. Dunn

Utica College of
Syracuse University

Boynton/Cook Publishers
HEINEMANN
Portsmouth, NH

Boynton/Cook Publishers, Inc.
A subsidiary of Reed Elsevier Inc.
361 Hanover Street
Portsmouth, NH 03801-3912

Offices and agents throughout the world

Library of Congress Cataloging-in-Publication Data
Dunn, Patricia A.
    Learning re-abled : the learning disability controversy and
composition studies / Patricia A. Dunn.
        p.   cm.
    Includes bibliographical references.
    ISBN 0-86709-360-9 (alk. paper)
    1. Learning disabled—Education (Higher)—United States.
2. Learning disabilities—United States.   3. Dyslexics—Education
teaching—United States.   I. Title.
LC4818.5.D85   1995
371.91—dc20   95-19316
                                                              CIP

Editor: Peter R. Stillman
Production Editor: Renée M. Nicholls
Cover Designer: T. Watson Bogaard

Printed in the United States of America on acid-free paper.
99 98 97 96 95 DA 1 2 3 4 5 6

For Joey and Larry

Contents

Acknowledgments

I would like to thank my husband Ken Lindblom for his encouragement, for his enthusiasm about this project, and for his logical and extremely useful readings. I would like to thank my sister Kathy for her wide and varied reading habits, and for her creativity and insight. I am grateful to my mother, Rita Dunn, for reading and commenting on this manuscript in its earliest draft and for her ever-present faith in me. I would also like to thank some good friends, Sister Judith Dever, Marie Jordan-Whitney, and Kathleen Thornton Chamberlin, for their confidence in me. I am grateful to Utica College of Syracuse University for giving me a summer grant to work on this book, and especially to Frank Bergmann for supporting all my scholarship at Utica College. I would also like to thank Lil Brannon and Peter Johnston, who gave me productive critiques very early on in this project. I owe a special thanks to Steve North, who helped me immensely with his close, careful readings and candid, thought-provoking observations. His commitment to the field and contribution to it has inspired me. I am also indebted to the many people who allowed me to interview them, especially the three students featured in Chapter Four, who gave so generously of their time and ideas. Finally, I am very grateful to Peter Stillman for his excellent suggestions and the chance to publish this text.

Introduction

One day Barbara[1] came to the university Writing Center because she said her phonetic spelling was interfering with her job as a secretary. She thought if she studied spelling rules and "spelling demons," she might write better. I watched this bright, articulate young woman as she tried to write *specifically*, a word she was using in a draft. It came out *scipbficlty*—the *b* squeezed in between the *p* and the *f* as an afterthought (see Figure I–1).

She kept writing this word over and over in different ways, hoping that it would eventually look right to her. As we talked about words and letters, Barbara also told me she frequently had trouble distinguishing *sign* from *sing*. While we examined the two words, she asked me, "Don't the letters look weird? Don't they jump around?" I had to answer, "No. Not for me." What alarmed me was

Figure I–1
Barbara's attempt at *specifically*.

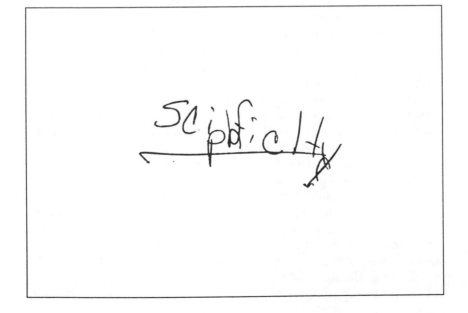

that after seven years of teaching high school English, five years of teaching four to five sections of composition per semester at a two-year college, and then three years of concentrated study in a doctoral program in Composition, I was stumped. Not only did I have no clue about how to help Barbara, I could not even comprehend the kinds of difficulties she was describing.

Shortly after that tutorial, I was walking to my office from the campus parking lot and telling a colleague I thought one of my students with unusual spelling problems and a tendency to transpose letters might be dyslexic. A woman walking in front of us (and apparently listening to our conversation) turned around and said, "Did I hear you say you thought a student of yours was dyslexic?"

"Yes," I said.

She smiled and informed me, "You know, dyslexia is really very rare."

Everyone has something to say about dyslexia and learning disabilities. Opinions regarding these terms are so entrenched that educated people are sometimes not even aware that equally educated people hold opinions completely opposite to theirs. What to call it, how to define and test for it, and how to remedy it have far-reaching implications for researchers, educators, psychologists, and parents, not to mention the students themselves. What labels and treatments are chosen by those in a position to choose them affect the self-esteem, the education, and perhaps even the personality of those on the receiving end of the treatment.

My reasons for investigating learning disabilities were both personal and professional, and had existed even before I met Barbara. During the five years I taught composition at the two-year college, I had encountered several students whose numerous, inexplicable errors were so puzzling to me that I did not know where to begin helping them. One student sometimes, but not always, wrote *has* for *as*. For example, "Has for me, I prefer to drive," or "It was bright has day." One-to-one conferences left both of us frustrated and discouraged. She knew perfectly well that *has* did not fit in that sentence, and she never made such errors when she spoke, yet she did not see it when proofreading unless someone read her draft aloud.

Another student in one of my literature classes had always made interesting, perceptive comments in class regarding whatever short story we were discussing. However, her essay on the same short story was an almost incomprehensible jumble of bad spelling and strange idioms, not at all reflected in her oral language. My professional conscience nagged me no matter how I graded her work. If I graded high because of her valuable contributions to class discussions, my allegiance to "standards" would scream, "But look at her papers! They look like a first grader wrote them. What would the academic dean say if she saw Tracy's papers and the *B* you gave her this quarter?" If I graded low because her essays were not "college level," my duty to fairness would start in: "How can you give her a *D*? She has more insights about those stories than anyone else in the class!" I simply did not know what to do for Tracy. Our one-to-one conferences were pleasant and chatty, and we discussed her papers until we were both satisfied she could recognize and fix any problems. Then in her next piece of writing, she would make another strange, but different, batch of errors.

At the same time I was teaching at the two-year college, my nephew Joey was reaching the age of two, and then three, and then four, without speaking the way I heard other children speak. His first (and for a long time only) word was *Up*, which could mean "Pick me up," "Put me down," "Look over there," "Carry me across the room," or "Give me back to Mom." At four, he was still speaking primarily in monosyllables, which were not always pronounced correctly and which he seemed to have a difficult time recalling.

When he was seven years old, he was speaking in short sentences, but they didn't come out quite right. For many months he would say, "No don't know," for "I don't know," and "I want go yours car," instead of "I want to go in your car." He was always producing odd combinations of words such as "I want need help," and "I no can't member" (I can't remember). We all kept giving him the benefit of the doubt, believing that in time he would pick up language the way he was supposed to. One incident, however, made me wonder if that would ever happen.

Most of the family referred to Joey's younger brother as "Beaner." One day Joey was attempting to say something, but could not remember his brother's name. "Give it um—um—what him name?" Someone supplied "Beaner." Embarrassed, Joey laughed nervously, hit himself in the head, and said, "I forgot Beaner's name. I don't know. My head sometimes." While Joey frequently had trouble recalling my name—I was sometimes "Mom, I mean Nanny, I mean Dad, I mean Aunt Pat"—he *always* said "Beaner" easily. This day, when he had trouble even with this frequently said word, I knew Joey's problem was not the same as when I might occasionally forget a student's name.

My sister had been doing a lot of reading about speech, language acquisition, and reading difficulties. She had heard people speak about children who were having problems similar to Joey's— problems recalling the words they wanted to say, problems pronouncing them, problems putting sentences together in conventional ways. As I leafed through some of the material my sister brought home from the library, I began recognizing some of the kinds of errors the college students had made. Most of the case studies and accounts of children and adults with language difficulties like Joey's and with spelling and idiomatic problems like Tracy's and Barbara's appeared in books and journal articles about *learning disabilities*, something I had heard of, but to which I had not given much thought. An older term was *dyslexia*.

The more I read about dyslexia and certain kinds of learning disabilities, the more I talked with my sister and with the parents of children in the special school Joey was attending, the more I observed his struggle with language, and the more I noticed the error patterns of several other students who came into the Writing Center, the more I became intrigued with this condition. Was it indeed a cause, or was it an outmoded label for a multifaceted problem? Could Joey be helped? What about Tracy and Barbara? I was determined to find out all I could, to try to separate fact from myth, and to use my professional judgment to analyze the remediation recommended by reading and learning disability professionals.

The helplessness I felt in listening to my nephew struggle to recall his brother's name, along with the frustration I experienced in not being able to help some of my students, suggested to me that the theories of writing I had been studying in my own field did not account for all types of errors. I felt there was a gap in Composition pedagogy, a crack through which a small but significant number of college students were falling. Although Composition Studies, traditionally, does not deal with learning disabilities, I felt it was a subject I needed to investigate. Why do some students have more difficulty than others in learning to read and write well? Is there a way to help them? While research in Composition has addressed these questions, the answers put forth, although impassioned, are appropriate to many, but not all, people. Meanwhile, more and more bright students such as Tracy and Barbara continue to experience frustrating difficulties with the words some of their classmates mastered in first grade.

I began my research from the perspective of a Composition specialist convinced of the sociological nature of reading and writing (and, for that matter, of any kind of research, "scientific" or otherwise). I am an instructor who uses a pedagogy based primarily on the assumptions that reading and writing form a whole process of discovery and cannot be separated into parts. However, I also began this exploration with a nagging question about why some students seem to have such a difficult time learning to read and write. When social factors, which, granted, can never be eliminated, do not *appear* to account for an individual's uphill struggle to become literate, is there a cognitive-based theory that would explain it? If there is a neurological reason for some people's problems, could there be a way to help them?

I thought that perhaps the learning disability (LD) field could provide the answers to some of my questions. I soon discovered, however, that the LD field was fraught with confusion and controversy. The very term *learning disability* is a problematic one that reflects the many disagreements surrounding it. Whether or not such a phenomenon exists at all is being debated. What the condition should be called is a constant point of contention. Throughout this book, I will use terms I have encountered in my research—*learning disability, specific learning disability, dyslexia*—terms whose meanings sometimes overlap and blur. Although I recognize that *learning disability* and *dyslexia* are problematic terms for many reasons, I will employ them for lack of a better phrase with which most readers would be familiar.

By *learning disability*, I am not referring to hearing loss, poor eyesight, or other physical challenges. There are also such things as attention deficit disorders (ADD) and difficulties with math (dyscalculia). Because I am a writing instructor, I am interested in language-processing problems, which will be the primary focus of this book. I mean by *learning disablility* or *dyslexia* the inexplicable difficulties some people have in learning to read and write. Chapter One provides a more detailed explanation and critique of this and other terminology.

This study will resurrect some painful, stubborn questions regarding what it is we think we are doing when we teach writing. It will, by necessity, touch upon areas not usually considered the concern of composition instructors. However, the students we teach often reflect and are the products of the philosophies and practices of our predecessors, people who in turn have been exposed to professional preparation and theories of writing different perhaps from those with which we in Composition are familiar. Composition Studies cannot be a self-contained field. The students it affects have been doing various kinds of writing since kindergarten, under the direction of many and various teachers. Therefore, any investigation into how writing development occurs becomes a complex and intricate web that extends throughout the educational system. We cannot, obviously, be familiar with everything studied by education majors, reading specialists, and special education teachers. However, if we are claiming to know how our students learn best to write, we need *some* awareness of what other professionals claim is best.

In this book I examine what I now see as gaps in the preparation and professional reading of Composition specialists. The controversy regarding the cause and treatment of linguistic difficulties is something all writing instructors should be cognizant of as more and more students enter college announcing themselves as learning disabled. Some say the percentage of disabled students in college has doubled in ten years (Vogel and Adelman 1992, 430), while others say it has tripled (Satcher and Dooley-Dickey 1991, 47). Although precise numbers vary, experts do seem to agree that LD students are entering college in greater numbers than ever before (Whinnery 1992, 31). This book is for educators willing to explore ways of knowing unfamiliar to themselves and also willing to re-examine what they have always believed about composing.

The main arguments in the LD controversy involve the causes of the difficulty and its remediation, as well as what research is useful. Many people believe that LD is caused by a neurological difference in the way some people process linguistic symbols. Others believe that dyslexia or LD is a myth, or at best an unnecessarily technical term for those who cannot read well because of the powerful negative social forces that shaped their opportunity and desire to read. Juxtaposed in Chapter One are the conflicting views of Samuel Orton, Gerald Coles, Albert Galaburda, Frank Vellutino, James Carrier, Marie Clay, Peter Johnston, and others. The ambiguous terminology of recent legislation regarding learning disabilities has also sparked different interpretations. Who will pay for needed accommodations? How might the new law impact classroom practices? These are also issues examined in Chapter One.

Chapter Two presents an overview of how learning disabilities are typically presented in the journals and conferences of Composition Studies. Most college composition specialists have limited knowledge of learning disabilities, stemming in part from the limits of their graduate school preparation. Composition Studies tends to discount neurological differences in people and instead emphasizes socioeconomic factors as the primary cause of writing difficulty. How we teach writing is a function of how we think people learn. Even if it is unacknowledged, even if the individual teacher is unreflective, we make an assumption about how learning occurs. As Ann E. Berthoff has pointed out, all practice is based on an epistemological grounding, whether or not it is consciously recognized (1981, 11). A writing teacher's practice, like any teacher's practice, is influenced by that individual's deeply rooted beliefs about learning. Whatever vocabulary is used to describe it, writing instruction today, as evidenced by the topics at writing conferences and in professional articles, is based more and more on a philosophy that students will develop as writers and readers the more they immerse themselves in and become engaged with occasions for meaningful writing. It is assumed that all people have more or less the same ability to use language and that students will develop facility with academic discourses and conventions as they have opportunities to use them. Chapter Two will show how most current Composition theory fails to account for a percentage of students who may not respond as well as others to teaching practices designed for the majority.

Regarding pedagogy, experts disagree on whether an explicit, multi-modal, phonics-based teaching method should be employed with LD students, or whether they should receive the same instruction as everyone else. If we are basing our philosophy of writing development on a particular theory of learning, and, of course, we must be, what evidence is there that this is a viable theory? Are there others? What are the conflicting arguments, theories, and research results touted on either side of this issue, and what are the risks involved in not being aware of the controversy? How might the pedagogy of a writing teacher utterly convinced that dyslexia is a real phenomenon differ from that of another teacher equally convinced that it is not? Contrasted in Chapter Three are the theoretical assumptions underlying whole language practices with the assumptions supporting explicit, phonics-based, multisensory approaches. The circumstances under which my nephew Joey learned to make linguistic connections are recounted, and these results are interpreted with regard to older students.

Chapter Four gives the perspectives of experts not often consulted in this controversy: college students labeled LD who are successfully completing programs designed primarily for people who learn differently than they do. The stories of these three students are for me the strongest argument for a rethinking of composition pedagogy, a stretching of multidimensional thinking, and an open-mindedness regarding what—and how—other people know.

The last chapter suggests ways in which writing instructors might adapt their theory and practice to include the learning styles of all students. It calls for educators at all levels and in all disciplines to reexamine their assumptions about reading, writing, and learning.

I used the word *re-abled* in the title of this text to argue that so-called *dis*abled people *do* have abilities, which have been disabled in part by a society and school system that insists on a way of learning convenient or familiar to a majority of learners, but which does not tap into the substantial intellectual resources of 1 to 5 percent of the population. Many "disabilities" have come about because of a hegemonic insistence on outdated schoolroom methods, inadequate measures of intelligence, and intolerance for differences. Reforming general education and broadening ways of learning will not only benefit all students. It will *re-able* those whose substantial talents have been underused for too long in a linguisto-centric education system.

Notes

1. The names of all college students and instructors mentioned in this book have been changed.

Chapter One

Learning Disabilities: The Controversy

For a crash course in the learning disability (LD) controversy, one need look no further than a venomous letter-to-the-editor exchange in the February 13, 1991 issue of the *Journal of the American Medical Association* (*JAMA*). The first letter, written by Gerald Coles, (Coles' book, *The Learning Mystique: A Critical Look at "Learning Disabilities,"* lambastes the entire LD field), is ostensibly in response to a report by Shaywitz, Shaywitz, Fletcher, and Escobar on LD diagnosis and gender that appeared in an earlier issue of *JAMA*. Shaywitz et al. (1990) had found that school referrals of LD students indicated a three- or four-to-one ratio of boys to girls who are reading disabled, while groups not referred by schools showed no significant difference in the number of males and females who were reading disabled. The authors explain that since boys in grade school typically are rated by their teachers as having more behavior problems than do girls, more boys than girls are ultimately labeled LD. The original article, aimed at physicians who recommend services to aid in many aspects of their patients' lives, advises pediatricians not to rely solely on schools for referrals of LD children, but to be aware themselves of identifying characteristics of LD, especially among girls. Coles' letter, however, and Shaywitz et al.'s reply to it, barely mention the original report entitled "Prevalence of Reading Disability in Boys and Girls." Rather, the correspondence serves as a microcosm of the broader, deeper chasm that is the learning disability controversy.

Coles' letter attacks not merely this one report but characterizes virtually all empirical LD research as being "quasi-scientific." He says any references to a biologically based cause for LD are rooted in "more belief than fact," a phrase that captures his book's argument

9

in a nutshell. Coles goes on in his letter to propose, as he does at more length in his book, that reading difficulties are caused by "defective school practices," which LD researchers virtually ignore in their effort to do what Coles calls a "pseudo medical diagnosis" (1991, 725–26). In their response to Coles, Shaywitz et al. write that Coles' difference of opinion is "primarily philosophical" and conveniently ignores years of neurological research that shows brain differences in LD and non-LD people. They also point to reading research by Frank Vellutino, Isabelle Liberman, and others that shows significant phonological coding differences between LD and non-LD students, differences that Coles, they say, does not fully recognize. While they acknowledge that bad teaching can influence the reading ability of students, they argue that this explanation does not account for why most students in the same class read well and only a small number of them do not. They say that Coles' proposed focus on educational practices would be too narrow a search for the cause of certain kinds of reading difficulties.

The essential arguments of each letter demonstrate the basic rift in the two main camps of the LD controversy: those who believe LD is an identifiable phenomenon caused primarily by biological differences, and those who believe that LD, if it exists, is caused primarily by social factors. These letters, which discuss students' reading difficulties and general educational practices, are also interesting for where they appear: in a journal aimed not at elementary, secondary, or college instructors or educational administrators, but at medical doctors. Although the issues are multifaceted, and the authors' views may be more moderate than these letters suggest, this exchange illustrates not only the basic research agenda of both sides of the controversy but also how far it extends into fields (and journals) not usually investigated by college composition professors.

This chapter is intended as an overview of the learning disability (LD) field and the controversies surrounding it. It explores terms, definitions, manifestations, causes, and diagnoses, as well as disagreements regarding how the legislation applies and what research is valid. There is also a controversy regarding teaching methods appropriate for LD students—whether they learn better in a whole language class or in one based on explicit, multisensory, structured phonics instruction. The differences between these two approaches are explained briefly in this chapter and examined at more length in Chapter Three.

What exactly is a learning disability and what do we know about it? How is it defined and diagnosed? Is there any basis to the theory underlying it? How many students are likely to be affected?

Is *dyslexia* or *learning disability* a real syndrome that can be identified and remediated, or is it simply a label for people who cannot read well for a host of sociological reasons? What does the research indicate, and how reliable is it? Do LD students learn in the same way others do? Attempting to explain the LD controversy is like unraveling a multi-colored knitted blanket the size of a football field. My purpose in this chapter is to give interested observers an overall idea of the complexity and extent of the controversy surrounding learning disabilities, the terms themselves a part of the dispute and often surrounded with derisive quotation marks.

The LD field has been influenced greatly by the Orton Dyslexia Society, which began in 1949 and has 37 branches and over 9000 members (Rawson 1988, 146). It holds yearly, national, and multi-day conferences, bringing together for lectures and workshops teachers, medical doctors, and psychiatrists. This organization has as its basic tenet the theory that one segment of the population is working from a different neurological framework and processes language in a way that is, while not necessarily deficient, at least different from those for whom reading and writing seem to come easily. LD theory, just now beginning to be addressed in Composition journals and conferences, has been of major concern in reading, special education, neurological, psychological, and medical journals for decades. *Dyslexia*, sometimes called by other, long-defunct terms, is a condition that has been more or less recognized since the turn of the century. Journals, reports, monographs, essay collections, and textbooks on this subject have been proliferating since 1896. *Learning disabled* is sometimes a generic label for anyone who has any psychological, sociological, or neurological impediment to learning. The causes and treatments of dyslexia and/or learning disability have frequently been the subject of professional debate, parental frustration, and student humiliation.

The Law

One aspect of the LD controversy, and the one perhaps responsible for the increased attention to other aspects—definitions, causes, treatments, etc.—is the recent legislation regarding all disabled or handicapped people, including those with identified learning disabilities. How will this legislation affect colleges and universities? This question can best be addressed by briefly explaining two applicable laws: Section 504 of the Rehabilitation Act of 1973, and the 1990 Americans with Disabilities Act (ADA). To a large extent, the 1990 ADA focuses on removing architectural barriers for physically challenged people and preventing discrimination not just in federal or state-owned facilities but also in the private sector (University of the State of New York 1991, 18). This includes private colleges because of the federal aid they directly or indirectly receive. It was the 1973 law that substantially altered how learning disabled people were treated with regard to education and that impacted the accommodations typically available today in higher education. The 1973 law mandated that "no otherwise qualified handicapped individual . . . shall, solely by reason of his handicap be excluded from the participation in, be denied the benefits of, or be subjected to discrimination under any program or activity receiving [f]ederal financial assistance" (Rothstein 1986, 229). The 1990 ADA places more emphasis on the requirements initiated in the earlier legislation and steps up the removal of architectural barriers. It insists on equal opportunity for all disabled people in all areas, including equal access to computer technology (Castorina 1994, 46).

Many have noted that the terms used in the 1990 ADA are ambiguous and will need to be more specifically defined by case law. Colleges are required to provide "reasonable accommodation" for "otherwise qualified" individuals, providing it does not involve "undue hardship." Obviously, the adjectives used here are subject to interpretation. At a time when many colleges are already facing financial crisis and the cost and need for accommodations rise, this interpretation becomes critical. Neither law specifically details practical applications in higher education. Because of imprecise terminology in both the 1973 and the 1990 laws, the following questions are currently being debated: If note takers, scribes, or readers for LD students are found to be needed accommodations, who will pay for them? Who will decide if students need them in the first place? How much do academic programs need to be altered for LD students, and who will say so? Who should be admitted to an academic program and what are legal means of ascertaining applicants' abilities? Recent judicial rulings as well as ongoing lawsuits address some of these questions. While some court decisions have helped clarify some guidelines, further litigation will be needed before institutions have a clear idea of what is expected. At a 1993 conference on disabilities, an Assistant Counsel for State University of New York Central Administration said, "The courts will do slowly what legislation should have done quickly" (Hasselback 1993).[1]

Case law continues to develop from the earlier legislation. In a unanimous decision on November 9, 1993, the Supreme Court upheld a lower court's ruling regarding a sixteen-year-old LD student. In 1985, her parents took her out of a South Carolina public high school, where she was found to be functionally illiterate and where administrators had proposed that she receive three hours of tutoring a week, a plan that lower courts had found to be inadequate. The girl's parents had placed her in a private academy specializing in LD, where she graduated successfully in three years. Even though the parents' decision was opposed by the school district, and the private academy was not officially state approved for special education, the parents nevertheless won the $35,700 judgment for payment of three years' tuition and board. In her opinion, Sandra Day O'Connor wrote that the Federal law mandated "free appropriate" education for LD students (Greenhouse 1993, B19.)

Another recent case may have implications for LD students and the institutions they attend. In a class-action lawsuit featured in the *Chronicle of Higher Education*, a quadriplegic student is one of several people suing the University of Miami for not providing paid note takers. As reported in the article, the student's mother sits in class and takes notes for him. While some institutions such as Miami-Dade Community College pay for separate note takers, other colleges have students' peers in the class take notes, sometimes on a voluntary basis, sometimes for a small stipend. At the university in question, volunteers are provided with carbon paper so that copies of their own notes can be given to those who are unable to take their own. The students filing suit claim, however, that the volunteer note takers are not reliable and that they, the disabled students, are "made to feel like charity cases" (Jaschik 1994, A39). Although that case is pending, others relevant to this issue already have been decided.

Katherine Raymond, Assistant Counsel for the City University of New York, speaking at a 1993 conference, said that note takers are a "clear requirement" of the ADA, and that institutions must provide them for students who need them, even if those students can afford to pay. Readers and extra time for exams should also be provided free of charge to students who need those accommodations. She spoke of one case involving a student with a language disability in which a culture course was substituted in one program for a language requirement. Raymond stressed that what courts look at most closely in these decisions is whether or not the institution has taken an individualized look at each person's needs and has documented evidence to that effect. Shelly Kehl, of the National Association of College and University Attorneys, speaking at the same conference, also stressed that judicial decisions involving ADA compliance frequently depend on whether or not a college has given careful, nondiscriminatory consideration to each case. She too advises that all institutional decisions and actions involving LD or other students covered under the law be documented. Robert Boehlert, Deputy Advocate Counsel for the New York State Office of the Advocate for the Disabled, stressed at the same conference that complying with the ADA is not a one-time action. Changes do not need to be made overnight. What matters, he said, is that "readily achievable" accommodations be accomplished first, and that there be in place a plan for achieving longer-term goals.

In an excellent article summarizing recent court decisions, Brinckerhoff, Shaw, and McGuire (1992) write that who pays for what services often depends on what is normally available to all students. For example, if all students are routinely provided with free tutoring or counseling services, then so must LD students be provided with those same services for free. Colleges may only charge LD students for services that go beyond what is normally provided for free. Colleges are also not usually required to provide for free such services as special LD tutoring programs or readers for students' leisure-time activities (424). They also point out that colleges are usually not required to pay for testing of potential LD students, but if the institution decides to challenge an earlier diagnosis of LD, then it would most likely have to pay for subsequent evaluations (421). Most experts agree that legally, college students themselves must initiate testing procedures or requests for accommodations.

Who pays for LD diagnosis can depend on the situation, according to University of Houston law professor Laura F. Rothstein, writing in 1986 for the *Journal of College and University Law*. For example, if other kinds of psychological testing are normally provided through a campus health clinic to any student, then LD testing should probably also be similarly available. On the other hand, if students usually pay for other psychological services, then they would probably also have to pay for LD testing (236). Rothstein predicted correctly that this issue would become more critical as these diagnostic evaluations become more expensive and that in most cases the students, not the institution, would be obligated to pay for the testing to document their disability (237).

Documentation of the disability is, of course, crucial to being entitled to accommodations for it. Rothstein cites case law establishing that colleges cannot be held liable for not providing accommodations to students who had disabilities of which the institution was unaware. The 1990 law places much responsibility on the college student to make the disability known through proper channels and to suggest appropriate accommodations for it. Rothstein continues: "Colleges and universities not only have no duty to inquire into the existence of a handicap, but they are specifically prohibited from making preadmission inquiries about handicaps except where the inquiry is for the purpose of remedial action or to overcome limited participation" (237).

As is obvious from these few examples, questions regarding this legislation rarely have simple answers. What seems to be emerging from case law, however, is that courts are carefully examining each case on an individual basis. While the law "does not require modifications that would fundamentally alter the nature of services provided by the public accommodation" (U.S. Equal Employment Opportunity Commission 1992, 21), institutions have been expected to demonstrate challenged educational requirements clearly and to document decision-making processes regarding the participation of LD students (Raymond 1993; Kehl 1993; and Boehlert 1993). The substantial questions and ambiguities concerning relevant legislation are just the tip of the iceberg that is the LD controversy.

Terms and Definitions

The terms *dyslexia* and *learning disability* have almost as many definitions as the number of people who employ them. Some people use them interchangeably to mean, in a general way, a difficulty in reading and writing. In fact, *dyslexia* means, literally, difficulty with reading. For many professionals and diagnosticians, *dyslexia* is a subcategory under the general heading *learning disability*, but because it is often referred to as *specific learning disability*, it is sometimes shortened and essentially equated with *learning disability*. Many, however, are vehement about keeping these terms distinct, and most books on the subject have lengthy introductions explaining how a particular author defines these terms. Related to and sometimes subsumed in these categories are the lesser-known terms *dysgraphia*, which means difficulty with writing, and *dysnomia*, or difficulty recalling the names of things. Dyslexia is sometimes called *developmental reading disorder*, and *dysgraphia* is sometimes called *developmental writing disorder* (National Institute of Mental Health 1993, 7–8). Although discussions of learning disabilities sometimes also include *dyscalculia* (difficulties with math), and *attention deficit disorder* (ADD), this book, intended for writing instructors, will not address those aspects of LD. In this text, I will employ the terms *dyslexia* and *learning disability* interchangeably to mean a difficulty with reading and/or writing that goes beyond what one might expect, given a particular student's apparent intelligence and educational background.

I have substantial objections to this nomenclature because of its connotation of dysfunction. Preferable terminology (if distinctions between people ought to be made at all) might refer to a difference rather than a disability—although any departure from "normal" inevitably connotes something negative in our society. Neverthe-less, *dyslexia* and *learning disability* are generally recognized and used regularly in legislation and public policy statements. This book's use of *learning disability* or *dyslexia* refers specifically to difficulty processing linguistic symbols.

For most experts today, *dyslexia* has become a somewhat unfashionable term and has been replaced by *specific learning dis-ability*, as defined in 1975 by the U.S. Congress Public Law 94-142:

> a disorder in one or more basic psychological processes involved in
> understanding or using spoken or written language but specifically
> excluding those children having learning problems from visual,
> hearing, or motor handicaps, from mental retardation, from emo-
> tional disturbances, or from economic, cultural, or environmental
> deprivation. (Senate Report No. 94-168, 1975, 1465)

As many have pointed out, this definition is problematic for a number of reasons. First of all, it uses negative terms such as *disor-der*, and it by definition excludes those children who might have a specific learning disability *and* another condition such as a motor handicap or an economic disadvantage. In order for students to obtain funding for LD tutoring, they must conform to this definition. They must be of average or above-average intelligence.

To deal with some of these definition problems, the National Joint Committee for Learning Disabilities, in 1981, defined the con-dition this way:

> Learning disabilities is a generic term that refers to a heteroge-
> neous group of disorders manifested by significant difficulties in
> the acquisition and use of listening, speaking, reading, writing,
> reasoning or mathematical abilities. These disorders are intrinsic
> to the individual and presumed to be due to central nervous sys-
> tem dysfunction. Even though a learning disability may occur con-
> comitantly with other handicapping conditions (e.g., sensory
> impairment, mental retardation, social and emotional disturbance)
> or environmental influences (e.g., cultural differences, insufficient-
> inappropriate instruction, psychogenic factors), it is not the direct
> result of those conditions or influences. (Hallahan et al. 1985, 14)

This definition has fewer outmoded terms and allows people to be both specifically learning disabled *and* affected by outside social factors.

As Michael Rutter (1978) observes, the term *dyslexia* is usually invoked as a syndrome caused by inborn cognitive problems when other factors cannot fully explain why a child fails to learn to read. The World Federation of Neurology uses the following definition, which Rutter criticizes as being essentially useless as a diagnostic tool: "[specific developmental dyslexia] is a disorder manifested by difficulty in learning to read despite conventional instruction, adequate intelligence and sociocultural opportunity. It is dependent upon fundamental cognitive disabilities which are frequently of constitutional origin"(12).

Rutter objects to what he calls this "negative definition" (12) because it implies that children of below-average intelligence cannot also have *specific developmental dyslexia*, that is, a constitutional impairment regarding linguistic development. It also implies that children with low IQ's cannot be taught to read, which is not necessarily the case. Marie Clay reports that some adolescent Downs Syndrome children with mental ages of about five years had reading levels of normal seven- or eight-year-olds (1987, 158). The World Federation's definition, which Leon Eisenberg calls "a non-definition of a non-entity" (1978, 31), also makes no provision for children from a lower socioeconomic group who may *also* have this "constitutional" deficit (12). Like the Public Law 94-142 definition, it attempts to give a label, and call it a reason, to a condition of not being able to read. As Martha Bridge Denckla points out, *dyslexia* (or *specific developmental dyslexia* and other variations on that theme), can be employed to mean "a symptom or it may be used with the implication that a specific neurologically based syndrome is being diagnosed" (1978, 243). In other words, *dyslexia* can mean simply that someone has a lot of trouble reading, or it can mean that *dyslexia* is *why* a person has a lot of trouble reading.

Others have had even stronger objections to these labels and definitions. Anne E. Bennison, in Barry Franklin's collection, *Learning Disabilities: Dissenting Essays*, links today's *learning disabled* category with the classification *feeblemindedness* which existed at the turn of the century. She says that "those labels have multiple interpretations at any given time, and that the concepts are applied differentially according to current social concerns." Bennison sees the LD label as an excuse to discriminate, and she calls for "a strong commitment to social justice" as a solution (1987, 26). Most contributors to Franklin's collection of dissenting essays say that *learning disability* is nothing more than the latest in a series of increasingly euphemistic terms for a group society does not know what to do with. They say expressions such as *feebleminded* and *brain-injured*, like *learning disabled*, blame the individual for problems that are societally caused.

Another well-written critique of the LD field is James Carrier's *Learning Disability: Social Class and the Construction of Inequality in American Education* (1986). As does Gerald Coles, Carrier sees LD as an attempt to blame the failure of a system not on the system itself, but on its children. In his essay, "The Politics of Early Learning Disability," Carrier explores the history of the phrase *learning disability* and explains that it had semantic advantages over previous terms because it implied "an accidental condition which was unfortunate and troublesome, but which did not implicate the child's basic mental ability or reflect adversely on the parents" (52). Carrier accuses traditional LD theory of being more concerned with "the desire to explain unequal educational achievement" (72) than by the desire to teach students to read. He brings up the powerful influence of teacher expectations, pointing out the probability that "the social class of pupils influences the way teachers treat them" (77).

With views similar to Carrier's, Gerald Coles argues that the learning disability terminology seemed to be a more attractive label for middle-class children than did *mentally retarded, emotionally disturbed,* or *disadvantaged.* Coles also argues that in some parts of this country, the LD category was used in various ways to initiate or maintain a form of racial segregation (1987, 203–07). In a recent *New York Times* article, Lynda Richardson corroborates this view: "Nationwide, black students are twice as likely to be in special education programs as white children, with much higher rates in predominantly white districts, according to Federal studies" (1994). The special education programs we have today for LD students, says Coles, are a result of frustrated parents who lobbied heavily for the term *learning disability* and for special programs to cope with such a thing. Coles points out school systems' penchant for assessing students and then being satisfied if students live up to (or usually down to) that assessment. He observes that it does not take long for children placed on the low end of the scale to become discouraged and for teachers to become disillusioned. He implicates destructive school atmospheres and criticizes the built-in notion that there will always be failing students and that the cause of their failure can be found in the children themselves. According to Coles, any dysfunction lies not in the individual child but in "social relationships and activities" (1987, 186).

Peter Johnston and Richard Allington (1991) also criticize what they see as a "sickness" approach inherent in the terms and programs regarding the learning disabled (985). They believe all students should be taught with solid learning principles, and that the "individualized" learning in special education classes is more often than not reduced to different worksheets for different students (992–94). They point out that "success" and "failure" are social constructs, and that an unpleasant experience with school may actually cause, rather than eliminate, a learning disability. Instead of the label *learning disabled*, they prefer phrases which indicate the social aspect of the problem, such as "children-with-different-schedules-for-reading-acquisition," or "children-we-have-failed-to-teach" (986). In a 1985 article entitled "Understanding Reading Disability: A Case Study Approach," Peter Johnston discusses adults' reading problems as being exacerbated by their early learning of an "inappropriate concept regarding reading or by an appropriate concept *not* being learned" (his emphasis, 158). Intense anxiety on the part of poor readers contributes to their avoidance of reading and to a resulting lack of practice. Johnston also points to studies which show that when students are told they are learning disabled, or neurologically different, they might conclude that nothing can be done, and thus they stop trying to read and write (170–71). Priscilla L. Vail, author of the popular mass market book, *Smart Kids With School Problems*, prefers the phrase *learning difference*. She emphasizes throughout her book that these children are smart, an adjective that perhaps partially accounts for the book's popularity with desperate parents.

Challenging the view that reading level is not a function of IQ, Michael Rutter says that IQ score taken at age five "predicted reading at age seven better than a psychological battery designed to identify children with special disabilities" (1978, 9). In other words, for Rutter, reading ability *is* seen as a function of intelligence, a theory not likely to be popular among parents of dyslexic children. They are more likely to welcome Katrina De Hirsch's view of IQ tests. While she says they are fairly good indicators, she ranks them only twelfth as predictors of reading performance, well behind measures that test time and space orientation in children, matching and letter naming, and gestalt awareness—tests that are usually part of a battery administered by LD experts (1984, 50–51). Determining a person's IQ is itself a related imbroglio, which I will discuss in more detail later in this chapter.

While *dyslexia* and *specific learning disability* seem to be the most utilized terms for this difficulty in learning to read and write despite normal or above average intelligence and an unremarkable social situation, the never-ending list of names reflects experts' desire to pin down once and for all this baffling syndrome. Hyla Rubin and Isabelle Y. Liberman use the phrase *language disabled* to refer to children with "phonological deficiencies in the accuracy of stored representations and in short term memory coding" (1983, 118). To distinguish it from environmental factors, it was also referred to as *constitutional reading disorders*. Note the plural. No one has been able to completely isolate one set of problems common to all dyslexics. There is also the more blunt phrase, *general reading backwardness*, which includes *all* poor readers without regard to IQ (Rutter 1978, 14–15).

Katrina De Hirsch differentiates four *disorders of learning*, but her third category, *disorders of printed and written words*, comes closest to what most people generally call dyslexia, and her definition is similar to the legal definition in that it limits the category to those with at least average intelligence who have had "adequate educational opportunities" (1984, 91). It should be noted that Marie Clay would question De Hirsch's assumption here of "adequate educational opportunities," since Clay believes that a school system's "inappropriate programme" is the primary cause of many children's reading problems (1987, 160). But for De Hirsch, nothing obvious, such as unfavorable educational or environmental conditions, can explain why these children have trouble. For her, and for many others who use the term *dyslexia*, this name by definition excludes social problems. It would seem that *dyslexia*, or the next most common appellation, *specific learning disability*, is reserved for that kind of reading trouble which is maddeningly inexplicable.

Manifestations

What are the symptoms and manifestations of dyslexia? Those reputed to be afflicted with it have tried to explain it. What people *say* about themselves as recognized dyslexics is important, but like other evidence in this troubled field, also subject to debate. Donald Lyman, a self-defined dyslexic who has taught many other dyslexics, describes his adventures with abstract written language: "Those typewritten *a*'s looked so strange to me that I was never sure which letter I was dealing with. I was always saying *how* for *who* or the other way around. I don't know why it happened but I sometimes mixed up *y* and *v*. Everybody laughed when I read that Tom went out to play in the vard" (Lyman 1986, 7). Gloria Tannenbaum (1989) quotes one child as saying, "The words dance around the page." I've already related how my student Barbara claimed that for her, letters would "jump around."

Some critics, however, question an individual's description of letters that move around, arguing that people are taught this response, and that the only way they would be aware of the concept of "upside down" or "reversed" letters is if they are told this by others. This objection to people's testimony could be equally applied, however, to the objectors. In other words, critics of such testimony are themselves influenced by what they have read or been told. If they have decided that reading problems are caused primarily by society, their objection to what students say about their reading is predictable. Although students' testimony regarding what happens when they read should be heard with the critics' objections in mind, children's voices should not be silenced simply because those with more authority choose to discount what they say. Gerald Coles refers to current beliefs in the LD field regarding word reversals "lore" and cites studies by F.W. Black (1973) and Kaufman and Biren (1976–77), among others, which show that "normal" children also experience reversals (Coles 1987, 30). Critics of Coles' diatribe against the LD field say that criticism of reversals is not news and in any case is not important to the diagnosis of LD.

Decades ago, when some LD experts theorized that dyslexic children saw things backward, practitioners sometimes employed various eye exercises to remedy the problem. Coles says many states still test for perceptual deficits and continue to use them as part of their definition of learning disability (1987, 37). In the last twenty years, Frank Vellutino has repeatedly concluded from his research that there is nothing wrong with dyslexics' vision (1987, 34). Coles cites Vellutino's research disproving old beliefs regarding visual perception problems. However, according to an article in the science pages of the *New York Times*, several recent studies add a new element to the vision debate, which had been considered long settled. Stephen Lehmkuhle of the School of Optometry at the University of Missouri discovered timing problems in the visual pathways of dyslexics.[2] In related research at Harvard, Margaret S. Livingstone also studied brain activity in dyslexics and reported that this group has a timing difference regarding visual information, and that this may affect reading ability (Rennie 1991, 26). One element of the vision question is apparently still open.

In other research, Vellutino and Scanlon write that it is dyslexics' short-term memory for linguistic symbols, not their vision, that seems to give them more problems than most of us experience (1991, 245), especially if the words are abstract, such as *were, at, through, where, when*, etc. Although this kind of empirical research has methodological factors which may not be transferable to real life (see discussion below), results regarding the recollection of concrete and abstract words have been somewhat replicable. Other researchers have raised the possibility of short-term, linguistics-related memory problems (Rubin and Liberman 1983, 118; Farnham-Diggory 1978, 108; Rawson 1988, 66; and Blalock 1982, 607).

Katrina De Hirsch (1984) points out that while dyslexic children have no problem remembering sounds in nature, such as the different sounds made by various animals, they seem to have problems associating the sound/symbol system of our alphabetic code (93). She has hypothesized that dyslexics have difficulty remembering letter shape (21). Frank Vellutino, however, found that both dyslexic and normal readers performed equally on tasks requiring them to remember letter shapes lacking meaning for them—in this case Hebrew words and letters for children not familiar with Hebrew. From this, Vellutino concludes that for both dyslexic and normal readers, "visual form perception seems to be comparable in the two groups" (1987, 36). On the other hand, when poor and normal readers are tested on their ability to recall colors, numbers, pictures, and words from their own language, the groups differ only on their ability to recall the words (1979, 254). Therefore, the problem is not visual perception or memory per se but rather "access to specific word meanings or meanings coded contextually . . ." (263).

Sylvia Farnham-Diggory believes this difficulty in remembering linguistic symbols may not necessarily be a defect, but simply a difference (1978, 95). Bernard M. Patten (1978) contends that it is a mistake to insist, as our present educational system essentially does, that everyone learn the same way. In emphasizing verbal thought, it is possible that we are squelching a very creative, alternative system of thought possessed by a certain portion of the population. Patten contends that Albert Einstein was one such individual. Gerald Coles (1987) criticizes what he calls this "affliction of geniuses" argument of the LD field—the "romanticization of learning disabilities" (107) achieved by citing all the famous people reputed to have been dyslexic. In his book he first summarizes three respected studies which concluded that learning disabilities are inherited. He then refutes them, referring to Einstein's reputation as a dyslexic as "LD lore." He criticizes biographies of famous and reputedly dyslexic people by claiming the authors did not adequately consider these children's old-fashioned, rigid teachers and their probable negative effect on students' learning (124). For those who attribute reading problems primarily to societal influences, teachers are inevitably implicated. Einstein's instructors, conveniently unable to defend themselves, are particularly handy scapegoats.

Approaches to Teaching

Two different approaches are used in schools to teach reading and writing—one a "whole language" approach, one a structured, phonics-based, often multisensory approach influenced by techniques developed by Samuel Orton, Anna Gillingham, and Bessie Stillman.

Although these two approaches do contain some elements of each other, they are each based on different assumptions about learning and are therefore philosophically and methodologically quite different. Which one is more appropriate is yet another part of the LD controversy.

Although whole language does allow for different rates of learning, it does not address learning differences arising from a neurological basis. The whole language philosophy, basically, is that exposure to meaningful texts, coupled with limited explicit instruction, will be sufficient. Robert Blake, in the introduction to his collection of essays on whole language, puts it this way: "Children are capable of intuiting the purposes of print if they are constantly exposed to all kinds of writing" (1990, v). Gordon S. Anderson, in *A Whole Language Approach to Reading*, writes that "Communication is largely accomplished and learned without any direct teaching or instruction" (1984, 1). Lucy Calkins, in *The Art of Teaching Writing* (1986), a text for primary grades, has a more moderate view of whole language. Her version of whole language *does* involve some explicit instruction (204). She advocates what she calls "mini-lessons," short (approximately three-minute) lectures on such things as topic choice, mapping or brainstorming strategies, the form of a sympathy letter, or story endings (167–93). Calkins' mini-lesson can even include a sounding out strategy: "I sometimes encourage children to stretch out a word, listening slowly to the component sounds" (174).

This kind of exercise is similar to the explicit teaching of phonics that is used by some teachers using a highly structured, multisensory approach, sometimes called the Orton-Gillingham (O-G) method. The difference is that in whole language teaching, phonics is not emphasized, and the words used come from the children or from high-interest texts. In O-G more time is devoted to explicit sounding out techniques, more attention is given to memory aids, and the words come, for the most part, from programmed lessons. Whole language does include phonics instruction, but it is presented in context, secondary to the whole meaning of the text. O-G methods attempt to include interesting materials, but content is secondary to the structure and controlled vocabulary they say is necessary for LD students to be exposed to (Bertin and Perlman 1980).

Whole language instruction, while it includes some explicit teaching, makes little provision for children who may need a multisensory cue or a mnemonic link to help them remember. While Calkins recognizes developmental differences, she attributes them primarily to family background differences: "I have also been in kindergartens where the children know *less* than I suspected. Usually these children come from homes without books and from families who do not read, from families where parents may not have time to talk with and listen to their children" (1986, 37). Her analysis of the problem is that the student's environment needs enrichment. Although Calkins may have documentation that these poor readers come "from homes without books and from families who do not read," she does not include this evidence in her argument.

Other reading researchers also emphasize society's influence on reading development. In their book-length study of poor readers, Jeanne S. Chall, Vicki A. Jacobs, and Luke E. Baldwin emphasize the sociological reasons children read poorly. While they recognize reading disorders of neurological origin, they go to great lengths to exclude children with such disorders from their study (1990, 17). Anyone reading their text, *The Reading Crisis: Why Poor Children Fall Behind*, might get the impression that most, if not all, problems are environmentally caused.

Each approach to teaching reading is geared to addressing what is believed to be the problem. The whole language approach is based on the idea that children exposed to and personally engaged in whole, interesting, relevant, meaningful, and interrelated acts of reading, speaking, and writing will implicitly come to know whatever linguistic structures are necessary. An O-G based, multisensory reading/writing method is based on the belief that some children will *not* as easily intuit the linguistic code and must be explicitly shown how it works. It is basically exaggerated phonics instruction, and strictly bottom-up—that is, students learn letters, phonemes (the smallest units of sound), and words in a formulated order. The sounds and letter shapes are constantly reinforced through all the senses and through whatever associative or mnemonic links the teachers or students can think of. Chapter Three includes a more detailed explanation of how these two approaches differ philosophically and practically, along with an account of one child's experiences with both methods in learning to write.

Causes

The idea that some people are born with a neurological setup that gives them more difficulties than others have when dealing with linguistic symbols has been proposed for almost a century. As early as 1895, James Hinshelwood, an ophthalmologist from Scotland, called this reading difficulty *congenital word blindness* and theorized that different parts of the brain handled different memories and processes. In 1912, Hinshelwood described an intelligent twelve-year-old, with good eyesight, who did well in math but had great difficulty learning to read (Farnham-Diggory 1978, 20). Gene transmission research, as reported in the September 18, 1991 issue of the *Journal of the American Medical Association* shows some support for the hypothesis that dyslexia is inherited. Whether this involves one primary gene or several groups of genes is still unclear, and the researchers qualify their conclusions by calling for more studies regarding the effects of environment on reading development. However, in a study of 204 families in three different states, researchers from the University of Denver and Yale University report that dyslexia seems to be inherited, at least in the majority of the families they studied (Pennington, et al. 1991, 1533).

Another key figure in the learning disability movement, which recognized children with specialized reading and writing problems that were congenitally (as opposed to socially) caused, was Samuel Orton, a professor of neuropsychology at Columbia University in the 1930s. Sometimes called "the father of dyslexia," Orton used his own term of *strephosymbolia* (meaning *twisted symbols*) to refer to this syndrome he noticed in his patients. Orton defined *strephosymbolia* as "The instability in recognition and recall of the orientation of letters and the order of letters in words" (Orton 1966, 122). Orton's compassion for children with this problem is evidenced in his call for more understanding and less ignorant treatment of them (Eisenberg 1978, 34).

Orton studied the writing and error patterns of these children and noted that many of them were left-handed or ambidextrous. Theorizing that language was handled primarily in the brain's left hemisphere in most "normal" people, Orton suggested that dyslexics had differences in the parts of their brains that handled language processes. It was likely, he said, that the right side of dyslexics' brains was attempting to handle a process meant as a job for the left side, or perhaps both sides of a dyslexic's brain were unproductively competing to process language, resulting in the reversals and mirror writing Orton reportedly observed in his patients.

Albert Galaburda's research into brain configuration and neuron lineup has also suggested that Orton's theory may have been partially correct, although as is usually the case when dealing with this subject, lab results can be and often are variously interpreted. According to Galaburda, who does postmortem brain analyses of people said to be dyslexic, the brains of dyslexics are different from those of normal people. Although both sides are needed for integration of words and meaning, and no one side is the pure custodian of the brain's language files, it is the left side of the brain in normal people that is the larger hemisphere. This is thought to be due to its development as the handler of language. Galaburda (1983) claims that in many dyslexics, the right side is as developed as the left, whereas normally the left side is more developed (45). Galaburda argues that in normal people, a certain amount of "neuronal death" occurs naturally in the right side of the brain while the organism is still in utero. However, in dyslexics, there is less neuronal death in the right hemisphere than might be expected. Galaburda suggests that perhaps that is why there seems to be "a disproportionate number [of dyslexics] with talents in music, visio-spacial abilities, and left-handedness" (51). These are talents believed to be handled by the right side of the brain. Galaburda summarizes earlier research by W. E. Drake that also showed neurological differences in the brains of dyslexics: "The first post-mortem report on the brain of a dyslexic patient stated that excessive numbers of neurons were present in the sub cortical white matter" (49). If this seems like too simple an explanation, it is. There are "normal" people who also have more developed right hemispheres, and "dyslexics" whose neurons are normal. Even Galaburda, who seems convinced that there are enough differences between the brains of dyslexics and those of normal people to warrant a neurological explanation for their language problems, calls for more study.

In his critique of the LD field, Gerald Coles (1987) devotes several pages to problematizing Galaburda's research. Sponsored by the Orton Dyslexia Society, Galaburda's autopsies involved the dissection and examination of the brains of people reputed to be dyslexic. Coles critiques this research, which he says involved only four brains, and challenges the original diagnosis of dyslexia in the subjects. One of the individuals, for example, although reportedly dyslexic, had earned a doctorate in engineering, a feat Coles says is unusual for a dyslexic. He also takes issue with Galaburda's findings of hemisphere differences, saying that it is unclear whether the perceived differences were due to dyslexia, as Galaburda claims, or to other medical conditions had by the individuals such as circulatory problems, brain hemorrhages, and epilepsy. Coles further points out that although these relevant details are available in the original reports, they are often omitted from subsequent summaries of such research as they appear in Orton Society publications (86–91).

In her book, *The Early Detection of Reading Difficulties* (1979), Marie M. Clay also criticizes what she sees as a long-disproven belief regarding how the brain works. Orton-Gillingham advocates often speak of people having a different neurological makeup. Clay's argument, while it does not totally eliminate the possibility of neurological difference, attributes reading difficulties to a learned, rather than an innate difference, which she believes can be remediated with proper instruction (1972, 964). Clay's Reading Recovery program is founded on this fundamental belief. Coles, too, says that differences in neuron lineup or hemispheres, if they exist and could be accurately measured, are caused by in-life experiences, not inborn differences. To argue this point, Coles points to rat studies which suggest that life experience can alter the brain's neuron patterns (1987, 175). Any neurological differences can be explained by what he calls an "interactivity theory": "biological makeup that appears to be or in fact is dysfunctional may be caused not by an inherent breakdown in the organic processes but by exogenous social and psychological conditions which reciprocally interact with biological functioning "(176). Barry Franklin criticizes similar cognitive research done in the 1930s by Alfred Strauss and Heinz Werner, who identified two types of neurological conditions they called "endogenous" (hereditary) and "exogenous" (due to trauma). Franklin questions the tests Strauss and Werner used to distinguish between the two "types" and finally dismisses virtually all research the LD field traditionally cites as its beginnings, therefore debunking the entire theory of a neurologically based cause (1987, 29–46). Kenneth Kavale and Steven Forness, in their book *The Science of Learning Disabilities*, are not at all subtle in their accusations regarding research in the LD field. They compare LD experts to "astrologers in the Middle Ages" and call what some LD professionals view as fact nothing more than "magical belief" (1985, 11).

Although the theory regarding hemisphere dominance has not been disproven, John Hughes cites research demonstrating that brain differences are also seen in good readers (1978, 234). Michael Rutter, in summarizing research done in at least six different studies, also disputes claims that handedness is related to dyslexia. In the same paragraph, however, Rutter admits that "a *confusion* between right and left is associated with reading difficulties," and that it is possible "that a *delay* in the acquisition of left-hemisphere dominance may be associated with some cases of reading difficulty. . . ." He adds that "the evidence on this point remains inconclusive" (1978, 9). For Ursula Bellugi, a neuroscientist and director of the Laboratory for Cognitive Neuroscience at the Salk Institute for Biological Sciences in La Jolla, there is no question that the left hemisphere is primarily responsible for language. In her continuing studies of deaf users of sign language who have suffered strokes, she has found that deaf signers with damage to the right hemisphere— the side thought to handle space perception—had trouble drawing the left side of a picture but could still use sign language normally. Those with damage to the left side of their brains could draw both sides of a room, but lost most of their ability to sign (Radetsky 1994, 66).

Results from tests with names like "positron emission tomography," "magnetic resonance imaging," and "roentgenographic computed tomography" are reported in journals such as *Archives of Neurology, Brain and Language, Psychology Bulletin*, and *Annals of Neurology*. According to routine summaries of relevant literature that appear in these reports, such tests indicate hemispheric differences between dyslexics and non-dyslexics. Coles, however, summarizes other studies challenging these findings. No matter how recent the research or how clearly documented the differences appear to be, Coles objects that the subjects' dyslexia diagnosis was not sufficiently established. Thus, he can discount any conclusions.

Do EEG's, CAT scans, MRI's, and other unpronounceable technologies show brain hemisphere differences in people? Available published answers to this question are not along the lines of "maybe" or "sometimes," but are deeply entrenched in definitive "yes" and "no" camps. The rhetorical stance of many LD-related EEG and CAT scan reports is, "Of *course* this technology shows brain differences in dyslexics. Everybody knows that." The rhetorical stance in Coles' (1987) chapter section regarding this research is, "Of *course* this technology has failed to show brain differences in dyslexics. Everybody knows that now."

This element of the LD controversy has a tiresome, school yard "is/is not" tone to it. What are English professors to do? Short of pitching in and buying our own roentgenograph and tinkering with it ourselves, we are forced to rely for our summaries of this research on opposing camps with apparent difficulties contextualizing their own conclusions. First, there are the neurologists, whose expensive machines become more valuable if they promise answers for desperate children, parents, and educators. Then there are critics whose backgrounds in clinical psychology may predispose them to look for familial and societal causes for any and all learning difficulties.

I originally wanted an answer to the above question because I felt it might influence my pedagogy. However, exasperated at least temporarily by the polemics, I have decided that the answer may not matter. EEG results are not needed to confirm for me that my nephew has linguistic recall problems that respond favorably to multisensory associations. (See Chapter Three.) They are not needed to demonstrate that a small number of my students speak far better and faster than they can write and that they possess talents it would behoove more linguistically talented students to develop. (See Chapter Four.) What these LD students themselves say about the way they learn best is as good a place as any to begin the restructuring of mainstream education at all levels that needs to be done to improve learning for all students. (See Chapter Five.)

Newer brain-related technology builds upon and extends the earlier, less sophisticated studies. Research studying the brain activity of individuals who are asked to perform linguistic tasks has been going on for decades, but new findings on Williams syndrome, a birth defect that occurs in one of 20,000 children, may reveal more insights on language development and the brain. Researchers now know that Williams syndrome, discovered in 1961, results from a missing gene copy on a chromosome. Children with this syndrome have low IQ's, extremely poor spatial abilities, and heart defects. However, they are highly sociable and can speak in grammatically correct, complex sentences, using sophisticated vocabulary. The admixture of strengths and weaknesses common in all Williams syndrome children is an area with possible implications for LD research because it raises questions about IQ, language development, and which areas of the brain handle different language tasks (Blakeslee 1994b).

Research by psychologists Rosaleen McCarthy and Elizabeth K. Warrington and reported in *Nature* has suggested that the brain may store and retrieve information partly according to category (i.e. animate and inanimate objects), and modality (sight, sound, etc.) (1990, 599). If individuals differ in their reliance on various modalities to recall words and images, it may account for different learning styles and differences in using written language, which depends primarily on the visual mode. The differences researchers report in the thinking patterns of dyslexics and non-dyslexics are also intriguing. For example, Judith M. Rumsey reports in the *Journal of the American Medical Association* that when subjects were asked to identify rhyming words, dyslexics performed at levels below that of the non-dyslexics, and the areas of the brain activated by this task reportedly differed from those areas activated in the brains of the non-dyslexics (1992, 915).

In what may be the most exciting new brain research yet, Paula Tallal and her colleagues at Rutgers University have discovered a different explanation for dyslexia: a difficulty one area of the brain has in handling fast-arriving sounds. For example, words like *boy* and *pet*, which begin with "stop-consonant syllables," require the listener to rapidly process the *b* and *p* sounds before those consonants melt into the vowels that follow them. These vowel sounds, which last only forty milliseconds, are much shorter in duration than the *m* sound in *ma*, for example, which can last more than one hundred milliseconds. Albert Galaburda has studied the "medial geniculate nuclei" area of the brain and reports that dyslexics' left hemispheres have fewer of the cells required to discriminate between these rapid sounds—the stop-consonant syllables. Glen Rosen of Beth Israel Medical Center and Holly Fitch of Rutgers have carried out related animal research. They found that brain lesions in a corresponding section of rats' brains caused auditory timing difficulties similar to those found in human dyslexics. (Curiously, it affected male rats only, not females.) If this auditory timing problem is indeed the cause of dyslexia, a treatment seems promising. Michael Merzenich from the University of California in San Francisco, along with Tallal, has developed computers that extend the sounds of the stop-consonant syllables, allowing dyslexics to hear and process them (Blakeslee 1994a).

Gerald Coles criticizes most LD research as being biased toward a confirmation of the researchers' preconceived ideas concerning a neurological cause. In his opinion, there is virtually no reliable evidence to support the claims and practices of people in the LD field. He ridicules many LD practitioners, painting them as unscientific quacks clinging ignorantly to unproven beliefs in a type of "amnesia" that allows them to recall only that which supports their view (1987, 31–32). Coles attributes virtually any learning problems to social, educational, and cultural forces. The research flaws Coles details concerning much LD research are serious, but whether or not researchers' alleged predisposition to find neurological differences should make us discount all research is debatable. After all, as mentioned above, it is impossible for any of us, including Coles, to step away from our own philosophical grounding and expectations, or even to be completely aware of them. The best, most well-designed clinical research has inescapable problems, which even Coles' exhaustive critique does not mention. A short examination of a sample research report will illustrate some of these problems.

Any one research project can be examined regarding a number of components: the appropriateness of its pool of human subjects, methodology, statistical analysis, interpretation of results, and conclusions. In order to illustrate the importance of careful scrutiny, I will examine briefly the methodological implications of one researcher's work, Frank Vellutino, whose reports have been widely circulated in many texts, among them his 1979 book *Dyslexia: Theory and Practice* and his 1987 article on the same subject in *Scientific American.* If there are uncontrolled and/or unacknowledged variables in the methodological approach, the resulting findings will be questionable, or at the very least, colored by such factors. Since his work is always of the highest quality, and since my own views of dyslexia are influenced by having read much of his writing, I will examine one aspect of one of his reports.

In 1987, Frank Vellutino and Donna Scanlon conducted research designed to test their hypothesis regarding poor readers' difficulties with phonemes, the smallest unit of sound. For example, "cat" has three phonemes: /c/, /a/, and /t/. Vellutino and Scanlon found that "deficiencies in phonological coding and phonemic segmentation are a direct cause of deficiencies in word identification" (1987, 321). Indeed, they conclude: "These results provide strong support for the contention that deficiencies in phonemic segmentation and alphabetic mapping are basic causes of difficulties in word identification" (339). Advocates of a structured, explicit teaching method often cite studies such as this as support for their phonics-based pedagogy. (See Chapter Three.) Such support, however, should be tempered by the following considerations of the research methods involved in this particular study by Vellutino and Scanlon. First, the tests for phonemic segmentation and alphabetic mapping occur in highly artificial testing environments. Second, in addition to the skills they were intended to examine, these researchers may have been inadvertently testing other skills not acknowledged by the researchers.

For example, one of the tests "presented the child with three pairs of rhyming words and required that, for each pair, he or she provide a third word that rhymed with the words in the set" (324). The directions to the children regarding such a task are not provided verbatim, but it is obvious that the children being tested must understand the word and concept of *rhyme* and *set*. They must also be passive or cooperative enough to perform this task without the strong positive motivation that might be present in a real-life reading situation with stories of interest to them. As part of the five- or six-day training period required of the children before taking part in the research proper, they were sometimes asked to "vocal[ize] syllables in reverse order. The stimuli used for these exercises consisted of both real words and pseudowords, presented both auditorily and visually" (334). The explanation given of the tasks required makes no allowance for the inquisitiveness of normal kindergartners who might be so preoccupied by what they might see as the absurdity of the tasks—saying words backward or repeating pseudowords—that they consciously or unconsciously refuse to answer seriously. The researchers, of course, have many logical, well-thought-out reasons for using these particular tasks, to which the kindergartners are obviously not privy. Real children might be bored or perverse enough to answer not according to the involved directions they were trained in but according to whatever contrary game they might conceive of during the course of the test, making their answers not wrong, but merely resistant.

In another task, children are tested on their memory of nonsense syllables linked with "novel cartoon-like animal pictures" (337). Although this is an ingenious way to simulate vocabulary acquisition, it may indirectly assess a child's willingness to perform such tasks. It makes no allowance for motivation on the individual child's part to associate the researchers' nonsense or pseudowords with unrealistic-looking creatures. A child who has trouble in this clinical setting might easily perform similar tasks at home involving, say, X-Men.

In their rather lengthy accounts of these and other research projects, as written up in the specialized professional journals, Vellutino and his colleagues are very conservative in their conclusions and careful not to make sweeping generalizations about the reading habits of all children based on this limited research. They acknowledge some (but not all) of the possible problems in the actual research—cautions that are less obvious in the subsequently-summarized accounts of the complete project likely to be scanned by reading and writing practitioners who have neither the time nor the inclination to decipher the more involved reports.

Similar objections regarding methodology could be raised about virtually every component of every study. If the generally high quality of Vellutino and Scanlon's research can generate a myriad of control problems, research conducted with less care can yield even more caveats. While control problems in empirical research should no doubt be acknowledged more frequently than is presently the case, and those that are duly explained in original reports should at least be mentioned in summarized references to the work, these problems should not become the basis on which all similar research is cast aside. Clinical research is always done in artificial conditions. Many people, therefore, object to any clinical studies on reading or writing, claiming that such research is not naturalistic. It is certainly true that the tasks subjects are asked to perform are not similar to real-life reading and writing tasks, and that components are difficult to control, even in a clinical situation. However, in a natural learning environment, nothing is controlled and few results can be satisfactorily documented. Such issues regarding the methodological implications of research traditions founded on different philosophical assumptions can and do result in standoffs, with involved parties often refusing, on theoretical grounds, to recognize any conclusions made by researchers with different methodologies. Stephen M. North and others have warned of the dangers inherent to this kind of methodological isolationism. (See Chapter Five for a more complete discussion.)

Laboratory testing is, by definition, not naturalistic. Granted, there are often unacknowledged variables that must be considered when discussing results of such empirical research. In spite of the fact that empiricists traditionally have not been methodologically self-aware, their best work is somewhat repeatable, and preserves the possibility that there are differences in the ways individuals process linguistic symbols, and by extension suggests that people learn differently. Pooling our resources, discussing—even shouting about—our different methodological assumptions would seem to be more in the best interests of our mutual students, who stand to benefit or suffer from whatever public policy results from interdisciplinary squabbling, or worse, from silent assumptions that we always know what we are doing.

The learning disability field has existed for almost a century. According to many professionals on one side of the controversy, there is a percentage of the population who, for reasons not related to intelligence (whatever *that* is), seem to have more problems in picking up spoken language or in learning to read and write than could be predicted. As convinced as the Orton Dyslexia Society is that dyslexia or learning disability is a real phenomenon, and a neurologically caused one at that, there is another group equally convinced that dyslexia for the most part is a myth, and that if children cannot read well, there are sociological or educational reasons to explain why. As we have seen, Coles' main criticism of LD research and conclusions is that its claim for a neurologically based cause uses "biologically reductionist explanations" to account for what Coles views as a sociologically based problem. The LD movement, according to Coles, serves society by keeping things as they are and focusing on the individual's need to change. Coles condemns the LD movement for requiring only minor "adjustments" in a dysfunctional school system rather than the large changes he sees as necessary. Coles believes learning disabilities are caused not by nature, but by the destructive effects of late capitalism and general "social inequality." They are "part of a larger failure of U.S. middle-class life to achieve post WWII promises and expectations." Attempts to explain reading difficulties any other way are, for Coles, "misguided" (1987, 194–99).

In his eagerness to implicate social situation rather than neurological make-up in determining a child's language difficulties, Coles chooses to highlight studies suggesting that family life greatly influences a child's speech patterns. According to the studies Coles cites, the "factors" supposedly responsible for children's linguistic problems include "the mother's effectiveness in teaching her children (whether there were sufficient positive messages and few negative ones)" (60). A child's failure to thrive linguistically is blamed on the primary care giver's failure to properly engage the child in conversation. If it is discovered that the child did indeed have an abundance of encouragement, then the reason for the difficulty must be that *too much* emphasis was placed on the child learning to speak and write. For anguished parents, the sociological view is a dilemma. Unless the parent (usually the mother) manages to provide some ideal balance of encouragement coupled with the right amount of laissez-faire, she may find herself labeled as the cause of her child's problems: "Family research has found that mothers hold the primary responsibility for a child's cognitive development" (146). Although for Coles, "suburban life" in a decadent Western capitalist society is the primary culprit responsible for the situation women find themselves in, he never addresses what assumptions may have preexisted for those researchers who "found" that mothers are responsible for a child's development. It seems that only those researchers whose findings Coles disagrees with have preexisting assumptions.

No one can dispute the fact that environment influences a child's language development. But if this theory is carried to an extreme, parents (especially mothers) will be haunted by the possibility that they must have done something wrong, that perhaps their children watched one too many episodes of Mighty Morphin Power Rangers or were yelled at too often (or not enough) when they spilled their milk. In this explanation, LD is caused by "parents either uninvolved or overly intrusive" (142). In other words, parents cannot escape indictment. If a parent says, "But I was always involved," then researchers can respond, "Ah *ha*! You must have been *too* involved!" If it is unclear what it was that the parent did or did not do to cause the child to be LD, this too fits the theory because "The specific ways in which family relationships are involved in the creation of learning disabilities remain to be determined" (146). How convenient: a one-size-fits-all explanation for LD, which, although it cannot be proven, also cannot be disproven.

Coles' primary aim is to protect children from a blame that might be more justly bestowed on their environment, but in looking almost exclusively to social causes for reading failure—a condition he readily admits no one really understands—Coles' accusations regarding a child's early experiences invites already distraught and confused parents to blame themselves for their child's difficulties. Although Coles ridicules other people's explanation for dyslexia (a neurological glitch) as being unproven, his own explanation (mothers and teachers not providing some ideally appropriate response to their children) has also not been proven and merely substitutes one hunch for another. In fact, recent research seems to challenge Coles' emphasis on the importance of one's parents' conversational habits. Hearing children of deaf parents—children who hear no speech at all in their early childhood—learn sign language as toddlers and then just as easily learn speech when they are eventually exposed to it (Radetsky 1994, 68).

The term *radical* is, in this field, a relative one. Coles' critique calls for an overhaul of society and chastises opponents for perpetuating what he views as a decadent and classist economic and educational system. Ironically, Orton-Gillingham enthusiasts view themselves as the radicals bent on reforming what they claim is an outdated *look-say* educational system that discriminates against children who have a right to learn differently.

The social-scientific research Coles employs as support for his interactivity theory—that learning differences are primarily socially caused—is no less tainted than the neurological research he rejects for being designed with the neurologists' preconceived ideas of what they would find. Coles' social-scientific studies feature families deliberately chosen for what the researchers already knew about them (1978, 142). As Michael Polanyi has explained in *Personal Knowledge* (1958), no scientific research—neurological or sociological—can be conducted without the background, expectations, and paradigmatic worldview of the researchers playing a part in the research design or in its findings. Such personal knowledge is not only desirable, but unavoidable and should be recognized and utilized for the insights it can provide.

While Coles painstakingly dismantles neurological research for setting out to find a neurological basis for learning disabilities, he accepts with nary a peep the psycho-social analyses made by sociologists whose profession is founded on the power of psycho-social relationships. In a postmodern world, it almost goes without saying that neurologists will set out, consciously or unconsciously, to find neurologically based cases for LD, and that sociologists will similarly set out to find socially based ones. That we recognize this does not mean we should summarily dismiss research results of these professionals, but rather that we should view all data with a critical eye on the particular researcher's educational background, funding, and methodological paradigm—*all* data, not just those collected by "them."

Even with all these factors considered (and whoever is doing the considering is similarly trapped by personal and educational schema), some research—both neurological and sociological—will be of a higher quality than other research. Useful discrimination between and among sloppy and careful studies, however, cannot occur if the critic is willing to condemn for tainted preconceptions only the folks on the other side of the campus. By limiting his impressive analytical and rhetorical powers to the dismantling of only one kind of research and then uncritically summarizing the conclusions of those whose results it benefits his argument to accept, Coles' own credibility is diminished and his substantial contributions to understanding LD are rendered less helpful. Those who wish to become better informed about the LD controversy cannot remove whatever sturdy lenses color their perceptions of what they read. They can, however, be aware that they are wearing such lenses when they examine all research, including that which confirms their own worldview.

After Coles' book was published, its argument was addressed by a number of professionals in the LD field. Several reviews appeared, as might be expected, in the *Journal of Learning Disabilities*. Virginia Mann, a cognitive scientist at the University of California, Irvine, agrees with Coles that "reversals" in reading are not, contrary to notions sometimes discussed in the popular press, indicative of LD. She disagrees with him, however, in what she sees as his dismissal of "language-based theories." She argues further that if a substandard educational background alone accounted for reading disabilities, many more students would be labeled LD than is presently the case, and enrichment programs would show more success than they presently do. She also points to the presence of dyslexia across many cultures as evidence against Coles' sociopolitical explanations of reading difficulties (Mann 1989, 283–84).

Albert Galaburda, whose autopsy studies were discussed earlier, disputes Coles' argument that brain differences between LD and non-LD people could develop primarily from social factors. Galaburda argues that while education is no doubt influential and can contribute to reading development or lack thereof, asymmetries in the brain "are visible in the fetal brain shortly after the middle of pregnancy" and therefore "could not have been caused by a detrimental educational system" (1983, 280–81).

A psychologist from Oakland University in Michigan, Keith Stanovich spends a large section of his review of *The Learning Mystique* praising Coles for drawing attention to an issue that needs to be addressed outside isolated professional fields. He writes that Coles is correct to debunk the "nonsense" that famous people such as Albert Einstein and Woodrow Wilson were dyslexic, and to stress the importance of adequate reading instruction, especially regarding phonological awareness. He further agrees with Coles that much "sloppy" research and testing results in many people being misdiagnosed as LD. Finally, he acknowledges that Coles, unlike many experts on both sides of the controversy, points out that brain differences are not necessarily inborn but may develop as a result of experiential influences (Stanovich 1989b).

Stanovich then goes on to point out what he sees as major flaws in Coles' theory of "interactivity"—the belief that social factors account for most major differences in reading abilities among children. He says that Coles' theory addresses "*generic* learning problems, not LD" (his emphasis, 288) and that Coles does not sufficiently address the primary definitional factor of discrepancy. In other words, Coles blurs generally poor academic achievement with specific learning disabilities, ignoring the fact that LD is traditionally defined by a discrepancy between IQ and achievement. If Coles had chosen to, says Stanovich, he could have attacked IQ testing and the discrepancy model, which do have serious flaws and which have been attacked as such, as we will see, by many in the LD field. How and if poor readers can be reliably distinguished from LD readers is an issue Stanovich says is presently "unresolved" in the LD field, and one that Coles does not adequately address. While Stanovich welcomes Coles' contribution to a needed debate, he feels Coles' overemphasis of the "interactivity" model overlooks differences between children who perform generally poorly in school and those whose problems are specifically linguistic (288).

Coles labels the motivation behind most LD research "misdirected thinking" which has led to "a fundamental misunderstanding of children's difficulties" (Coles 1987, 15). What he does not explain, however, is how anyone can "misunderstand" what even Coles admits no one really understands: "Little is known about the neurological and mental processes involved in successful learning —indeed, how any child actually learns to read remains, on the whole, something of a mystery—" (xiv). Curiously, this statement is not fundamentally different from a rarely cited opinion by Samuel Orton, the man usually thought of as being totally opposed to Coles philosophically. Orton said that specific reading difficulties could be due to "both the hereditary tendency and the environmental forces which are brought to play on the individual" (Orton 1966, 127).

Interestingly, both Coles and Orton recognize the possibility that learning disability may be a construct of *both* an inborn difference *and* the individual's social experiences. From these assumptions, each man heads in extreme and opposite directions. However, when these more moderate views of Coles' and Orton's are carefully studied, it would seem that they are not as far apart in philosophy as condensations of their work often make them appear. Writing instructors wishing to explore the LD field should not rely on secondhand summaries of either Coles' or Orton's work but should read for themselves from a variety of sources before dismissing or embracing any recommendations.

IQ and the Discrepancy Model of Diagnosis

There has been much debate recently both in LD journals and in general interest publications regarding the diagnostic procedures for LD. If there is one element common to most definitions, it is the discrepancy between intelligence quotient and linguistic achievement. Only children of average or above-average intelligence who have trouble reading are eligible to be called dyslexic. The disability must be *specific* if it is to be called dyslexia. That is, if a child is below average in intelligence and has trouble reading, or if the cognitive disability seems to affect the child's performance regarding other tasks, then he or she might be labeled something else, but not LD. In addition, IQ testing of young children presents some methodological problems similar to those discussed in regard to clinical research. Children wary of what they view as a strange or threatening testing atmosphere may score poorly on IQ tests, not because they *cannot* answer correctly but because they *will* not. Unless test administrators are alert enough to distinquish between valid and less valid test results, children with misleadingly low IQ scores may be slotted into a disastrously inappropriate educational track.

Kenneth A. Kavale and James H. Reese (1992) discuss further the problems inherent in the discrepancy model of LD diagnosis. As has been seen, LD students are supposedly of average or above-average intelligence. But, what happens if a student falls a few points below the numerical gauge of average intelligence or has a gap not quite severe enough to meet the discrepancy requirements? As Kavale and Reese point out, since scores are recognized by most professionals as being inexact, it makes sense to include students just short of the cutoff points in order to provide educational resources that may greatly improve their skills (81.) On the other hand, if cutoffs and categories are too fluid, it blurs the distinction between "real" LD students and people who simply cannot read well. This blurring is what several researchers are presently discovering. As many have observed, the point spread between expected and actual reading achievement can vary widely from state to state, with some school districts strictly adhering to an "average" IQ and a strict discrepancy cutoff, while other districts, so as not to deny services to borderline students on the basis of somewhat arbitrary numbers, include students with below-average IQ's or with discrepancies not strictly within prescribed boundaries.

The results of Yale research on LD diagnosis and the comments about it overflowed from professional journals to appear in several general-interest publications. John Rennie in *Scientific American* (1992) and Geoffrey Cowley in *Newsweek* (1992) discuss the work of Sally Shaywitz, who claims that poor readers cannot be reliably distinguished from LD students, and that all poor readers, labeled or not, display similar problems such as difficulties with phonological processing. Shaywitz would like to see help available to all poor readers, not just to those who meet what she views as an arbitrary discrepancy gap. Other experts disagree with her, objecting to her subject selection and other methodological procedures. As Anne Marshall Huston points out in a letter in the *Chronicle of Higher Education*, LD diagnosis ideally includes more than a simple discrepancy between the scores of two tests (1992, B7). In practice, however, whether or not an individual is labeled LD is heavily dependent on IQ score.

Based on her own research and on her analysis of other studies, Linda S. Siegel, of the Ontario Institute for Studies in Education, concludes that dyslexic children and poor readers differ only in IQ, not in reading behaviors. As did Shaywitz, Siegel says that regardless of diagnosis, poor readers experience similar phonological processing problems (1992, 618). That is, they have trouble recognizing sounds from the phonemes contained in words. To put it more simply, they have trouble sounding out words. Siegel would instead prefer that a reading disability diagnosis be based solely on reading score, with no special category for dyslexics (627). While Keith Stanovich has some objections to Siegel's conclusions, he agrees with her basic findings that it is very difficult to show differences between LD students and plain old poor readers. He questions the judgment to withhold specialized reading instruction from students who might fall a few points below the number line drawn regarding amount of discrepancy needed for LD labeling. Stanovich, who would rather examine discrepancies between listening comprehension and reading comprehension, says it is "nothing short of astounding" to use IQ scores, themselves so controversial, in diagnosing LD (1989a, 487).

As might be expected, Siegel's conclusions, published in a special series in the *Journal of Learning Disabilities* regarding the IQ controversy, have also sparked sharp disagreement. Peter G. Cole, of Edith Cowan University in Australia, takes issue with Siegel, contending that if the IQ discrepancy model is no longer used, then mentally retarded students could be labeled LD (1993, 9). Peter Cole's objection itself raises a serious ethical issue. Who would object if students with below-average intelligence could benefit from reading instruction intended for their officially more intelligent peers and designed to address problems with phonological coding? If IQ measurements are themselves controversial and inexact, then all categories blur to some extent, including *mentally retarded*, which by definition excludes students from LD labeling and designated funding. While mentally retarded groups are entitled to different government funds, one wonders if any amount of money could possibly compensate for the negative stigma associated with that category.

The LD label is in many ways a failed attempt to spare some children the discrimination against retarded people that is blithely accepted in this society. LD students endlessly fight the stereotype that they are "stupid." They are well aware of how this culture views mentally retarded children. Although providing "special" schools or programs for "special" children was intended to help them, and there are unquestionably professionals in those fields who do a heroic job doing that, the categorizing of our children has overall deficits so severe that any good this system is doing may not be able to override them. Students so isolated, whether categorized as LD or as something even less accepted in society, are ostracized academically and socially, while "regular" children are made to feel superior to these other children and learn nothing about what integration with them might teach. It may be time to remove all the labels and treat everyone the way we would all want to be treated— like normal people. Parents wary of such an inclusive mainstream may fear that their "gifted and talented" children will function only as tutors to LD or retarded (gasp!) youngsters. There are, of course, stories of how extremely disabled or disturbed children, when "dumped" into a regular class, disrupt learning for everyone, especially when there is inadequate training for teachers. There are also stories of how inclusion has demonstrated that all children have much to teach each other about the perspective, the creativity, and the talents to be found beyond linguistic skills.[3]

The present education system, in spite of serious, enduring questions about intelligence measurements, insists on sorting, separating, and labeling all students based on those measurements. Those with the lowest IQ scores are the groups most isolated in restrictive environments—resource rooms, special education classes, or even different buildings from those in which "regular" classes are held. This practice is no doubt directly responsible for much of the ridicule and rejection many youngsters must endure, and it is nothing short of appalling that so little effort is made to help "normal" children and their parents understand the normalcy of "special" children.

Ostracizing children socially and educationally from the mainstream is what recent legislation was intended to prevent, by requiring that LD students be placed in the "least restrictive environment." That is, they are to be included as much as possible in regular classes and receive only those special services that specifically "meet their needs." However, the people who most often decide what constitutes this least restrictive environment are specialists with an arguably vested interest in the concept of LD labeling and special services. This is not to single out one group of professionals. Advocates of mainstreaming may have vested interests in having students mainstreamed. No one is immune, including the author of this book, from advocating for students what may indirectly benefit themselves. There is a dangerous cycle regarding LD, however, in that what may harm students the most may be both expensive and well intentioned: restriction and isolation in the form of "special" services. On the other hand, without these services, many LD students who are barely coping now with a reading-based education system might fail altogether.

It would be better to change the mainstream than to continue the divide-and-treat-differently model that has developed—for mostly noble reasons—in recent decades. Even as I argue for more inclusionary classrooms, I am not arguing that we teach all students in the same way or make the binary leap in thinking that because diagnosing LD is such a tricky business, we therefore should conclude that LD does not exist. We must not simply and comfortably adopt, or return to, pedagogical models of reading and writing based on theories that all human beings naturally and easily intuit linguistic processing skills. While we need to mainstream, we also need to change the mainstream—to make it wide enough to accommodate tributaries from diverse terrain, and to remove unnecessary boulders so that all can flow through it more smoothly. To divert what may be some of its most creative elements weakens the flow and constricts what might be productive meanderings until it dries to an overfiltered trickle. We need to make general education flexible enough, broad enough, and creative enough to challenge all students, regardless of IQ measurements.

Now is an ideal time to alter the mainstream in these ways. Writing across the curriculum, in spite of funding problems, is evolving toward more sophisticated concepts of critical thinking and discourse analysis, and is having an influence throughout educational levels. This results in more collaboration between faculty and students in different disciplines, which can only further communication and exploration of discipline-specific, as well as individualized, ways of knowing.

Summary

In summary, experts disagree with each other or are admittedly baffled by the causes and manifestations of learning disabilities. However, in spite of the varying and problematic definitions, and the conflicting and often outlandish reasons given to explain it, I believe there exists for some people a learning difference in regard to linguistic symbols that is a real phenomenon. Its nature and cause remain inexplicable.

If it is even partly true that normal, intelligent people sometimes think or process language differently, then writing teachers may want to rethink current practices that are based on what is believed to be the learning process of the majority, but not this minority. Trouble with written language becomes a "disability" only in a society that values a certain kind of literacy. To insist that everyone think the same way is to truncate the thoughts of those who may be the most creative people. In describing his experiences as a dyslexic child, Donald Lyman speaks of a "lost world" of "wordless memories" (1986, 27). His trouble, he says, was with symbols: "This was my learning disability—an inability to make sense of a representational world, a world in which an object as named was more important than the object itself" (28). Bernard Patten, rather than labeling dyslexia a deficiency, calls it a "visual form of thinking," which he sees as a possible improvement over "auditory" forms. He observes, "Our present verbally oriented schools should not prevent geniuses with visual or other forms of thinking from achieving their full potential. Indeed, the total thinking power of even an average person can also be expanded" (1978, 224). In other words, the dyslexic's "difficulties" may be unrecognized assets. This is, of course, an extreme view of what dyslexia entails, but it raises interesting questions about privileging in our schools what might be called a "linguisto-centric" view of thinking.

Why is this controversy important to college composition instructors? First, the proliferation of reading and writing research notwithstanding, there is certainly enough disagreement in the field to keep the question open as to whether neurological differences might account for linguistic difficulties in children and in adults. Second, estimates of people who might have this difference in learning vary so widely that we cannot afford to ignore the numbers of adults who may be showing up in college composition classes. While occasional general interest articles put the dyslexic population at close to 20 percent, most experts say that is much too high a figure. A 1993 pamphlet distributed by the National Institute for Mental Health says that between 2 and 8 percent of children are dyslexic. Frank Vellutino (1990) believes that between 1 and 5 percent of children are what he calls "different" in how they learn to read. Even the most vehement critics of the LD field do not totally rule out a neurological difference.

Marie Clay, who dismisses most claims of learning disability by emphasizing the role of appropriate instruction, recognizes that some small portion of the population may indeed be different: "Diagnostic teaching can reduce the number of readers who become disorganized because their experiences have been inadequate for their needs, and *then we can discover the nature of the residual group of children who may perhaps be organically impaired*" (my emphasis, 1972, 161). And Gerald Coles, who has written most prolifically about the problems of LD empirical research concerning neurological difference, admits "there is a modicum of evidence suggesting that a very small portion of the children identified as learning disabled do have some degree of neurological dysfunction that may interfere with learning and academic achievement" (1978, xvii). It is precisely because experts in this field are so opposed, and opinions are as strong as they are divided, that composition specialists need to join the fray. Even if only one student—a member of what Clay calls that "residual group" who may have a difference in learning not related to dialect, social class, or educational background—appears in a composition class, the instructor owes it to that student to be informed. We need to read widely, to argue, and to conduct our own research.

As will be discussed in Chapter Two, writing instructors are not sufficiently prepared, either in graduate school or through their professional affiliations, to sort through the impassioned rhetoric of the LD controversy. The Works Cited section in this book reveals only a small portion of the material written about the learning disability field. Composition specialists cannot be expected to explore thoroughly all aspects of this complicated subject. However, one danger of relying on thumbnail summaries or critiques of Orton's theories, is that they will reflect the speaker's enthusiasm or scorn for the ideas being discussed. A neutral position about serious issues is, of course, virtually impossible for anyone to achieve. In order to form an educated opinion on the LD issue and to discover how it may impact on their teaching, composition specialists are encouraged to read from different sources, to talk with different people, and to form their own interpretations. They need to listen both carefully and critically to people from a variety of fields, and they need to trust their students' experiences as learners and their own experience as teachers.

Notes

1. The conference, entitled "Higher Education for Persons With Disabilities: Challenges and Opportunities," was sponsored by the University of the State of New York and the New York State Education Department. It was held at Empire State Plaza, Albany, New York, November 30, 1993.

2. "Reading Problems Tied to a Deficit of Timing in Visual Pathways." *New York Times,* 13 April 1993.

3. For newspaper reports reflecting different views of mainstreaming or inclusion, see the following:

Bryce, Jill. "Special Education Pupils Mix Well into Mainstream Classes." *Daily Gazette* (Schenectady, NY), 20 June 1994.

Fallick, Dawn. "Inclusion: How Inclusive? Placement of Special Ed Students in Regular Classes Raises Complicated Issues for All." *The Record* (Troy, NY), 3 July 1994.

――――. "Special Education Students Not Only Ones Affected: Critics: Gifted Students Being Slowed." *The Record* (Troy, NY), 5 July 1994.

――――. "Including Children Makes Dollars, Sense for School Districts." *The Record* (Troy, NY), 6 July 1994.

――――."Inclusion: Everyone Helps Everyone." *The Record* (Troy, NY), 4 July 1994.

――――. "Troy: Teachers 'Extremely Pleased' With Mixed Classes." *The Record* (Troy, NY), 4 July 1994.

Chapter Two

Gaps in Composition Theory and Practice

Any discussion of Composition Studies and learning disabilities should be contextualized by a brief look at the historical developments in both fields. In the previous chapter, we saw how clinical research in reading and learning disabilities has explored the prevailing belief, promoted by Samuel Orton, that reading difficulties are caused primarily by dysfunctions in children. Preoccupation with brain hemisphere differences and visual acuity left little room for the possibility of inadequate educational opportunity and inappropriate reading instruction as causes for reading failure. Today people such as Gerald Coles, James Carrier, Marie Clay, Peter Johnston, and others, view the traditional LD field as one which overemphasized neurological differences at the expense of what they see as very strong sociological and educational forces shaping children's desire and opportunity to read. Indeed, these neurological differences continue to be emphasized by proponents of the structured pedagogies of Orton-Gillingham offshoots such as DIS-TAR, Slingerland, Lindamood, and Alphabetic Phonics. (See Chapter Three.) Those who rightly point to the sociological and educational barriers that some children have had to contend with often feel they are placing themselves against the historical grain of reading research.

Oddly enough, Composition Studies, a younger field, provides a kind of mirror image to the reading field in that it has traditionally concentrated on social differences. It has had its share of empirical research, of course, but most influential voices—Shaughnessy, Britton, Berthoff, Freire, Rose, Shor, Elbow, Macrorie—have in various ways concentrated on sociological, rather than neurological, approaches to writing. As Stephen North observes in *The Making of*

Knowledge in Composition (1987), the large group he calls the Experimentalist community "has not exercised anything like a proportionate influence on the field" (144). Although there have been well-known studies such as Britton's *The Development of Writing Abilities*, North believes its influence was due more to its "philosophical underpinnings" than to its results (145). North sees Elbow and Berthoff as being highly influential in the composition field, as is Shaughnessy, though he believes "her attitude is more valuable than any of her findings *per se*" (53). As will be seen in this chapter, graduate school programs in composition have those names high on their required reading lists.

Although these writers may be vastly different in their philosophies, none of them considers neurological learning difference as an explanation for writing development. For Shaughnessy, poor writing is primarily a function of inexperience and lack of proper opportunity, instruction, and practice—all sociological factors. For Britton, poor writing can be overcome by using personal, expressive writing as a way toward a more authoritative, academic voice. For Elbow, writers' inhibitions and blocks can be overcome by freewriting, practice, and peer-group responses. These are, of course, somewhat reductive views of these influential figures, but whatever their various approaches, not one of them seriously considers neurologically based processing differences in people.

This is not a criticism of their work. Traditionally, Composition Studies has not dealt with learning disabilities, and these specialists are merely reflecting what have been the main concerns of the field, focusing on the "normal" student. Those first-year students whose writing exhibits qualities radical enough to be obvious in entrance exams or placement essays are often sent to remedial programs outside the jurisdiction of English departments. For many reasons, then, most people in Composition Studies are not directly exposed to the LD controversy presented in Chapter One.

The first half of this chapter will show what Composition Studies *does* say about learning disabilities, first highlighting the concerns of the mainstream Composition field—what is studied in its graduate programs, written about in its journals, and discussed at its national conferences. It will show that although LD is mentioned occasionally, the idea of neurological difference to explain writing difficulties is rarely discussed in detail. This chapter will also provide an overview of what might be called a subset of Composition Studies: basic writing. In the journals that deal with students in this group, the subject of LD has made somewhat more of an inroad, but unless instructors are teaching a basic writing class, they may not have time to read the *Journal of Basic Writing* or the *Journal of*

Developmental Education. Although Composition deals with students at all skill levels, theorists seem most puzzled by "basic writers." Recommendations for this group are usually based on what composition specialists believe is lacking: experience, familiarity with the language, or proper instruction.

If there *is* a language-processing difference, it is likely not be to be addressed. Those few students who are diagnosed LD are generally considered outside the expertise of composition specialists and within the domain of those with masters or doctorates in learning disabilities. However, real life is not always so tidy that LD students appear neatly in the classrooms and offices of LD specialists. Recently, more of these students are showing up in first-year writing classes and may or may not wish to be segregated from their peers. If even one LD student is a member of a college writing class, mainstream or basic, then Composition as a field should educate itself about the needs of that student. The second half of this chapter will examine the theoretical assumptions underpinning the practice of some of Composition's most influential voices—Shaughnessy, Bartholomae, Berthoff, and others—and show what gaps remain in those assumptions.

Graduate School Preparation, Conference Topics, and Professional Journals

One way to predict what books and articles have shaped present mainstream college writing teachers' theories and practices regarding Composition (and LD) is to see what books and articles they were exposed to while in the process of obtaining their degrees. Although many English professors undoubtedly extend their reading interests beyond the required texts of their graduate school days, it is safe to assume that what they read and discussed then continues to influence what they presently think and write about Composition Studies.

Richard L. Graves and Harry M. Soloman, in an article that appeared in *Freshman English News* in the spring of 1980, summarize the results of a survey they did of the texts used nationally in colleges and universities to prepare students to teach college writing courses. In "New Graduate Courses in Rhetoric and Composition: A National Survey," they point out the proliferation of new curricula in basic writing, and they observe what a cursory reading of basic writing materials will also reveal: "New courses in basic writing are a testimony to the influence of one person and one book. The person is Mina Shaughnessy; the book is *Errors and Expectations* "(4). Their survey also revealed that most Composition and Rhetoric programs listed the following writers as being important: James Moffett, Janet Emig, Edward P.J. Corbett, James Britton, Ken Macrorie, Charles Cooper and Lee Odell, Aristotle, and Cicero.

In its spring/summer issues of 1981 and 1984, the *Journal of Basic Writing* published two special editions in which distinguished professors and administrators from representative institutions wrote about their programs and included required reading lists. Virtually every article listed Mina Shaughnessy's *Errors and Expectations* as being required reading for graduate students in Composition and Rhetoric. Since Shaughnessy's book does deal with basic writers but does not address dyslexia or learning disability, it is not surprising that composition teachers graduating from programs so heavily influenced by her work should know very little about the LD field.

Among the programs described in these two issues of the *Journal of Basic Writing* are the doctoral programs in Composition and Rhetoric at Wayne State University, Queens College, University of Louisville, University of Massachusetts, Ohio State University, Penn State, University of Iowa, and Idaho State University. They all list basically the same readings, attesting to the influence of Shaughnessy, Elbow, Britton, Emig, Macrorie, Moffett, Vygotsky, and Bartholomae (especially Bartholomae's "The Study of Error"). In addition to listing specific full-length texts, most programs also recommend that their students read individual essays published in the major composition journals such as *College English, College Composition and Communication (CCC)*, and occasionally the *Journal of Basic Writing*. Although the authors of these essays point out the importance of writing teachers being cognizant of Black English vernacular, Aristotle's works, Shaughnessy's and Bartholomae's versions of error analysis, and a cognitive theory of process writing, nowhere do they consider learning differences.

The theories and research emphasized in Composition and Rhetoric graduate schools are, not surprisingly, reflected in the session topics at the professional conferences and in journal articles, a brief look at which confirms how much (and how little) those in Composition Studies know about the LD controversy. The following two works demonstrate the sometimes opposite approaches taken by writing teachers faced with a problem totally foreign to them.

At the 1978 Conference on College Composition and Communication (CCCC), Alan S. Loxterman spoke about learning disabilities in his presentation, "College Composition and the Invisible Handicap." One of his students, John, received poor grades in English because his writing was filled with spelling errors. He was sent to a writing lab for programmed instruction via filmstrips and tapes. Although he reportedly improved somewhat, he still received a poor final grade because of his errors. In another case, Norman Lavers (1981) wrote in *College English* about a student he encountered who made excessive spelling errors. Lavers read what he could about dyslexia, but when he discovered "a vast and contradictory literature," he dismissed the traditional view and set out to find "the mechanisms of what my evidence told me was the neurotic source of the particular spelling disability I was dealing with" (713). After consulting with a psychoanalyst about his student's problems, Lavers came to believe "that some students, especially males, unconsciously develop this problem to covertly express aggression against parents" (714). This teacher's solution was simply to ignore the spelling errors, an approach he claimed was effective. Neither one of these essays provides enough information about the students' work to determine whether or not they improved. The two examples, however, illustrate the frustration, bordering on desperation, that composition instructors may feel when confronted with surface errors of the magnitude LD writers can produce. Whether they send students to a programmed writing lab or subject them to Freudian analysis, it is clear that these two composition instructors knew little about what to do or where to turn for help.

An informal examination of recent Conference on College Composition and Communication (CCCC) programs demonstrates that learning disabilities have received little attention. Most experts on LD present not at CCCC but at the Orton Dyslexia Society's conference, usually scheduled in March. Ironically, in 1990, several professionals writing extensively about LD research and teaching practices—Charles A. Perfetti, Keith E. Stanovich, Isabelle Y. Liberman, and Phyllis Bertin—all spoke in New York City on March 22–24, the same dates as the Chicago CCCC.

A sampling of the workshop titles at the 1990 CCCC reveals current interests in the field: "Using the Diversity of the 'Urban Culture' to Teach Reflective Essay Writing to Developmental and Remedial Students"; "Essential Skills and Knowledge for Teaching ESL Students"; and "Valuing Diverse Discourses in Our Classrooms and Professional Journals." Although there are many references to "diversity" and "difference," there are no allusions to learning disabled or dyslexic students as being among those who are different. There is a section for "Basic Writing," but many of the speakers listed in this category assume that all BW students come from *under*privileged social backgrounds. They do not allow for students placed in developmental writing classes because of multitudinous surface errors due to a neurological learning difference.

The 1991 CCCC reveals a similar pattern, although Paula Gills delivered a paper called "Serving the Needs of Linguistically Handicapped Students in the Writing Center: A Challenge for the '90's." And there was one session by Allen Einerson and Adelaide Bingham of the University of Wisconsin, Whitewater entitled, "Again the Issue is Literacy: How Students with Learning Disabilities Perceive Writing." This rare use of the terms "learning disabilities" indicates at least a recognition of the syndrome. The 1992 and 1993 programs had a section on "Diversity," but LD was not mentioned in any of the listed papers. Under "Basic Writing," in the 1993 program, Nancy R. Ives had a paper called "Learning Disabled Students in the Composition Classroom." Among other things such as process writing, collaboration, computer training, and sentence-combining instruction, Ives recommends a peer tutoring system in which the tutor is in a Special Education or other teacher-training or writing program.

At the 1994 CCCC in Nashville, there seemed to be a slight increase in interest in LD-related topics. The program had a new category called "Issues of Difference," in which at least four papers in the eighteen sessions listed dealt with LD in some way. Kathleen A. Patterson had a paper called "Teaching Disability Studies in the Freshman Composition Classroom." Sue Fisher Vaughn's presentation, "The Impact of the Americans with Disabilities Act of 1990 (ADA) on the Writing Class," focused on accommodations used by her students, among them the use of peer partners. Linda Houston's presentation on learning differences, however, spoke of one LD student who did not work with peer tutors because he felt they did not understand his frustration. He would instead voice tape his paper and revise and edit orally. In the discussion that followed Houston's presentation, it was pointed out that for many LD students whose primary mode of functioning is through dialogue, the typical classroom's emphasis on being quiet and listening hinders their progress. Anne Mullin's presentation, "Of All Places: Students with Learning Disabilities in the Writing Center," included a list of resources, a checklist of typical signs of LD, and advice for LD students from her colleague Liz Scheid on strategies for reading, writing, note-taking, etc. In the days and weeks following the Nashville conference, many Internet users requested copies of Mullin's handouts. While the proportion of papers on this subject was still minuscule, this noticeable increase in attention to LD at the 1994 CCCC may be a reflection of the 1990 ADA's becoming effective, or it may be a result of the high number of students labeled in the 1980s beginning to show up as first-year college students. The 1995 CCCC proposal form has an area cluster called "Writing and Difference," in which are included issues of race, ethnicity, class, gender, orientation, language, and nationality—but not learning difference. At the 1995 CCCC in Washington D. C., Anne Mullin spoke about the use of color-coded felt pieces and other forms of "non-verbal representation" designed to help LD students with their writing. She credited Linda Hecker and others at Landmark College for their work with these objects, called "manipulatives." Unfortunately, the approximately four minutes allowed for Mullin's presentation in the new forum format did not give her much time to elaborate.[1]

Probably the best gauge of a profession's interest in a topic is what appears in its journals. Here, LD fares better than at conferences, but those Composition professors attempting to learn about LD from their own journals would not obtain a thorough view of the subject. Very occasionally there will be an article such as Carolyn O'Hearn's "Recognizing the Learning Disabled College Writer" in *College English* (1989), which laments "the absence of scholarship in this area" (295), but most pieces on basic writers in this professional journal, if they are included at all, deal primarily with the social background of this group.

Not long ago, when LD summaries occasionally appeared in Composition journals, the authors usually related their surprise at discovering the existence of legislation that bars discrimination against students with any kind of handicapping condition. Alan Rose, in his article, "Specific Learning Disabilities, Federal Law, and Departments of English," which appeared in the fall 1986 *ADE Bulletin*, quotes from the U.S. Code and discusses what it might mean in college English departments. He expresses a concern that accommodation for LD students not result in a lowering of academic standards (26–29).

Two people in Composition Studies who are recognized as experts in basic writing, Mike Rose and Andrea Lunsford, have had articles on that topic published in major NCTE journals, but neither one mentions brain research being done in learning disabilities or comments by students describing the instability of letters or words as they attempt to internalize them. In "Remedial Writing Courses: A Critique and a Proposal" (1983), Mike Rose refers to an article on learning disability which appeared in a 1975 issue of the *Journal of Basic Writing*: Patricia Laurence's "Error's Endless Train: Why Students Don't Perceive Errors." He mentions some of the reasons Laurence gives pertaining to why students cannot find their own errors, but someone reading only Rose's summary would have no idea that Laurence's article was about learning disabilities, nor would they see her reference to Katrina De Hirsch's research involving students whose envisioning of words is unstable (Laurence 1975, 32).

In an article in *CCC*, "Narrowing the Mind and Page: Remedial Writers and Cognitive Reductionism" (1988), Rose critiques, among other theories, what he calls "hemisphericity" (277). He claims that EEG studies are inconclusive and should not be used to make sweeping generalizations concerning whether people are primarily left-brained or right-brained. While he acknowledges neurological research that establishes "different areas of the brain contribute to different aspects of human cognition" (275), he points out the methodologically problematic areas of brain research, suggesting that it could be "culturally biased" (295) (but so, of course, is one field's critique of another field's research methods). Rose's summary, in a well-known composition journal, provides information on neurological research that college writing teachers are unlikely to encounter in their usual professional reading. He wisely cautions against using ambiguous, sometimes biased research results to create reductive categories regarding types of writers. His main purpose is an admirable one—to turn attention to individual students' texts in order to analyze their thought processes more accurately. The problem, however, is that instructors reading about neurological research exclusively in Rose's summary will get the general impression that such research is not really worth investigating. The interesting possibilities of such research, however flawed it might be, are not probed. He does not explore what it might mean that different parts of the brain *do* handle different tasks, nor does he encourage instructors to do so.

Andrea Lunsford, in a *College English* article, "Cognitive Development and the Basic Writer," acknowledges Mina Shaughnessy's influence on her and limits her discussion of cognitive research to Vygotsky, Piaget, Odell, Chomsky, and Britton. Lunsford makes no distinction between basic writers and learning disabled students (neither did Shaughnessy), and to remediate them, she recommends (as did Shaughnessy) simply more practice (1979, 41). In *College Composition and Communication*, Lunsford has another article, "The Content of Basic Writers' Essays." While Lunsford recognizes that the writing of these students is often more interesting, albeit fraught with errors, than the sometimes sterile texts of "normal" students, she nevertheless views basic writers as somehow being more limited than other students. She ends her essay with a quote from Wittgenstein, which she says applies to basic writers: "The limits of my language are the limits of my world" (1980, 288). Lunsford's assumptions about her students' "limits"—ideas published in major journals read by composition teachers and graduate students—may be assumptions which subtly limit what writing instructors believe their students can do.

In the January, 1990 issue of *College English*, Paul Hunter has a review of recent texts, all of which critique the LD field. In "Learning Disabilities: New Doubts, New Inquiries," Hunter gives a positive response to the views offered by Gerald Coles, James G. Carrier, Kenneth A. Kavale and Steven R. Forness, whose works ridicule the "socially created facts of the LD field" (94). Although these texts have already been discussed in the Chapter One, it is important to note here that anyone reading only Hunter's review of this material and not the three books themselves, the vast amount of LD material they critique, or the reading field's response to these critiques, would certainly come away from this single article in *College English* with a very limited view of learning disabilities. In the Comment and Response section of the February 1991 issue of *College English*, Patricia J. McAlexander takes issue with Hunter's review of those three texts. She especially objects to Hunter's claim that Carrier, Coles, and Kavale and Forness "dismantle virtually every fact [he] had ever read about learning disabilities." She says, "the 'dismantling' of the LD field is not as great as the review suggests." Further, "the four authors do not as fully reject a neurological basis for learning disabilities as might be assumed from the review" (224). To challenge Hunter's claim that the sociological aspect of LD is new, McAlexander points to Vygotsky's work, which years ago took that into account. (As discussed in the previous chapter, even Samuel Orton considered social factors in his analysis of a student's predicament.) Finally, McAlexander calls for English teachers to "maintain a middle position between the two extreme reactions of defensiveness or sudden disbelief in learning disabilities" (225).

Also in a 1990 issue of *College English* was an interesting essay called "Of Brains and Rhetorics," by Jeffrey Walker. He summarizes brain research of the twentieth century, relating it to what neurologists say about language and thinking and how that relates to rhetoricians. Contrasting the neurological research of the 1970s with the most recent research, Walker reports that traditional left- and right-brain theories are usually reductive, and that the brain really utilizes both sides (308). In other words, it is too simplistic to say that one side of the brain handles creativity and the other handles logic. At the same time, however, other beliefs about left- and right-brain functioning have held up. The relegation of the speech cortex to the left side has been supported by current research, as has the traditional theory that damage to the left hemisphere results in aphasia. Walker points out the importance of brain research to those who teach writing, but cautions those reading neurological reports to do so with skepticism because any results are "frequently ambiguous" and "still fraught with methodological and interpretive problems" (315). Walker's is one of the few essays in *College English* that deals with brain research. Therefore, his view of the issue is likely to influence many of that journal's readers, especially if they read no further. However, writing instructors should not rely exclusively on Walker's perceptions of such work and should judge for themselves continuing neurological research outside Composition. For example, in a 1992 *Scientific American* special issue devoted to the mind and brain, neuroscientists Antonio and Hanna Damasio explain that while language processes involve both sides of the brain, it is primarily the left hemisphere that handles phonetic and syntactic structures (89)—a point that may be relevant in error analyses and other aspects of Composition Studies.

Research in the Teaching of English (RTE), an NCTE quarterly, regularly publishes a lengthy annotated bibliography (Durst and Marshall 1988, 434–52). Although this annotated bibliography concerns itself with research that has to do with the teaching of writing, it does not include LD studies that might impact on how writing teachers perceive differences in their students. Included in this list of works are many studies of a sociological nature and research regarding the effect of family life on academic progress. One such example is Gene Frank LoPresti's 1987 dissertation, "Four Basic Skills Students: A Naturalistic Study of Reading/Writing Models They Bring to College." LoPresti blames parents and former teachers for students' low-level linguistic skills: "The study . . . revealed how home environment can inadvertently encourage behavior antithetical to academic success . . ." (585A). He does not raise the possibility of a learning difference. In the 1988 *RTE* annotated bibliography, there are several projects concerning basic writers, but they are not differentiated from LD or dyslexic students. Those terms are not used. Although many studies from this issue of the *RTE* Annotated Bibliography on Research in the Teaching of English could be listed, suffice it to say that some research arguably vital to the study of composition and/or basic writing, the research done in the LD field, is not included.

One would expect to find more essays on learning disabilities in those journals that deal specifically with basic writers or remedial writing programs. The *Journal of Basic Writing* contains, obviously, many more essays about basic writers than do *College English*, *College Composition and Communication*, and *Research in the Teaching of English*. Graduate students and composition teachers who limit their professional reading to *CE*, *CCC*, and *RTE*, would have missed the following articles in the *Journal of Basic Writing (JBW)* which might concern a number of their students.

In 1985, Frank Parker had a summary of the LD controversy in his essay, "Dyslexia: An Overview." In it, he gives typical problems evidenced by dyslexic students and explains that the deficit is a linguistic rather than a perceptual problem. He summarizes Vellutino's research, as well as that of Geschwind, Liberman, and other LD experts whose work appears in publications *not* likely to be read by teachers of writing: *Advances in Neurology, Journal of Verbal Learning and Verbal Behavior, British Journal of Educational Psychology, Journal of Educational Psychology, Educational Research, Cortex, Science,* etc. Also in the *Journal of Basic Writing* is Amy Richards' essay, "College Composition: Recognizing the Learning Disabled Writer" (1985), which summarizes ways of using error analysis to distinguish between writers who are simply inexperienced and those who are truly learning disabled. In this same journal is an essay by Patricia J. McAlexander and Noel Gregg, "The Roles of English Teachers and LD Specialists in Identifying Learning Disabled Writers: Two Case Studies" (1989). Although many people who write for the *Journal of Basic Writing*, the *Journal of Learning Disabilities*, and the *Journal of Developmental Education* speak at the Orton conference, McAlexander and Gregg presented a portion of the material from this article at the 1989 CCCC in Seattle. However, there it was included as part of a panel entitled "The Challenge of Problem Spellers."[2]

One influential writer whose work appeared in the *Journal of Basic Writing* is David Bartholomae. His important essay, "The Study of Error," was published in *CCC*, won the 1981 Richard Braddock Award, and is cited second only to Shaughnessy's *Errors and Expectations* in the Composition and Rhetoric graduate programs as the most recommended piece on basic writing. Bartholomae's influence in Composition Studies is further demonstrated by the fact that he delivered the keynote address at the opening general session of the 1988 CCCC convention. In "Teaching Basic Writing: An Alternative to Basic Skills," Bartholomae's essay that appeared in the spring/summer 1979 issue of the *Journal of Basic Writing*, he criticizes what he calls the "basic skills pedagogy" of most remedial writing classes and refers to error as sometimes indicating growth (88). Bartholomae states at the beginning, "This paper draws heavily on Mina Shaughnessy's work" (86), and like Shaughnessy, Bartholomae seems to realize that there might be something going on that prevents some students from "manipulating a pen" as easily as others. However, Bartholomae never introduces the idea of a linguistic processing problem, other than to mention "the few who are learning disabled," a condition he never defines or explains. There is, of course, a danger in classifying students according to the kinds of errors they make, especially since "learning disability" and "dyslexia" remain in some sense hypothetical phenomena. But to exclude them from discussions of error analysis is possibly to exclude from help those students, even if they are only a few, who make the "bizarre" errors no one has yet satisfactorily explained. For that matter, it is to exclude— even as a possibility—the chance that there are more such students than we have traditionally believed.

The *Journal of Basic Writing*, although not as well-known as *College English* and *CCC*, is still read by many college writing teachers, especially those who teach basic writing. Since some essays on learning disabilities do appear in *JBW*, at least those who occasionally scan that publication would have some background on LD. Even further out on the periphery of Composition Studies is the *Journal of Developmental Education*, in which writing teachers would find articles such as Belinda D. Lazarus' "Serving LD Students in Postsecondary Settings" (1989). In it she quotes from Public Law 93-112, which states that "all postsecondary institutions benefiting from federal funds must provide equal access to educational programs for all persons regardless of their handicapping condition" (2). She explains the implications of this law regarding college writing courses, and provides a summary of practical instructional alternatives and evaluation accommodations for LD students in composition classes. Unlike Bartholomae, Lazarus makes a clear distinction between developmental students and those who are learning disabled (3).

An important essay for all composition teachers appears in the *Journal of Developmental Education*: Judith A. Longo's "The Learning Disabled: Challenge to Postsecondary Institutions" (1988). Another branch of the LD controversy is evident here. Longo points to what she sees as the "incurable" aspect of LD, in the hope of eliminating repetitive, traditional teaching methods she claims will not work. This "permanent" diagnosis of LD, however, is what others view as especially problematic. Peter Johnston and Richard Allington suggest that such a diagnosis may by itself discourage students, slotting them in a destructive, self-fulfilling role of failure (1991, 999). As we will see in Chapter Four, however, some students find the LD label somewhat encouraging because it helps them understand their frustrations in a reading-based educational system. Longo (1988) also cites comments from questionnaires filled out by college writing instructors revealing their ignorance of learning disability and their associating it with a lower level of intelligence. One professor said, "We cannot allow everyone into college—the integrity of the B.A. degree cannot be challenged." Wrote another, "I am trained to teach bright students, not handicapped ones" (14)—note the binary opposition, with "handicapped" juxtaposed to "bright." Longo points out the effect such thinking can have on teachers' expectations and students' self-esteem (14).

Although Shaughnessy, Lunsford, and Bartholomae write frequently about basic writing classes, and their articles appear not only in basic writing journals but also in the more well-known NCTE publications, those articles do not include many references to neurological research or the depth of the controversy surrounding it. Composition instructors have not been sufficiently exposed, either in their graduate training or in their professional reading and conferences, to the critical issues in the LD controversy, except in what is usually a cursory, dismissive way. They have not been sufficiently encouraged to learn more about LD, to conduct their own investigations, or to collaborate with others and pool their professional resources.

It may be time for composition specialists to learn more about what admittedly may be only a handful of students per semester who have a learning disability or difference. Even the latter term is not neutral because *different* means *not normal.* Although we can never eliminate semantic implications when attempting to discuss this small group of students, perhaps we need to expand our definition of normal to include those whose intelligence is not primarily linguistically based. Even though the LD field is a bottomless ocean into which composition specialists have rarely ventured, we may need to get our feet wet, since we *do* claim to know about "basic writers," and we know that influential people have attributed their problems to defects in experience, opportunity, or inclination. We need a theory to account for those few students whose writing or reading problems cannot be fully explained by environmental factors. Granted, we may not find an ideal way to test, teach, or even name such students, but we owe it to them to track down every clue available about learning. We need to examine theories, however controversial, put forth by those in other disciplines. A more detailed analysis of the views of selected Composition professionals will show how their theoretical assumptions attempt, but fail, to account for the problems of *all* students.

Theoretical Assumptions

This section examines the theoretical assumptions of those experts who, for various reasons, seem most to represent contemporary writing theory. Mina Shaughnessy's *Errors and Expectations*, a book about "basic writers," is, as I have suggested, the most influential one on that subject. David Bartholomae is, by his own admission, deeply influenced by Shaughnessy, and his essay, "The Study of Error," is cited repeatedly in graduate programs in Rhetoric and Composition. James Britton's and Janet Emig's pioneering studies have greatly affected contemporary research. Ken Macrorie and Peter Elbow are representative of those teachers who endeavor to help students express their individual selves through writing. Elbow's work especially is well-known enough to have reached commercial bookstores. The last part of the section concerns itself with a mix of theorists who, although they may contribute different philosophical or political perspectives, are nevertheless all concerned with the social construction of knowledge and with the power of writing. The theorists included—Ann Berthoff, Lil Brannon and C.H. Knoblauch, Pat Bizzell, and Ira Shor—are all interested in writing as a way of knowing and as a way of changing the world. It is not my purpose here to create rigid categories for Composition theorists. Rather, I want to explore the pedagogical implications of what these influential writers believe about learning.

Mina P. Shaughnessy's 1977 book *Errors and Expectations* is the most comprehensive analysis of student error patterns that exists in the Composition and Rhetoric field. In her perceptive study, Shaughnessy exhibits a sensitivity to the individual differences among "basic writers" (BW), and calls upon teachers to scrutinize student texts not merely to correct errors but to discover *why* the student made a particular series of errors. Because Shaughnessy's work is so comprehensive, and because it has had so much influence on other scholars trying to understand the reasons why students make the errors they do, this section analyzing her work is quite lengthy. What are the reasons Shaughnessy gives for the errors her students make? How do the reasons she finds for the errors affect their remediation? What might learning disability professionals say about the kinds of errors Shaughnessy finds in her students' papers? One of Shaughnessy's main points is that the remediation of an error must be dictated by the reason the student is making it. If there is a gap or a missing link in her analysis of a problem, then there would be a resulting gap in the solution to that problem.

Convinced that students' problems are primarily related to their inexperience as writers, Shaughnessy reiterates this premise throughout her book. Unlike some teachers who blame students' errors on laziness or stupidity, Shaughnessy gives them credit for intelligence and motivation, but says their mistakes are caused mostly by their position as apprentice writers in a sophisticated academic system. She realizes what part the frustrating and sometimes paralyzing

effects of fear and repeated failure might play in the student's problems with writing. She has worked enough with basic writers to
realize something many people still do not: that the number of
sentence-level errors students make can*not* be used as a measure of
their intelligence. Finally, while many composition experts mini-
mize the need for basic writers to focus on grammar and syntax,
Shaughnessy empathizes with those students who feel that they are
controlled by the English code—a feeling probably unfamiliar to
some writing teachers who have possessed for many years an ease
and control of the written language (13). Although this section is a
critique of Shaughnessy's work, a question about what she has *not*
considered in her otherwise comprehensive study, it is also a recognition that hers is a most sensitive, compassionate study of basic
writers and their texts. *Errors and Expectations* is divided into
chapters which address the various error patterns basic writers
make regarding spelling, syntax, vocabulary, and the like. I will be
following a similar format in this section. My aim will be, in each
case, to present first Shaughnessy's analysis of the particular error
pattern, and then to discuss alternative explanations LD experts
might offer.

Shaughnessy concludes, and perhaps rightly so for many students, that the writing instruction given in their former schooling
must have been of poor quality, that the opportunities for writing
must have been infrequent, and that what few occasions existed for
writing must have been "strained" and "artificial." She reports,
however, no investigations involving former teachers or administrators to back her assumptions, no sample course outlines, curricula,
or assignments confirming students' lack of writing experience.
There are no quotations or summaries from interviews with BW
students in which they might have indicated that their past writing
experiences in school were inferior to those, as Shaughnessy
assumes, of more "practiced" students. Although she may indeed
be correct in assuming that inferior teaching accounts for the problems of her basic writers, by viewing her students' writing problems
ever and always through this unsubstantiated premise, she risks
recommending solutions based on "more practice" when that may
not be the entire problem. As we have seen, Shaughnessy's indictment of the teacher as a cause of her student's problems has been
echoed by Gerald Coles and others who conclude that learning disabilities are socially caused. By contrast, Beth Slingerland, who pro-
motes a structured, multisensory approach to teaching reading and
writing for LD students, argues against blaming the classroom
instructor (1982, 34). Noel Gregg also differentiates between the
groups *basic writers* and *learning disabled*, contending that while

the former group should improve by simply practicing linguistic structures (Shaughnessy's advice), the latter group needs more explicit, multi-modal instruction as to how those structures function (1983, 334–36).

Shaughnessy notices that many basic writers have a handwriting that is a combination of print and script (1977, 15). Her solution to BW students' notoriously poor handwriting is more practice (16). Again, she is assuming that these students have not been properly trained, or else their handwriting would be better than it is. Although a more fully developed definition and history of *dyslexia* and *learning disability* is included in Chapter One, it is important to note here that as defined by the U.S. Congress Public Law 94-142, *specific learning disability* excludes those children whose disabilities are caused primarily by "environmental, cultural, or economic disadvantage" (Hallahan et al. 1985, 14). Although evidence supporting a neurologically based theory is controversial, no one has yet disproven it, nor has anyone yet shown that sociological factors account for all differences.

Some students intersperse capital letters seemingly haphazardly throughout their texts. Shaughnessy attributes this partially to students' reading of "sermon literature or Bible passages that follow seventeenth-century conventions of capitalization" (38). Carolyn O'Hearn, in one of the rare essays on learning disabilities to appear in *College English*, "Recognizing the Learning Disabled College Writer," also discusses the kind of haphazard capitalization used by many students O'Hearn would categorize as learning disabled. She cites unusual capitalization habits as being clues, albeit not always reliable ones, that the student may be LD (1989, 300). Shaughnessy's attributing mistakes with capitals to a hand-to-eye slipup, and O'Hearn's attributing them to a learning disability, may not appear to make much difference. However, since prescriptions are based on diagnoses, these different explanations could indeed have important implications for teaching. Shaughnessy, thinking the student merely needs practice to become more physically coordinated, might assign more writing or conventional exercises. Instructors who believe as O'Hearn does that LD is a neurologically related phenomenon might experiment with alternate, multisensory, or mnemonic methods of teaching. (See Chapter Three.)

Besides studying errors in handwriting, Shaughnessy also looks at punctuation problems, which she attributes to "inexperience" (1977, 16), or in some cases, to "carelessness" (27). If we are reluctant to implicate the basic writers themselves, Shaughnessy allows the culprits to be previous high school or grade school teachers who failed to teach these conventions (27). However, the study by Noel

Gregg suggested that although normal, basic, and learning disabled writers all made errors involving comma omissions and verb tense, the type and frequency of errors for the learning disabled students was qualitatively and quantitatively different from the errors made by the basic or normal students (1983, 335). Gregg cites other researchers who also found that learning disabled students make "significantly higher" numbers of punctuation errors on their compositions than do normal or basic writers (337). On a different test, Gregg found that while basic writers made conventional errors such as sentence fragments and errors in verb tense and parallelism, learning disabled students made more errors in spelling and dropped letters. As is the case with all such studies, Gregg's results are subject to interpretation, but they raise enough questions about learning differences to warrant further investigation. Gregg concludes that the errors involving parallelism and verb tense might, as Shaughnessy suggests, indicate a lack of instruction, but that the number and types of errors made by the other group indicates learning disability.

Amy Richards also comments on the high frequency of errors— LD students making sometimes twice as many spelling errors as other students. Richards, like Gregg, says that LD students make different types of errors than those made by basic writers. She distinguishes between unpredictable errors and common ones such as *summer* capitalized by mistake; *boy's books* for *boys' books*, etc. and points to apostrophe mistakes that are not merely simple misplacements (as in *boy's* for *boys'*). She says that LD students are known to produce oddities such as *The bu's came* instead of *The bus came* (1985, 74). Richards believes that composition teachers should be alert for papers such as these, for they signal problems much more complicated than lack of experience.

While Shaughnessy is correct when she says, "Not all BW students have the same problems" (1977, 40), she partially contradicts this statement when she asserts, as she does throughout her book, that BW students are simply inexperienced. *If* students are merely inexperienced, then the solution is to immerse them in meaningful writing situations, where their natural ability for language will develop. Some experts, however, might challenge this idea of a universal, "natural" ability to handle linguistic abstractions, or, at least, to handle them well.

In her chapter on syntax, Shaughnessy reproduces students' sentences in which prepositions, contractions, pronouns, and irregular verb forms are frequently misused. She acknowledges something that some LD experts have suspected for a long time, that nonspecific, nonconcrete words such as *by*, *of*, *it*, and *be*, have proven especially difficult for some writers. Unable to explain why students make these errors, Shaughnessy nevertheless concludes that students need better proofreading skills (48). According to research conducted in the LD field, those students labeled LD frequently make errors of this type. Their short-term memory for linguistic symbols seems to give them more problems than most people experience, especially if the words are abstract, such as *were, at, through, where, when,* etc. The theory in LD circles is that these students, because they have more difficulty than others with abstract language, are particularly stumped by words such as *of* and *be* because no concrete picture can be associated with them. Vellutino and Scanlon have said that dyslexics seem to have more trouble with abstract than with concrete words (1991, 247–48). As discussed earlier, conclusions about people's recall of concrete and abstract words should always be scrutinized because the clinical studies from which they are drawn often have design flaws which render them controversial. However, the number of studies that replicate, to a certain extent, findings regarding differences in abstract and concrete recall suggests a problem exclusive to dyslexics.

Continuing with her analysis, Shaughnessy says the many *that* and *which* errors made by basic writers are made because "they are not used in the writer's mother tongue" (65). While this may be true for students whose first language is not English, it cannot account for these errors in the papers of all students who might be LD. While Shaughnessy would recommend practice, LD students might better benefit from learning an associative link to find the words and phrases they want to use but cannot remember. To remediate students on the premise of dialect interference is useless if it is the abstract nature of the word that is the problem.

Interestingly, Shaughnessy discusses some problems her basic writers have which, although they are called by different names in the LD field, are the same problems LD students are reputed to have. She gives the example of the student who cannot reverse an awkward clause or successfully transpose a sentence because he cannot produce the "right" word, citing James Moffett's example of the student who must write "what is left in the cup after you finish drinking" because he does not know the word "dregs" (73–74). Shaughnessy here is more perceptive than Moffett in that she considers the possibility that although the student might have the word in his vocabulary, he hesitates to use it because he either cannot spell it or is unsure of the proper context, or is so overly concerned about proper usage that his thoughts are truncated. Therefore, says Shaughnessy, the student uses a "circuitous syntactic route," a long-recognized syndrome in the LD field called "circumlocution."

Although she has discovered that basic writers have trouble producing a word that would best fit their meaning, she does not attribute it to the specific linguistic *recall* problems believed to be experienced by LD students. (One student who came to the Writing Center for help told me that his written vocabulary was much poorer than his real vocabulary because he could not recall the words he wanted when he wanted them.)

Recognizing this difference in cause might greatly affect how the teacher views the student. It is well established in educational psychology that teacher expectations influence student performance. If teachers assume a student is using simplistic words because he or she *does not know* more sophisticated ones, they might also make inaccurate assumptions concerning the student's intelligence, which might in turn impact how they treat that student and what expectations they overtly or subtly convey. If, however, teachers are acquainted with the LD theory that poor vocabulary might be due to poor recall and not to ignorance of words, they might be more inclined to treat the student with more respect and to have appropriately higher expectations. This resulting change in teacher attitude might do wonders for a student's self-esteem, which might in turn enhance that student's attitude toward school and even writing performance. Charles T. Mangrum and Stephen S. Strichart, in their book, *College and the Learning Disabled Student,* stress the importance of professors' attitudes and point to research which, although limited, "tend[s] to suggest that many professors do not accept these [LD] students" (1988, 174). It is difficult to measure attitudes or student sensitivity to them. However, it seems obvious that if writing instructors with no background in learning disabilities assume that the myriad of incomprehensible errors are caused by their students' slow-wittedness, or even by their "inexperience," they will behave in a different way toward them. The formal and informal terms used for such remedial classes, from "Bonehead English" to the only slightly less pejorative "Basic Writing," reveal what society thinks of people who cannot spell or punctuate correctly. Although the phrase "learning disabled" is also problematic, suggesting perhaps another set of unhelpful assumptions, it at least raises the hope that teachers will view writing problems for this group as a *specific* language difficulty, the way they themselves might have math or spatial blocks.

Shaughnessy presents a good summary of the debate concerning when and if grammar should be taught in writing classes. She rightly points out that English teachers can become overly concerned with surface errors and that often an appearance of many mistakes is simply the result of a student repeatedly making two or

three types of errors. However, her contention that these errors will
"be rubbed off by time" (1977, 121) simply may not be true. For
example, the seven-year-old child who says, "You my way," for
"You're in my way," and "No can't how do dat" for "I don't know
how to do that" when no one else in his family speaks that way,
defies the hypothesis that all people equally absorb the forms and
conventions they hear used around them. Although the errors made
by this child and by many LD students may indeed be "rubbed off
by time," it may take a lot more time for some students, time they
may become too frustrated and discouraged to devote to a task they
see "regular" students doing so easily. If LD students require more
explicit or multisensory instruction, and are denied it in the belief
that more general practice will suffice, then the few years they have
left in college might be wasted practicing writing strategies not
suited to their ways of learning.

Preceding a lengthy section on grammar exercises, Shaughnessy
says that students need to be "introduced to the grammatical concepts of sentence, inflection, tense, and agreement," because it will
provide them with "a conceptual framework within which to view
[their] own difficulties in those areas" (137). Again, she is assuming, without substantiation, that basic writers make the errors they
do because they are inexperienced, because they have had poor
teachers in the past, and because they have never properly been
"introduced" to grammatical concepts and terminology. If she is
correct, then her fifteen pages of exercises may do some good. If,
however, basic writers *have* been previously exposed to these kinds
of grammar worksheets, the same way their peers in the "regular"
classes have, and their reason for making mistakes is related to
something else, then this "introduction" may be fruitless, even
oppressive.

Regarding spelling errors, Shaughnessy recognizes that many
students deliberately reduce their vocabulary, in some cases
because they cannot spell the sophisticated word they want. She
also points out that bad spelling is not associated with intelligence.
Regarding the misspellings of words that contain the schwa sound,
Shaughnessy points out the difficulty that many BW students have
with such words. Because that sound is represented in so many
ways, Shaughnessy reasons that the basic writer has trouble with it
because "he has not *seen* the words often enough as a reader nor felt
the spelling of them as a writer to be able to make the right choices"
(her emphasis, 167). Again, what she does not consider is that these
students have seen these words as often as their peers, but it is perhaps more difficult for them than it is for others to internalize the
standard spelling.

Peter Johnston has shown that adults with reading difficulties have essentially devoted their lives to avoiding situations that involve reading, and the resulting lack of practice makes a bad situation worse (1985, 159). While this lack of practice no doubt contributes to spelling and other problems, it does not answer the "chicken or the egg" question concerning the original cause of the difficulty. In addition, adult poor readers who have avoided reading have probably seen the words they are tripping over more times in print than has the eight-year-old who reads them effortlessly.

In her chapter on vocabulary, Shaughnessy discusses the "uncanny connections," the malapropisms that BW students often make. As an example, she gives the sentence: "The program uses a new *floormat* (format)." To remediate this kind of error, she assumes the students do not know what the two words mean. "The differences between *floormat* and *format* . . . are memorable once they have been pointed out" (1977, 191). However, students have confided to me that inadvertent slips such as these are embarrassing to them, that they realize immediately they have made a mistake, and that the word seemed to slip out as if of its own accord. To avoid such uncontrollable humiliation, these students limit their vocabulary to a very basic one. Having to listen to a teacher explain the difference between *floormat* and *format* must be extremely exasperating to students with this problem. One danger of assuming, as Shaughnessy does, that the student's vocabulary is poor, is that the teacher may encourage traditional vocabulary-building exercises concerning words the student already knows but confuses or blends with other words in ways that embarrass her. So she avoids them. Also, as mentioned above, teacher assumptions and expectations are subtle but powerful factors in determining how and what students learn. It is probably better that a teacher overestimate a student's vocabulary than underestimate it.

Another assumption Shaughnessy makes—that students are not familiar with "the reader's need for specificity" (202)—might dictate a lesson on the importance of specific examples in backing up a statement. While this might not do any students any direct harm, there is the chance of boring or frustrating students who have heard this admonition many times before. They may already know that they are supposed to use specific nouns or adjectives, but they cannot recall the words they want fast enough or accurately enough to use them in their writing. Indeed, students previously may have been exposed to "writer's strategies" for being specific, but the strategies that work for their English teachers may not work for them.

It is important, for the self-evident value of teacher expectation and student self-esteem, that students perceive the instructor's respect for their intelligence and past academic experience. Students may not need word exercises or lessons in specificity, but instead ways of coping with a recall problem, such as leaving a blank where the desired word should go and then filling it in later with the help of a thesaurus or a peer. Shaughnessy claims that a writer may know the right words but "does not seek them out" (204). If the teacher conceives of the student as lazy or uncaring, that will be obvious to the student. It may be that the student has tried all too much to seek out the word in her memory file, but has severe problems doing so. What Shaughnessy repeatedly fails to address is the possibility that the student does have an adequate vocabulary, has struggled probably more than anyone realizes to locate that exact word in her mind, but for reasons we can only yet guess, is unable to do so.

Throughout her extended analysis of errors, Shaughnessy exhibits insight and intelligence, doing her compassionate best to locate the student's meaning behind a web of misused words and tangled syntax. Although it is an unarguable fact that we all learn language through use, some people may have a knack for learning it much faster or in different ways than others. Shaughnessy's primary remedy, more practice with writing, is based on an assumption that students are inexperienced. And many of them may be. However, if the problem for even a few of those students is not inexperience but too much experience—that is, too much prior experience with failure at writing—then her solution may cause only more frustration for everyone.

Shaughnessy, like others cited in this book, admits: "We do not, in short, understand how people learn to think or be logical" (237). It follows then that we must remain open to ways of thinking that might differ from those with which we ourselves are familiar. From her extensive study, Shaughnessy learned that her basic writers "are, in some respects, a unique group from whom we have already learned much and from whom we can learn much more in the years ahead" (291). In order to learn from them, however, we need not to have made up our minds what is wrong with them before we really listen to them. We cannot, without some kind of evidence, conclude that they have had poor academic background and little experience with writing. If they have had experience, and they continue to have difficulties more severe than those of their peers, then perhaps we need to add neurological difference to Shaughnessy's list of possible reasons. While this will not solve their problems, it will allow us to view these students in a more positive light and force us to work with them in finding new and more creative ways to help them recall and use what they might already know.

Although Mina Shaughnessy's is perhaps the most well-known and influential study of error in the Composition field, it is not the only one. Other selected experts in our profession have also puzzled over beginning college writers and their development. While some, such as Shaughnessy and Bartholomae, do detailed error analyses, others argue in more philosophical or theoretical terms their reasons for underdeveloped writing.

Shaughnessy's influence on David Bartholomae is evident in the fact that he recommends reading student texts almost as a detective might, searching for clues regarding the causes of their errors. In "The Study of Error," Bartholomae says that basic writers do not have "arrested cognitive development, or unruly or unpredictable language use" (1980, 312). While it is refreshing that Bartholomae credits basic writers with intelligence, it is somewhat odd that he rules out "unruly or unpredictable language use" as a problem when so many of his student John's errors were *not* from dialect interference, or from "some intermediate system" of an idiosyncratic grammar code. Bartholomae can only call these errors "accidental." To call "accidental" what happens to most of us only occasionally but to a few of us all the time is to dismiss, as Shaughnessy does, the very real possibility that some people do have learning differences.

Bartholomae, like Shaughnessy and others, admits that we know little about "the natural sequence of learning" (313) by which people become better writers. What he never problematizes is the word "natural." Because Bartholomae does not understand why writers make what he calls "idiosyncratic" errors, he assumes it involves an "intermediate system" of misunderstood or misapplied rules. However, the reason a writer makes these unpredictable errors, instead of being due to Bartholomae's "intermediate system," could instead be due to an unstable internal image of the words in the writer's mind. Unless we arbitrarily discount what some students say about letters looking "weird" or "not standing still," we should also add to Bartholomae's list of problems the possibility of a learning difference. If writers make mistakes because of their own rules, then it makes sense to teach the conventional ones. If, however, they already know the rules but make mistakes because their internalized pictures of the words keep shifting, then reteaching the rules will not help. In his explanation of "interference," Bartholomae seems to realize that writing requires an accurate, automatic internalization of how a letter "looks" in the mind, but he does not consider how this internalization might be different for some students than for others.

Bartholomae notes that the errors John made with verbs "almost all involve *s* or *ed* endings, which could indicate dialect interference or a failure to learn the rules for indicating tense and number" (318). While it is dangerous to make assumptions about one student based on the errors of another, I think it appropriate here to discuss Ryan, a student I had in the Writing Center who, like John, also made numerous errors involving verbs and nouns with s endings. He had brought in a typed draft for revising, and when he read his piece aloud, he found most of the s errors, which he corrected in pen. Curiously, he sometimes wrote the added s backward, and then seemed embarrassed for doing so, making the unsolicited comment that he had "always done this." His speech gave no evidence that his writing errors were due to dialect interference, and he obviously knew the rules concerning plurals and agreement because he was able to correct his own work when he read it, or when I read it the way it was written. Thus, Bartholomae's hypothesis concerning an intermediate system of misunderstood rules could not be applied here, since Ryan had no problem editing orally. While it is still possible these errors could be called "accidental," it seems more likely that there may be a processing or retrieval difficulty experienced by Ryan that we can only partly understand.

Bartholomae spends several pages attempting to explain why John could not see the difference between *frew* and *few*, even when it was written on the board. He finally concludes that this error, as well as John's substitution of *when* for *went* is no more than "an accidental error, a slip of the pen" (321). Bartholomae says that while some teachers might have interpreted John's use of *chosing* for *choosing* as evidence of grammar rule difficulties, his error analysis has shown that this mistake is "only" an accidental error (322). While Bartholomae's discovery may prevent a teacher from conducting another fruitless lesson in grammar, his dismissal of "accidental" errors may be a reflection of his own ease in correcting them. He says a student's omission of a needed word in a phrase ("I would to write about" rather than "I would *like* to write about") can be easily dealt with: "It is an accidental error and can be addressed by teaching editing" (323). However, teaching editing to students with stable mental images of words may be quite different from teaching editing to students (such as my student Ryan), who say that their mental picture of a word keeps shifting. I agree with Bartholomae's statement regarding these accidental errors, that "This is an important area for further study." In further studies, however, it is vital that we remain open to seeing all possible reasons for error and listen to what our students say about what goes on in their minds when they write a word.

Patricia Bizzell, in her article, "What Happens When Basic Writers Come to College" uses and supplements William Perry's view of development. Bizzell says that learning new discourse conventions gives the student access to "a whole new world view," which is different from implying, as she claims other theories do, that the basic writer's thinking is inferior. As a solution to basic writers' problems, Bizzell recommends "a series of interviews to tell us how they [the basic writers] mediate between their home cultures and the academic culture as they move on through their college educations" (1986, 300). A problem with Bizzell's proposed research is that the assumption has already been made on the researcher's part that it is the "clash" between the student's home and school cultures that is causing his or her problems. She does not mention the possibility of a learning disability. By devoting so much of her essay to a discussion of "discourse communities" and "new world views," she makes it obvious that she is limiting her analysis of basic writers to their social background.

James Britton, like other modern Composition theorists, never questions the idea of writing development as a "natural" activity that occurs for all students in the same way. To illustrate the ease with which a child develops as a writer, Britton, in *Prospect and Retrospect*, uses as a case study a child named Clare. Although an *E* for her at first could face "right or left or up or down," she merely needed to be reminded how to do it correctly. When she was three and a half years old, and instructed on how to write the letter *R*, she said, "*R*—that's easy—just a girl's head and two up-and-downs!" (1982, 60). Britton uses this example, and Clare's estimation of picturing this letter as "easy," as evidence for his assumption concerning the "natural" development of language. What he does not consider is that what may come easily to Clare at age three may not come so easily to other children two to three times her age. Compare Clare's remark, "That's easy!" to a comment by another student, this one a nine-year-old dyslexic: "For other kids, learning to read is like a feather. For me, it's like a ton" (Rome and Osman 1977, 44). For Clare, who "continued to read and write stories for many years" (Britton 1982, 61), writing, especially her own successful writing, was its own reward. Once she had internalized the shape of that letter, it obviously always looked the same to her. We cannot help but wonder, however, if she sometimes mentally visualized an *R* as a *B* or a *p* as a *q* or *b*, and if her experience with letters and words were as frustrating for her as some children claim it is for them, would she have as happily continued writing her stories.

Britton's premise in his chapter "Spectator Role and the Beginning of Writing," is that story writing should be encouraged in children because when they write stories in which the world they create "is a world they control," the satisfaction they experience encourages them to write more (63). He also believes that beginners should start with stories rather than with transactional (informative) writing because "a story makes fewer demands" (63). In other words, Britton is associating the pleasure and ease with which a child controls language with the development of the child's writing abilities. He uses this premise to support his promotion of expressive writing as the proper way to begin writing instruction.

Although he sees the importance of a child's facility with language as vital to that child's use and resulting mastery of that language, he fails to consider that not all children will have that ease and control with written language, whether or not they are encouraged to write stories. There *is* great pleasure in watching one's words transform a page into an imagined world one can control. There must, however, be an equal and opposite pain if one cannot control what forms appear on the page. Britton's pedagogy is dictated by his belief that people learn to write implicitly. How teaching might be different for children who do not as easily process the formation of letters, words, etc., is something that he does not consider because he assumes all children learn the same way—like Clare. For Britton, "[writing] development comes from the gradual internalization of the written forms . . ." (110). If, however, some children have a neurological difference in the ways the letters become "internalized," or if the storage and retrieval system governing these internalized patterns goes slightly awry, Britton's remedy of "more reading" and "more writing" may only bring more frustration to some LD students whose writing teachers fully accept Britton's model of learning, or view it in strict binary opposition to other models. Of course, Britton's view of learning is valid. It may need to be supplemented, however, by other views in order to include the perspectives of all individuals.

Another influential work in the Composition field is Janet Emig's 1971 study, *The Composing Processes of Twelfth Graders.* Emig's study is often read in graduate programs in Rhetoric and Composition and is cited as a landmark study in the field. (See North [1987], 197–203, for a thorough discussion of Emig's study.) Like Shaughnessy, who also blamed the "poor instruction" of the past for many of her students' problems, Emig blames teachers she has never observed for her present students' distaste for writing. In the makeup of her sample of student volunteers—interested students who were "good" at writing—Emig has probably eliminated those students who might have had a learning difference. In *The Composing Processes of Twelfth Graders,* Emig makes conclusions about "bad teaching" similar to those of the critics of the learning disability field, who dismiss claims of neurological difference on the basis that it is the (former) teacher's deficiency that accounts for the student's present difficulties with reading and writing. Interestingly, in a 1978 essay, "Hand, Eye, Brain," Emig advised English professors to educate themselves regarding the physiology of writing, ending the essay with a call to investigate "what is truly organic about writing development" (120). Her advice to administrators of English doctoral programs to develop "closer ties with departments of biological sciences" has gone unheeded.

Ken Macrorie, in his 1984 book, *Searching Writing*, speaks of the human mind functioning much like a "connector" that somehow knows just what to do: ". . . ordinarily, it will work for you like a fan sucking in leaves and then blowing them in the direction you point it" (2). By using the generic "you," Macrorie reveals that he is talking about the mind functioning the same for everyone. If the mind fails to connect, it is only when "pressures become heavy." He does not allow for those who discover repeatedly that although they intend to write one thing, they end up writing something else.

A generic audience is similarly the target of Peter Elbow's recommendations. Attempting to free his students from the inhibiting restraints of early proofreading and too much attention to grammar, he invites them to "free write" about themselves or anything else that interests them, without stopping, without attention to sentence structure, form, syntax, or grammar. Elbow's emphasis is always on fluency first, overcoming writing anxiety—what he feels is the ultimate culprit responsible for bad writing. Correct grammar is, however, necessary in a final product, but Elbow does not give much direct advice in this regard, except to get an editor or to try to convince a couple of friends to help proofread. The main purpose of Elbow's *Writing Without Teachers* (1973) is to convince people to write without paying much attention to form, because it is precisely that excessive attention to form which makes them write poorly in the first place. For most students in Elbow's class, freewriting would lead to fluency and confidence, thus eliminating many problems with incoherence and grammar. For learning disabled students also, freewriting would undoubtedly make writing a more pleasant undertaking than one in which a teacher waited with red pen poised. Elbow expects, however, that surface errors will ultimately disappear once the student develops fluency and confidence. But for those students for whom the written language presented more difficulties than could be overcome through confidence, Elbow's pedagogy would offer little help except the advice to get a couple of friends to help proofread.

For Ann Berthoff, who holds that there is no reality beyond language, writing becomes primarily a means of "making meaning." Writing, according to Berthoff, is "a non-linear, dialectical process . . ." (1981, 3), during which students should be encouraged to "interpret their interpretations." Her recommendations can, no doubt, challenge writers at all levels to rethink and reconsider, to open their minds to become critical of their own ideas as well as those of others. If, however, there are students for whom writing is not their best way of making meaning, Berthoff's maxims offer little help, or recognition of a difference.

In *Rhetorical Traditions and the Teaching of Writing*, C. H. Knoblauch and Lil Brannon also recommend pedagogical approaches that support the idea of writing as something done naturally by people (1984, 15). Their philosophy of writing is a consistent, humane, and liberatory one. It advocates an approach to teaching writing by providing a challenging yet nurturing environment with alert, facilitative readers. They correctly point out that people learn best by writing about important subjects, aimed at a real audience, an idea that has sometimes become lost in pedagogies that stress grammar exercises and strict adherence to artificially imposed models and forms. By de-emphasizing correctness and encouraging students' further involvement with their own ideas, Knoblauch and Brannon's pedagogy would no doubt reassure LD students that they have valuable things to say, giving them real motivation to keep trying. It would also challenge them to rethink their ideas, providing for LD students (perhaps for the first time) a reaction to *what* they are saying rather than *how* the initial sentences appear. It would, however, provide no special help for or recognition of anyone having extreme difficulties recalling or writing the needed words.

Ira Shor opposes typical practices of public school life. In *Critical Teaching and Everyday Life* (1980), he writes about his classroom practices designed to promote Paulo Freire's philosophy that students need to be made critically aware of what Freire and Shor see as capitalism's oppressive powers. According to Shor, this will both change the world for the better and improve students' writing. He believes that if students are allowed to choose topics of interest to themselves, their writing will naturally improve, and that practice and political commitment will automatically erase most problems with code or form. In Shor's "liberatory classroom," students are nevertheless expected to abide by conventions of written English. The terms used to describe these forms and conventions are slightly different, and the emphasis is placed on the student's experience, but the fairly rigid expectations are still there: all students will learn, and all students will make progress in proportion to their interest in doing so. Shor makes no provision for students who might *want* to learn but whose neurological makeup makes it very difficult for them to do so. A student having severe problems with the code of written English might initially have a rewarding experience in Shor's classes because Shor gives the impression that content matters more than form. That student, however, if he or she is experiencing unstable word images, may ultimately be faced with very painful "voicing" sessions—Shor's editing cure designed for the problems of the majority only.

Both Shor and Elbow expect (but do not emphasize) that students' writing will ultimately conform to conventions of academic writing. Whether the student resorts to Shor's "voicing" or Elbow's "couple of friends," his or her piece must be grammatically correct. If this presents an impassable barrier, it will remain one. Whether these teaching practices are based on the theory that bad writing is caused by noncritical subject matter (Shor) or by a crippling fear of the blank page or surface correctness (Elbow), they are both based on an assumption of language use as an easy, natural occurrence that will develop through interest and use. Elbow admits that his practice is based on what worked for him as a writer. Composition instructors basing their pedagogy on the models provided by Shor or Elbow will undoubtedly make similar assumptions about writing development and will not consider or provide accommodations for a written-language block so many people say is a real phenomenon.

These influential theorists base their practices on certain beliefs concerning language, writing, and human development. Professionals in the Learning Disability field would agree with Composition theorists that context and social situation are important in learning. They would also agree that practice must be informed by an analysis of how people learn—the difference being in assumptions regarding what is "natural." The theory and practice of Composition Studies, as articulated by its most influential voices, is extensive. It makes an attempt to be critically self-aware and inclusive of many diversities. However, its glaring blind spot concerning learning disabilities has reached a critical point and needs to be addressed immediately in graduate schools, professional journals, and national conferences. To better understand all writers, Composition Studies needs healthy inquisitiveness, open-mindedness, and an ability to tolerate "both/and" theories of learning.

Notes

1. In her handout at this forum, Anne Mullin referenced Karen Klein's and Linda Hecker's article, "The Write Moves: Cultivating Kinethestic and Spacial Intelligences in the Writing Process," in *Presence of Mind: Writing and the Domain Beyond the Cognitive,* edited by Alice Brand and Richard Graves, Portsmouth, NH: Boynton/Cook, 1994.

2. Patricia McAlexander, Noel Gregg, and Ann Dobie now have a book entitled *Beyond the 'SP' Label: Improving the Spelling of Learning Disabled and Basic Writers* (Urbana, IL: NCTE, 1992).

Chapter Three

Multisensory Teaching Methods: Tutoring Joey

As the previous chapter has shown, present mainstream Composition theory and practice does not allow for the percentage, however small, of students who might have a neurological learning difficulty. Most pedagogies, whether Mina Shaughnessy's, Peter Elbow's, or Ira Shor's, operate under the unquestioned assumption that writing is natural for all and mainly requires interesting and engaging opportunities in order to develop. If, however, we admit the possibility of dyslexia or specific learning disability, how would our teaching methods change? Since learning disability is such an elusive phenomenon, and since no two LD students have exactly the same set of difficulties and/or talents, it is impossible at this time to prescribe a set curriculum. What helps one person simply may not help another. What works on a one-to-one tutoring or mentoring basis might not work in a classroom situation, and vice versa.

One element of the LD controversy concerns what instructional approaches are more effective for LD students. As whole language practices become successful and established ways of teaching reading and writing in primary and secondary schools in districts throughout the country, parents of LD students especially question whether the assumptions about language acquisition upon which whole language practices are based are appropriate for their children. Whole language relies heavily on high-interest texts and motivation on the part of students to learn. It assumes that if people are immersed in meaningful opportunities to use language, they will, with some well-placed instruction, develop the skills necessary to become literate. In contrast, the structured pedagogies influenced by Orton-Gillingham (O-G) rely more extensively on structured, explicit phonics instruction, often in conjunction with multisensory links, or mnemonics. Designed primarily for LD students, O-G methods operate under the philosophy that some children, in spite of a high motivation to read, have neurological frameworks less suited to linguistic tasks than those of others.

The differences between these two methods might suggest differences that could be applied to pedagogies used with college students. In this chapter, I relate my experiences tutoring my nephew Joey, and what might be discovered from how and when he made progress in learning to write. This account illustrates first, what "multisensory" means and second, what role it plays with children like Joey. It also shows the importance of an intense interest in learning. In Chapters Four and Five, I will attempt to translate what these two conditions mean for college teachers of LD students.

As little as has been written in the Composition field concerning learning disabilities, there is even less written on how college teaching methods would change if instructors believed some of their students learned differently. Quite a bit has been written, however, on how elementary and special education teachers use Orton-Gillingham (O-G) and other multisensory methods to teach students they believe are linguistically learning disabled. These methods are different from those based on the belief that exposure to meaningful texts coupled with some basic instruction is enough for students to learn.

Readers interested in the various offshoots of the O-G method are referred to Diana Brewster Clark's book, *Dyslexia: Theory and Practice of Remedial Instruction*. She explains the packaged programs available to teach reading, writing, and spelling through very explicit, sound/symbol instruction. She also recommends programs that are more appropriate for various age groups. There are many such programs, such as the Slingerland method, Alphabetic Phonics, Recipe for Reading, Preventing Academic Failure, and the Lindamood program, which Clark says is intended for teaching phonics to older students (1988, 200). These programs and others follow certain generic principles, which recommend proceeding from the simplest unit of instruction to the more complex—from sound symbols, to syllables, to sentences. Those students who easily absorb linguistic forms may be excruciatingly bored by such rigid phonics instruction. However, as Katrina De Hirsch points out, for frustrated LD students, ". . . phonetic techniques provide a feeling of mastery and security where in the past they have relied on guessing only" (1984, 109).

Isabelle Liberman argues the need for phonics instruction by discussing the logograms of the Chinese language. Logograms are not part of an alphabetic sound/symbol system, but represent whole words, necessitating whole-word memorization. This process is reputedly easier to learn at first, but becomes increasingly complicated as more and more logograms, or whole words, need to be memorized. Liberman says, ". . . children who learn to read English words as if they were logograms will never be able to read a word they have never seen before in print" (1983, 87).

A comparison of these two approaches may not be a direct help for college composition teachers, whose students come to them (for the most part) already knowing how to read. I present these differences, however, so that creative college teachers can adapt whatever ideas they can glean from creative elementary teachers who attempt to help their students find alternate paths to learning when conventional neurological paths might be somehow blocked, impeded, or otherwise occupied.

In their text, *Preventing Academic Failure: A Multisensory Curriculum for Teaching Reading, Writing and Spelling in the Elementary Classroom*, Phyllis Bertin and Eileen Perlman agree that different students require different, more explicit teaching methods. Explicit teaching means, for example, that LD students must be told that the sound /a/ (short vowel for *a*) is responsible for the sound /a/ in *apple*. Merely seeing the word and hearing it pronounced may not be enough for these students to figure it out on their own. The code that most students deduce without direct instruction must be explicitly pointed out, perhaps more than once, and cued with a mnemonic link (1980, 1–4).

A critical part of this method involves the use of several senses. Unlike other reading programs which assume that if children *see* a letter or a word enough times in context they will internalize and therefore learn to use it, the O-G method gives students the opportunity to use their other senses as a kind of backup system. Therefore, if they cannot visualize a word, their auditory or kinesthetic sense can sometimes help them out. This kinesthetic association is somewhat like the way people touch type. If asked, we might not be able immediately to say where a particular letter is located on a keyboard. However, if we were typing, our fingers would "know" automatically where to go. For example, I have known how to type since I was thirteen, but I cannot say where *c* is unless my fingers are positioned over the keyboard. A friend of mine told me that one day at work he forgot the password that he had to key into the computer program in order to access secure files. His mind could not recall the required sequence of letters and numbers, but when he put his hands over the keyboard, his fingers somehow "remembered" the password.

Large-muscle memory is also employed. When a letter or word is introduced, students are taught to "skywrite" it—that is, to write it in large, imaginary letters in the air, using the large muscles of their arms as they simultaneously say the word or letter aloud. Theoretically, once the large muscles are involved in learning, the muscle memory will aid students when they cannot "picture" the word in their minds. It is a part of this kinesthetic pathway—muscle memory—that enables us to ride a bicycle even though we may not have ridden one in years. We might not be able to explain how to balance ourselves, and perhaps if we thought about it too much, we would fall off. But if we get on a bike, we can ride it. In much the same way, experienced golfers may find when they pick up their clubs early in the season that they recover their golf swing more easily if they do not think about it or analyze it too much. Sometimes it is better to relax and allow muscle memory to restore the sequence of movements that will result in a long drive. Similarly, if students cannot remember how an *a* looks, but they begin to "write" it with their hands and arms, the muscles will automatically form the letter correctly. Almost eighty years ago, Maria Montessori discovered the benefits of a type of multisensory teaching. She taught a retarded girl to sew by having her weave mats, an activity that involved a similar over-and-under motion, only on a larger scale. Through a muscle memory, the girl was able to internalize the required motion. Montessori also emphasized the importance of observing the individual student before constructing a pedagogy (Berthoff 1981, 148–51).

Other aspects of writing, spelling, and reading which dyslexics reputedly have trouble with are addressed in Bertin and Perlman's approach (see Bertin and Perlman 1980). Dyslexic students' notoriously bad handwriting can be a result of many factors, but one which O-G teachers work on is the child's difficulty knowing where to begin forming the letter. Dyslexic children sometimes put their pens down any old place on the paper, not necessarily on the left side first, and not necessarily on the writing line. For that reason, first and second graders in the Bertin/Perlman program are given desks with vivid green tape on the left side—because many dyslexic children cannot reliably distinguish left and right. They also are introduced to each letter through skywriting and then given large newsprint textured paper, with four blue horizontal lines approximately four inches apart. To help the child learn which line to start on, the left side of the paper has a person drawn next to it. The top line, where capital letters hit, is the person's "hat line." The middle line, where lowercase letters hit, is the person's "belt line," and below that is the "writing line." Cursive letters such as *f*, which go below the writing line, hit the imaginary person's "shoe line" (34). When students are directed how to form the letter, they are given explicit instructions using these identifiable landmarks on their paper. For example, the cursive, lowercase letter *i*, is one of the "rocket letters." It begins "on the writing line, goes up like rocket, away from the green, to the belt line and comes back down." Then there are the "tall letters," such as cursive *l*, *h*, *k*, and others, which "begin at the writing line, swing up to the hat line, turn and pull down." For *h* and *k*, students are instructed to "aim to cross at belt line." While this may seem unnecessarily precise for most people, LD teachers claim this method works for dyslexics, for whom each line on a piece of paper either looks the same or shifts unless it is associated with this concrete image of a person with a belt, hat, and shoes (or some other associative link). These teachers claim that if students put their pencils in the same spot each time they begin to write a letter, the letter will come out right. If they begin on the wrong side, the letter will come out backward or upside down.

Students are not taught handwriting separately but in conjunction with the sounds and words that go with it. For example, the sound /u/ would be said aloud and handwritten at the same time. Words using the short /u/ sound would be used in sentences such as "The gum is in the mud." This is what LD teachers mean by "controlled vocabulary" and "structured readers." If they have just gone to much trouble to teach students that /u/ stands for the sound in *mud* and *gum*, they would not want *u* suddenly pronounced like the sound in *rude* or *dude*. That would come in a different lesson, once the children had adequately learned the short /u/ sound.

Review by means of a "card pack" (flash cards) is an important part of any O-G based method. Consonants are written on white cards; vowels on salmon-colored ones. The students say words and sounds out loud as the teacher holds up cards, assuring the multisensory aspect of the learning. It is also important that these students obtain positive reinforcement and reminders about how much they *do* know, and how much they *can* read. For this reason, the "card pack" never includes new material, only the phonemes and words with which the class is already familiar. Students who have repeatedly failed to learn to read are delighted when they can read, on their own, the most elementary words or sentences. (I once watched an articulate twelve-year-old boy, a product of an O-G private school, take about two full minutes to read one sentence on a blackboard. I was horrified at his extreme difficulty, but he and his parents were beaming. Before he attended this school, he could not read at all.) In the O-G-structured, multisensory method, there is no invented spelling, on the theory that LD students cannot afford to have their mistakes reinforced, or their minds will be getting even more conflicting messages.

Students, parents, and teachers who attend the Orton Dyslexic Society meetings and those of other related associations claim that explicit and multisensory instruction succeeds in teaching nonreaders to become literate when years in conventional reading or writing programs did not. These testimonials might be considered a type of lore, which, to use Stephen North's definition, is "concerned with what has worked, is working, or might work in teaching, doing, or learning writing." Lore may not be backed up by theory or research, but it is "essentially experiential" (1987, 23).

Lore can also be very powerful. A class I took in New York City from Phyllis Bertin was filled with elementary school teachers taking this class on their own time, some at their own expense, to learn a teaching method that they had heard, through word of mouth, was one that "worked." Similarly, classes on whole language teaching methods are filled with teachers eager to learn what they have heard "works." Both sides have their lore; both sides have their devotees. Many whole language teachers swear theirs is the method that works. These LD teachers are utterly convinced their way is the only way their students will ever learn to read.

As discussed in Chapter One, this structured, bottom-up approach to teaching is another part of the LD controversy. Skeptics say that the explicit sounding out of words might be the very activity dyslexics are least likely to do well. Peter Johnston and Richard Allington say that the multisensory techniques promoted by LD enthusiasts are not proven, and that the exaggerated decoding skills may actually cause the slow reading observed in LD students (1991, 999). Even Katrina De Hirsch, who aligns herself primarily with the O-G school of instruction, recognizes some potential problems in teaching phonics to children who have trouble synthesizing multiple factors (1984, 55). Diana Brewster Clark also favors multisensory teaching but mentions the possibility that some LD children might experience "sensory overload" when confronted with the multisensory tasks that O-G methods require (1988, 49). She also writes, however, that "practitioners using these [multisensory] programs appear to be highly supportive of multisensory instruction" (51). And one study reported that multisensory, O-G methods were used successfully even with college students (Guyer and Sabatino 1989, 430).

When I first began the formal research for this book, I interviewed Frank Vellutino at his office. Something he said at that time intrigued me: "You'll learn more [about this learning difference] from tutoring one student than you'll learn from anything you'll read about it." This has turned out to be true. Much of what I have learned, the information that has most convinced me that LD exists, has come from what my nephew has said and written, during the tutoring sessions I spent with him and in his everyday life. There is no question in my mind that his is a problem remembering linguistic symbols. Although his problems are unique, the pattern of his difficulties seems to be very much like the problems of dyslexics I have read about, heard about, or talked with. At present, there is no way I can prove this. But my observations have convinced me of his need for special instruction—not O-G and not whole language—but an elusive combination of both. I am not suggesting that anecdotal evidence regarding one seven-year-old child proves anything about college composition students. (After all, even those adult students who may be experiencing handwriting problems are not likely to embrace techniques of skywriting, green tape on desks, or little men with hats and belts.) Observing firsthand Joey's frustrations with linguistic recall, however, has persuaded me that were he taught to read exclusively by having to remember words visually, his reading and writing problems would remain or become more extreme as he grew older.

The experiences I had with Joey are, perhaps, tangential to what college writing teachers need to know. I include them because they played a crucial part in making me aware of the need for experimenting, for individualizing curriculum, for listening to the student, and for combining instructional approaches. As I explained in the Introduction, I had an important personal stake in finding a teaching method that might help Joey learn to read and write. He had been read to since he was an infant, and he loved stories, always giving the books his rapt attention and knowing the plots by heart—even if he used many circumlocutions such as "the thing that . . ." to explain the story. However, by the time he was six years old, he could read only the words "Stop," and "McDonald's," (and it was possible he wasn't really recognizing those words, but the octagon shape of the sign and the colorful logo of the restaurant). In spite of Joey's long attention span, his apparently positive attitude toward stories, and the interesting, "meaningful" texts from countless bookstores and libraries, he was clearly not absorbing, as the whole language people said he should be, the phonological keys to his native language.

Partly out of a wary curiosity, partly out of desperation, I enrolled in Phyllis Bertin's O-G-based course for elementary teachers wishing to learn a structured, multisensory approach to reading and writing. My sister purchased the textbook, the large newsprint paper, the card packs, the wall cards, the controlled readers—

everything the LD teachers said dyslexic students needed in order to learn how to read and write. I came back to Albany to try this out on Joey.

At first, he was fascinated with the large paper, especially the imaginary man on the left side of the paper with his hat, belt, boots, and so on. For the first week Joey would stay interested for twenty minutes or so, and he learned the /a/ sound in *apple*, although he really did not master printing the *a*. In the second week, it was harder and harder to keep Joey's attention. The novelty of the blackboard and the large paper had worn off, the game of "playing school" was getting old, and I think he was discouraged with his difficulty in writing the letter *a*.

The next sound in this O-G-programmed lesson was the hard /c/ sound, which Joey could not pronounce anyway—he always said *cake* as *tate*, and his phrase "You only kidding," came out as "You only tidding." Perhaps because of his frustration, perhaps because of the rather dry material, the structured phonics lessons became a chore for both of us after about two weeks. The expensive wall cards and readers remained in their boxes, and I considered other options.

One day I decided not to prepare anything or to bring any of the programmed O-G materials. Joey always had with him some dog-eared flyers that catalog all the old and new Transformers and Autobots so that kids will pester their parents to buy them. Joey was interested in a particularly vile beast called "Skalor," whose claim to fame was that he "smelled." Joey took delight in repeating the slogan, "Skalor Smells!" and pointing it out in the flyer (no doubt so that I'd know it the next time I went to the toy store).

Flying on inspiration, I wrote "Skalor Smells" in giant letters on a piece of paper, using a red marker for the *S*'s and black for the other letters. I also wrote *S* all around the words, saying *S* as I did so and also making the *S* pass for the symbol of fumes rising from the words *Skalor Smells*. Joey had always responded to any multisensory help he could get in trying to remember something. For example, he used to call his bicycle his "motorcycle," although more often than not he would ask us, "What I call this?" and we would say, "Motorcycle." Two minutes later he'd say again, "This my— What I call this?" One day my sister said "motorcycle" at the same time demonstrating for Joey the American Sign Language sign for "motorcycle," which is a person's fists pretending to rev up the hand grips of a motorcycle. She said "Vroom Vroom" as she did it. Joey would imitate the sign and say the word. After a while, whenever Joey asked, "What I call this?" all we'd have to do is to show him the *sign* for "motorcycle"—the fists revving it up—and somehow that would trigger his recall and he would grin proudly and say, "This my *motorcycle!*" This example of using several senses to stimulate Joey's memory is what made me try the *s* "fumes" and to make such a fool of myself saying, "*S*" and "*Phew!*" and "*SSSSkalor SSSSmells!*" as I wrote it all over his paper. Joey would giggle uncontrollably and repeat the *s* sound and the phrase after me.

The result of my rather undignified performance was that Joey was now extremely interested in *S* and the disgusting (or, as he would say, gisdusting) images it could be used to create. He would attempt to copy my giant *S*, but it usually came out looking like a lower case *e*. (See Figure 3–1.)

This is because he started at a different spot each time and went in the wrong direction. Instead of forming the *s* from right to left, he'd start his pencil going from left to right—sometimes producing something that looked like the number *2*. (See Figures 3–2, 3–3 and 3–4.)

I decided to capitalize on his interest in the letter before he got too discouraged from writing it wrong—which he always instantly recognized as such—and teach him to write it correctly. I took his hand and arm and helped him "skywrite" giant imaginary *S*'s, saying each one as we did it. After we were skywriting the letter for several minutes, Joey giggling the whole time, I put the pen in his hand, and we wrote the *S* large on scrap paper, again saying it and having him say it as we wrote it. Sometimes, I would outline it in

Figure 3–1
Joey's first attempt to write *S*.

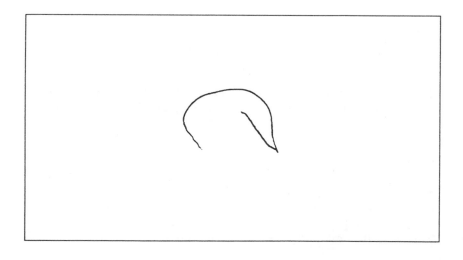

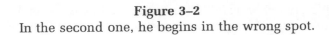

Figure 3–2
In the second one, he begins in the wrong spot.

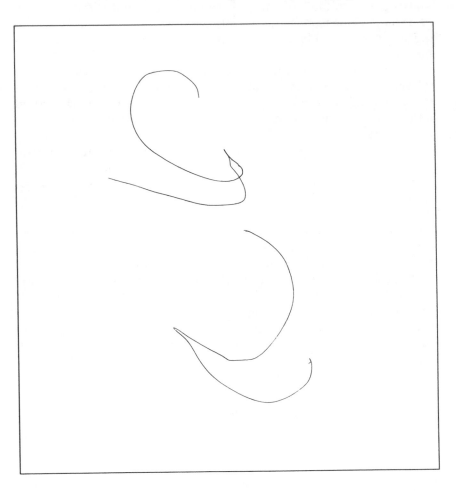

dots and have him trace it as we said it aloud (see Figure 3–5). His progress after having done both skywriting and tracing the dots can be seen in Figures 3–6, 3–7, and 3–8.

As you can see from the copies of our work, Joey sometimes would begin to write *S* incorrectly, so he would cross it out. Sometimes his *S* would look more like a *C* with a tail of a kite attached to it, but eventually he reached a point where he could write it correctly on his own three out of four times. Now, whenever he starts to write *S* backward, which is not often, I say, "Say it out loud as you write it, Joey, and you'll write it right." He does, and he does.

Figure 3–3
More false starts attempting *S*.

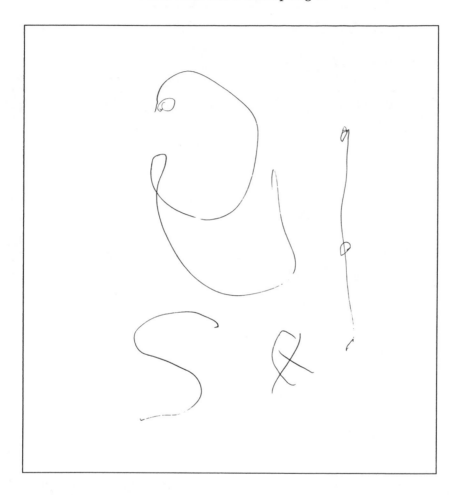

After Joey could write *S* with some confidence, he had more interest in other letters and in writing. One day Joey had a renewed interest in *Skalor Smells* and decided that he wanted to write *SMELLY*. (Figure 3–9). His first attempt at *S* is a rather primitive one, which he could see for himself. The corrected one is next to it. His *M* is a series of jagged peaks and valleys. His *E* is a bit disconnected, but still recognizable. Running out of room at the right side of the paper (which happens to him a lot), Joey wrote a nice *L*, which he had to squeeze in between the *E* and the *M*. His second L appears below the first. The *Y*, a rather forced, strangled affair, is

Figure 3–4
More attempts at *S*.

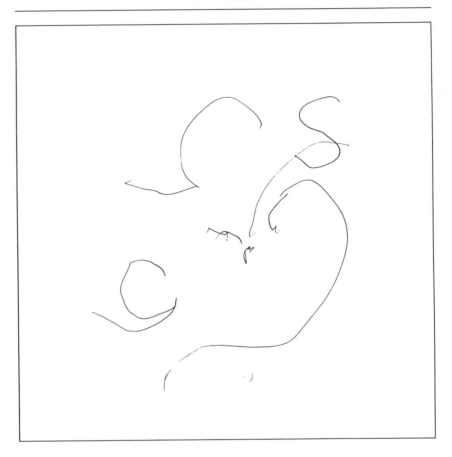

below the second *L*. Joey and I are probably the only two people in the world who would recognize these markings as the word *SMELLY*, but to us they represented a triumph. (The creature on the left side of the paper is Joey's self-portrait.)

The second attempt at *SMELLY* began with Joey writing his famous backward *S* (Figure 3–10). He immediately recognized it as wrong and began again. His *M* is much better this time, but he still ran out of room on the page. He wrote the *E* and finished the word writing the letters in order—*L L Y*—but they go from right to left.

His next attempt (Figure 3–11) is even more recognizable, but his spacing problems are obvious. In the next example (Figure 3–12), he finally wrote all the letters to *SMELLY* in order from left to

Figure 3–5
Tracing the dots after skywriting.

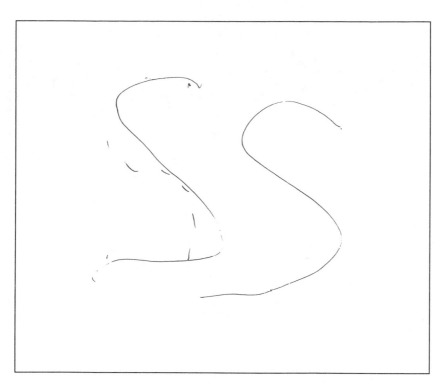

right, the only glitch being an extra "arm" on the *E*. The last attempt
(Figure 3–13) looks fine except for a slightly deformed *Y*. That
"text" was displayed proudly on his parents' refrigerator for many
weeks.

I took the time to relate this rather involved anecdote because it
reinforced what Frank Vellutino had said about learning more from
tutoring one student than from anything available in professional
journals. From Joey I learned several things. First, from watching
him struggle to articulate thoughts he clearly had but could not find
the words to express, I knew that he had extreme linguistic recall
difficulties. I also found out the hard way that O-G methods were by
themselves inadequate, as were practices based on whole language
assumptions of language acquisition. No matter how fascinating,
books and an intense desire to read and write would not be enough
to provide him with the phonological keys necessary for literacy.
Intriguing stories alone do not provide sufficient clues for children

Figure 3–6
Still some errors, but getting better.

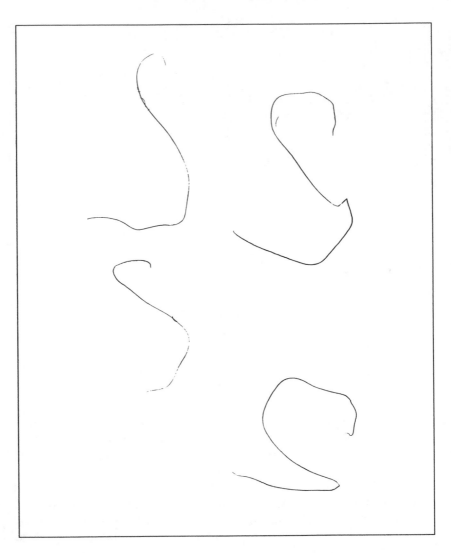

like Joey, who loved the books but could not read a word. (His four-year-old brother, by the way, *is* learning to read just by being exposed to books he likes.)

Similarly, programmed lessons and out-of-context instruction, however well prepared and presented, are not enough because the child is not engaged in the learning. Joey did not *care* that /a/ is the

Figure 3–7
Getting better.

sound in *apple* because he is not particularly interested in apples. He *wanted* to learn *S*, however, because it would help him write about smelly Skalor. He subsequently learned *T* rather easily because it was the first letter in Transformers and in Teenage Mutant Ninja Turtles. Incidentally, the first time he remembered to say the *tee* in *teenage*

Figure 3–8
Now he begins in the right spot.

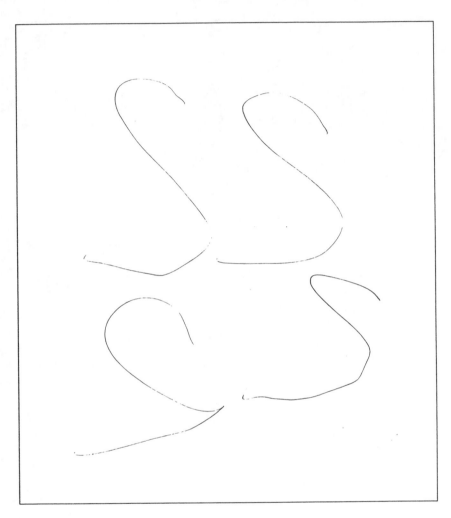

was through a multisensory, associative link: his mother had to pan-
tomime the act of drinking tea out of a cup. This way of learning is
consistent with what Vygotsky writes in *Mind in Society* regarding
human beings' penchant for building monuments to remember
events or tying knots in handkerchiefs as reminders: "The very es-
sence of human memory consists in the fact that human beings ac-
tively remember with the help of signs" (1978, 51).

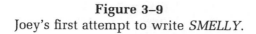

Figure 3–9
Joey's first attempt to write *SMELLY*.

What I learned, and am learning, from Joey is that when he learns, it seems to be through an individualized combination of multisensory techniques, such as skywriting and auditory and visual association, coupled with an intense interest in what the symbols stand for—in this case, the infamous Skalor. I should qualify my conclusions here by pointing out that they are based on my experience as one tutor working with one student. However, there

Figure 3–10
Second attempt at SMELLY.

does seem to be a need for *both* meaning-based and multisensory instruction, not perhaps for all children, but certainly for learning disabled ones.

A successful educator who seems also to have used different pathways to learning is Paulo Freire, often cited for his liberatory learning methods, but not often recognized as a teacher who combined his politically based pedagogy with a highly structured, explicit approach similar to that used in the O-G methodology. As

Figure 3–11
Getting better. The spacing is off.

Figure 3–12
Still trying. Too many "arms" on *E*.

Figure 3–13
Joey's triumphant writing of *SMELLY*.

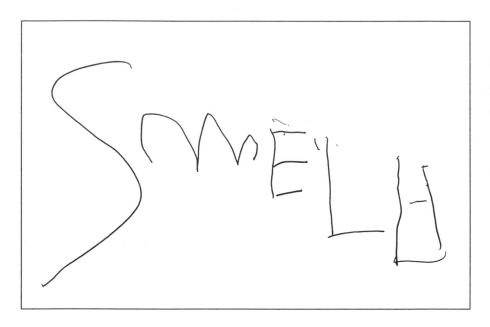

we have seen, a typical lesson in O-G begins with a review of sound symbols which are written on flash cards called a "card pack." Students are introduced to new words, which they are then asked to use in a series of sentences or in a paragraph. Freire too has exercises in his workbooks that present words such as *hoe, sowing, source,* and *knowledge,* followed by a paragraph and sentences in which the students use those words (Freire and Macedo 1987, 71). Like Orton-Gillingham, Freire uses careful sequencing of words, wall charts, word lists, and direct instruction about syllabification. His "generative words" are carefully chosen not only for their political interest but for the range of phonemes they will provide as a building block toward multisyllabic words. Orton-Gillingham relies on carefully presented "sounding out" techniques. So does Freire. Like Orton-Gillingham, Freire uses flashcards, called "discovery cards," on which are written the high-interest, politically and emotionally charged words that would get his adult students' attention. These words were chosen both for their critical importance *and* for their phonological advantages—they could be broken into phonemes, quite explicitly, and used to build other words in the reading vocabulary of the peasants he studied. In the same way O-G methods use the visual and other sensory inroads to learning, Freire uses slides and oral discussion to supplement the visual reading. (For a more in-depth discussion of Freire's classroom methods, see Freire and Macedo's *Literacy: Reading the Word and the World.*)

How, then, do theories about reading acquisition and the illustration of a little boy's symbolic mastery of his Transformer villain Skalor impact on college writing teachers? What is suggested is the importance of *both* explicit, multisensory teaching methods *and* engaging, student-centered texts to the learning of LD students. Simply exposing students to "great works" or to provocative political essays and providing opportunities for them to write will likely *not* be enough for LD students to develop sophisticated written discourse. On the other hand, structured grammar and spelling exercises not connected to anything meaningful in the students' lives are likely to be a waste of everyone's time. Joey learns, and probably LD college students learn, when multisensory links and a high interest in the subject combine. Chapter Four gives the perspectives of three LD college students and their stories of how they learn. Chapter Five suggests how writing instructors might develop interesting, multisensory, flexible class sessions and assignments for students who learn differently.

Chapter Four

Learning Differences: The Perspective of LD College Students

After reading dozens of books and hundreds of articles by experts in the LD, reading, and writing fields, professionals who had themselves studied LD and conducted classroom and laboratory research, I still had almost as many questions as when I began my research several years ago. I also realized that these experts, for all their education and experience, were most likely not learning disabled. Like me, they were researching a phenomenon that happened to others, not to them. In a way, learning disabled college students are the most expert people of all in this controversy because they have lived amidst its chaos for a long time. No matter what the various Ph.D.'s were currently deciding about the existence and extent of learning disabilities, I wanted to hear from young people whose lives had been influenced, for good or for ill, by being labeled LD.

Michael Polanyi and others[1] have argued for the validity of personal knowledge and experience. However, if these things were really valued, it would not be necessary repeatedly to cite testimony to that effect by respected scientists. The fact that personal knowledge cannot stand by itself, the fact that such high-level approval, a dropping of the biggest names, inevitably accompanies accounts of personal experience, almost by way of apology or permission, shows dramatically that personal knowledge is most definitely not valued for itself. It must always be "theorized," and "contextualized" by other, more academically acceptable evidence. The constant need to claim (even as I am doing here) that something matters because Polanyi or Bakhtin or Vygotsky says it does has a kind of "This is so because my mommy or daddy says so" ring to it. It should go without saying that the personal experience of our students matters, that what they say about themselves is credible, that their stories are true, that what they know about the way they learn, what they must do as they read, write, and study, is informed by years of life experience.

Students have been silenced, their stories discounted. Some critics of the LD field claim that what LD students say about their experiences with reversals and unstable letters should really not be taken seriously. It has been argued that these students' perceptions of what happens when they read or write has been heavily influenced by what they've been told, shaped by what they've read, and molded by the professionals with whom they have spoken. But whose perceptions have not been so shaped and molded? If these critics' doctoral studies and reading lists were shaped primarily by one or another side of the LD controversy, if they read basically from a fairly closed set of journals, and if in their professional lives they are surrounded principally by like-minded researchers, then the judgments of these experts should be heard with similar caveats. Without question, students' perceptions are influenced by others. But so are the perceptions of anyone who dismisses what students claim, or who says that students' perceptions about their learning styles are less valid for having been so influenced. If there is no objective knowledge, then there is no objective knowledge for LD students, for scientists, for theorists, for philosophers, for anyone. What's good for the student is good for the theorist. It evens the game a bit if we remember that those with twenty years of education are just as influenced by schema as are students. Young people's versions of their experiences should be just as valid as the version given by the most credentialed among us.

That said, I present in this chapter the stories of three college students who are currently labeled LD. I asked to interview these particular individuals because I felt fairly confident they would not be embarrassed speaking about their experiences. I deliberately chose students I knew were open and apparently comfortable about being labeled. They were neither randomly selected nor meant to represent all LD students. In fact, all three were quick to point out that LD people are all different. It may indeed be likely that these three are somewhat atypical: many LD students drop out of high school, never attempt college, or leave after initial frustration with their first semester. These three are successful, confident college students who are maintaining a *B* average in competitive majors (criminal justice and occupational therapy). Each is officially labeled LD and takes advantage of available academic support services. They all seem to possess a metacognitive awareness of where their strengths and weaknesses lie, and they all seem to have come to terms with the way they learn. Although they would prefer not to draw attention to themselves as different learners, they have found ways to ask for, even insist upon, accommodations they believe they need to succeed.

All three are white middle-class, only partially representative of Utica College, which has a student body that is currently about 15 percent African American, Asian, or Latino. According to Steve Pattarini (1994), the Director of Academic Support Services at Utica College, 13 percent of the forty-five students labeled LD this year are from this latter group. As the students interviewed will attest, being labeled LD throughout elementary and high school can be a curse or a blessing, but it does guarantee certain legal rights. There are, undoubtedly, many LD students at Utica College and across the country who are not officially labeled as such. (See Coles 1987, 203–07 and Chapter One of this book.) According to a recent *New York Times* series on special education, the labeling of students in New York City is influenced by discriminatory practices based on race, gender, and class. (See Dillon 1994; Winerip 1994; and L. Richardson 1994.) Marilyn Wessels, the president of a New York-based organization called "Schools Are for Everyone," reports that her state has one of the worst records nationally for placing LD students in the least restrictive environment (Nelis 1993, B10). The three students I spoke with were not isolated, as so many LD students still are, in separate classes or separate institutions. Their experiences may be quite different from those of students who *are* so isolated from the mainstream.

These students, therefore, do not purport to represent all LD students. They cannot speak for other people with similar linguistic processing difficulties who may be first-year students on the verge of giving up. They cannot speak for returning students (or those who never return), who attended elementary and high school long before LD was routinely diagnosed and people could receive the help they needed, or for those who were labeled but relegated to unenlightened programs that did not expect much from them. They cannot speak for LD students who may have other problems stemming from socioeconomic factors or racial discrimination, which may have prevented them from being included among the officially labeled group, or perhaps caused them to be labeled and then separated so completely from the college-bound groups that they never considered higher education. They cannot speak for the percentage of illiterate prisoners, some of whom may have been helped by an LD label they never received, or harmed by a label that doomed them. Nor can these students speak for the children and adults socially imprisoned by the shame often accompanying reading and writing difficulties.

The purpose of these interviews was to give several individuals labeled LD a chance to explain how having a learning disability affects their lives. These three happen to be fairly confident, mature, and self-assured about their strengths. Whatever demons may have plagued them earlier about whether or not they would finish college have been for the most part expelled. These three students refer to themselves as "lucky," and all three express concern about those LD students younger than themselves who may not, for whatever reasons, have the same opportunities they did. It is hoped that these three narratives will somehow help educators gain a broader perspective on the learning environment of students of any gender, race, or class, labeled or not, who may have a learning difference.

I asked the first person, Nick, to speak with me because I had worked with him several times in the Writing Center on both global and surface revisions of his papers. I also knew him from a literature class I had taught several years ago. The second person, Monica, I knew only slightly, but I was aware that she was a strong supporter of accommodations for LD students. I did not meet the third person, Janine, until the day of the interview, but I was aware that she had asked to take the college writing exam in the academic support office, rather than in a lecture hall, an accommodation for LD students. I had seen an essay of hers that caught my attention because of its peculiar error pattern, and I wanted to ask her about it.

It is important to hear these people's stories in their own words. For the sake of brevity, I have summarized some sections of the interviews, but others are transcribed word-for-word so that readers can hear, first of all, these students' determination, their sense of humor, their passion for what they believe, as well as their experience with frustration—a word used by all three of them. The interviews, conducted individually, ranged from an hour and a half to over two hours, and each person's speech was intense and fast, so fast I had to rewind the tape over and over in some sections in order to transcribe what they said.

It was during this transcription process that I realized these students sometimes omitted words, or used the wrong word or the wrong tense. I did not notice this during the interviews themselves. I suspect I unconsciously filled in left-out words, or "heard" words that they meant, but did not actually say. As I listened to them speak in person, my impression was that each student was extremely eloquent, grammatical slipups were barely noticeable, and the stories and examples they related were vivid and detailed. It may be that all people make occasional mistakes in speech that are obvious only in a transcript of the conversation, or it may be that the errors these students occasionally made provide insights into their written work. The purpose of these interviews was to hear these students' experiences, not to analyze their speech, so when I began transcribing the interviews, I was automatically fixing any slipups I heard, in order to make the transcript more readable and to more closely convey the overall quality of the students' speech patterns. As I heard more and more errors on the tape, however, and began to recognize that these oral errors fit the pattern of errors these students said they made in their written texts, I decided to go back and transcribe exactly what they said. In most cases, I have supplied in brackets the word I think they meant, where applicable, and sometimes I have simply used *sic*. Often the student heard the error and rephrased the sentence. I view these occasional slipups as perhaps a significant footnote to the compelling experiences they relate. The names of all three students have been changed as have those of any teachers or professors they discuss.

Nick

The first person I talked with was Nick, who currently maintains a *B* average in college and participates in many social activities—dramatic productions, fund-raisers, and residence life workshops—all of which capitalize on his speaking skills, none of which involve a lot of reading and writing. He had been a physical therapy major, he told me, but the technical, complicated vocabulary of the major muscle groups had plagued him beyond his frustration level, so he switched to criminal justice, where he said he could learn more through listening.

His writing, while sophisticated in ideas, organization, sentence structure, and vocabulary, is typically peppered with surface errors. These written errors often involve subject-verb agreement, such as *rights that an individuals has*, and *powers has*. He often uses plurals when he should use possessives, or vice versa: *the students ability* for *the student's ability*; *courts* for *court's*; or the possessive *college's* instead of the simple plural, *colleges*. His writing also exhibits frequent spelling errors that may be simple typographical problems, or they may be connected to an impaired ability to envision them mentally: *discission* for *decision*; *untied* for *united* ; and *ablošhed* for *abolished*. Very often, he writes the wrong word: *supple* for *supply*; *quilt* for *guilt*; *behave* for *behalf*; *tear* for *tier*; *sold* for *solid*; *well* for *will* and so on. (See Chapter Five for further discussion of errors and cues to learning disabilities.) These wrong word errors remain difficult for him to eradicate because the computer's spell checker reads them as correctly spelled words. Although Nick has been no doubt told that he is being careless or lazy because so many surface errors appear in his late-stage drafts, I can safely say, from watching him edit, that he is neither. He has to look at a sentence again and again before he sees an error, and he may read the right word out loud, even when the wrong one is on the page. While everyone does all these things from time to time, Nick's writing has many more of these kinds of errors than is usual, even when he is doing his best work, even when he has proofread it carefully many times.

I learned much from my two-hour interview with Nick because his narrative provided a unique perspective not available in the scholarly research. Although Nick's elementary school teachers wanted him to be tested for LD, his mother did not want him to be stigmatized. In his early years of high school, another teacher wanted Nick to seek help, but he was too proud to risk going to the "resource room," a place he refers to in an autobiographical essay as the "reject room." He remained in a regular classroom, using what professionals might refer to as "compensatory strategies." He calls them "survival instincts." By listening carefully in class and craftily arranging group study sessions, Nick managed to get average grades through high school. Then he experienced several incidents, detailed below, that made him decide to get tested for LD, and ultimately labeled and provided with special services.

Because he was not officially labeled LD until his junior year in high school, he had limited, but insightful, experiences in that "resource room," a place where LD high school students are sent for extra help after they have been singled out from their classmates. (Christopher Lee, in *Faking It* [Lee and Jackson 1992], calls his high school resource room "the stupid trailer.") In highlights of the interview, Nick talks about the students in this room, as well as about specific moments in his life that most shaped who he is today. He talks of ongoing problems and painful moments in his current college career that are related to his disability. Since his telling of his story is more vivid than my summary of it would be, I have reproduced substantive sections of the interview transcript, with some retrospective commentary of my own.

P: How did your being labeled come about?

N: That's an interesting story. I was labeled end of junior year in high school. I was labeled LD very young, but my mom refused to recognize that, and later my ninth grade teachers wanted to test me again, and I refused, and my mom respected that. Then, in junior year, a chemistry teacher sat me down and said, "Look, you have the knowledge and ability to go to college, but you're not going to be able to do it without additional support." I admire her as a teacher. She was probably one of the most intelligent teachers I've ever met. And so she pushed me toward it. So I, respecting her, agreed to it. I was tested, and they found a discrepancy in the English/reading/writing area, and therefore, I went through the official process.

P: Do you think that it has helped you or hurt you—being labeled? Do you think it helped or hindered you early on by *not* being labeled?

N: Ah—regarding early on. It helped me *not* to be labeled, I feel, because I had to work, because I didn't have that support, so therefore I had to come up with ways to learn in class because I never took notes. I never—I didn't have the skills of the regular, normal students, so therefore I learned to overcome my disability on my own.

P: What did you do?

N: I never missed a class, never missed school. In my whole high school career, I think I missed like maybe ten days. Class time was where I learned everything. I would just ask questions, and I just listened. Studying-wise, I always studied in groups, and everyone else would talk, and I would just pick it up auditorially.

P: That's interesting. How did you get the groups together?

N: Oh, just friends, you know. When you have a disability, you learn to be—ah—deceiving, and you just, you know, like, "Well, do you want to study in a group?" I like studying in a group, and usually everyone likes to study in a group because you can chat and have a conversation when you study, so it's not as boring, so most people are willing to study in groups. And if they weren't, then, I usually didn't study at all. [laughs]

P: Now, these people in the group—they were not aware of your . . .

N: [laughs] No. Some of them were aware of my situation just because it was such a small school, and they knew I went to the resource room. Well, they knew I had a problem because in class, I wouldn't ever read. The teacher would ask me to read, and I refused. But they never asked anything. They thought that I was just being myself: stubborn. That was before I got labeled.

P: Would you say that when you were studying in groups, a lot of your knowledge came in through listening?

N: Oh yeah. Definitely. I learn auditorally, and I think that was because of my disability, but also I had to adapt and overcome. I couldn't read in the books; I mean, I didn't read the books. I never did.

P: You never read the books?

N: Oh no. I never read one. I read one book in high school, and that was a book I read leisurely.

P: What was that?

N: *Friday Night Lights.* It's a sports book. It's about a football team in Odessa. It's quality. I like that. And that's the only book I read in its entirety.

P: In all of high school?

N: Yeah. I never read a book in high school.

P: That's amazing.

N: It is. Actually, it's sad, in my eyes. It's really sad that I was able to do that, and teachers never picked up on it.

P: And nobody knew?

N: No. 'Cause, you know, you're in class, and teachers discuss the books, and they're not going to test you on something they don't talk about, so you just pick up what they talk about in class. And you just—just—I don't know—you learn. You're able to see what teachers test on, I think.

P: Tell me more about those adaptive strategies.

N: [laughs] I don't know if they're—like—strategies. I don't know. They just came to me, and I guess it was—ahh—I don't know, survival instincts? —because I knew that if I didn't learn it somehow, I was going to fail, and my mom would have killed me. I mean, that's basically what it was. But even though I was able to do that, I wasn't getting great grades. I mean, I was getting all right; my high school average was about 70 percent. My stepfather said that I could do the work, and I said, "Yeah, yeah, whatever," so he bet me fifty bucks one semester that I couldn't get on the honor roll, which was 85.

P: That you *couldn't*?

N: That I couldn't. He bet me fifty bucks that I couldn't. I said I could. And I did. I got an 85. But then the next semester I was like—I didn't do it. You know, it was sad because I proved that I could do it. But he showed me I could do it, but I didn't learn my lesson. I was just like, "Whatever. Give me my fifty dollars and that's it." So I did get decent grades, but it wasn't what I could've got.

P: You said you never read entire books, only sections. How did you know what to read to get by? How did you figure that out? How did you know what the tests would be like?

N: Oh—teachers are funny. They give you answers. I don't understand why, but I guess it's their human nature. They don't want you to fail. So they will—actually, they spoon-fed me. I mean, I knew what was going to be on the test. Pretty much in general you know this chapter is going to be stressed, this chapter, blah, blah, blah, and you just learn when the person stressed it. I had a very energetic English teacher my senior year, and you just knew when she got really excited about it. When she went ecstatic and went running around the room, you knew that was going to be on the test. Just stuff like that. Other than that—teacher stressing things—they say, "This is important."

P: So would you just take that from class? Would you go back to the book at all? Read some stuff?

N: Just listen.

P: Just listen?

N: Just listen. Yeah.

P: So how did you handle the reading comprehension on the Regents? Were you used to reading chunks like that?

N: I—luckily I was able—I got labeled. I was able to take the Regents exam untimed. If I didn't take it untimed, I would have never passed. So that was a tremendous help because I never would have been able to finish the reading. Like—a paragraph that takes most students, say, five minutes, would take me twenty minutes. My reading deficit is bad. That exam I was really nervous about because I didn't think I was going to pass. But I did.

Several points here are noteworthy. First of all, while parents may occasionally be criticized for refusing to have their children tested, or accused of denying them what is viewed as needed help, it should be recognized that at least some of the time, parents know more about their children than do education professionals. This is not to say children should not be tested for LD or given extra help, but parents should not be automatically condemned for disagreeing with their children's teachers regarding proposed programs about which they may have many legitimate questions. While it may be argued that Nick may have become a better reader by getting labeled early on, it might just as easily be argued that, left to his own devices, he was able to discover how best to hone his auditory skills, closely observing human behavior and reading people's expressions. He found out for himself the benefits of what is just now becoming a respected educational tool: collaborative learning. Group projects, discussion-based classes, and study groups would be inexpensive, relatively easy ways of restructuring much of what happens in college classrooms. These student-centered approaches, which can be used for everything from memorizing definitions to analyzing discourse, would no doubt enrich college experience for everyone. For LD students, these approaches might make the difference between success and failure.

It should also be noted that his mother's high expectations ("because I knew that if I didn't learn it somehow, I was going to fail, and my mom would have killed me") also no doubt motivated him to find these alternative methods. Using reverse psychology, his stepfather also motivated Nick, at least temporarily, to make the honor roll. What made him not try for it the next semester is not clear. Perhaps it was simply too time consuming.

Although not being labeled early in his educational career may have worked to Nick's advantage in some ways, he reached a point when the label became useful. Without it, he could not have taken the English Regents exam untimed, an element he feels was necessary for him to pass it. Nick said that he scored almost 300 points higher in an untimed SAT than when he took a timed version. In the next section, Nick speaks indirectly about the power of attitude. In the same way his mother's high expectations and stepfather's reverse psychology motivated Nick to find alternate ways of learning, the perceived low expectations of some of his teachers invited him to do less than his best.

P: If you could speak to writing teachers, are there any specific dos and don'ts you would tell them regarding LD students?

N: I guess there's numerous dos and don'ts, but probably the number one don't would be to look at them differently—because a student usually is uncomfortable with their disability anyway, and any time a teacher almost looks down upon them and says, "You don't have to do this quality of work because you have a disability," that, in my mind, says that they don't think that we can do the work, so therefore they're not making us do the work. Therefore, they set a lower standard, and that perpetuates a continuously low quality of work. I see that happen continuously in high school as well as college.

P: Can you think of examples?

N: High school I can think of tremendous examples where many of my friends, because they're in the ah—resource room—that's what most high school uses [*sic*]—teachers allow them to have late assignments in, allow them to do assignments poorly because they assume that because they're in that room that gives them permission or the ability to do that quality of work. Specific examples? I can name numerous times when I myself have gotten away with not my best work because teachers would look at it and say, "Oh, that's all right. It's because he has a learning disability." And, you know, I used it to my advantage sometimes in high school. I'm that way sometimes, but you know, when I look back on it, I say they should have forced me to do the equal work, compatible to everyone else in the class, because I was capable of doing it. It just took me longer to make that final copy, to get that finished work.

P: If they allow late assignments, if they allow more time, how can you not be singled out?

N: I think it turns with writing assignments outside of class. They shouldn't get any extended periods of time unless the circumstances are substantial. They can say, "No, we want it at the same time, but I will work with you." They *should* get extra time for in-class exams. They might need an extra half hour to think it out.

P: I don't know if you can judge this, but what happens when you read? Why do you think it takes you that long to go through a passage?

N: Oh, that's very simple. I can't read the words. I can't read them. Like, for example, in a paragraph, there's probably—there's my law journals. Like, I'm a college student. It's junior year, and there's probably in a paragraph of law, out of one of my cases, I couldn't read probably ten to fifteen words. Like, I can't read them. Like, I don't know what they say.

P: Is it the vocabulary?

N: No, because—see, again. An example I can give you is, I used to help out at a nursery type school. I used to do community work there. I mean, literally, I was reading a book to the student, a little—I mean, it's like a third—it's like a book—and I couldn't read one of the words, and I had to make it up.

P: A third-grade book?

N: No. I don't even know what it was. It was like—kindergarten. I wrote a story on it, and that was like, one of the reasons I got tested, because I made up this word, because I couldn't read a kindergarten book, or whatever it was—a kiddie lit book, and I couldn't read it. So it's not just the vocabulary in the law book. It's everything. I can't pronounce things. Like the way I learn something is like if someone said the word before, so I know the word—what it sounds like? I can't—like names are really difficult for me. Like reading names off a sheet. I've never heard the words before, so therefore I always pronounce them incorrectly.

P: Can you tell me about that story you mentioned?

As Nick recounted this incident, his speech became halting and agitated, especially when he tried to remember the name of the book.

N: The story that I wrote—about the kindergartners? Yeah, well, what happened was, when I had to write my admissions essay for college, my resource room teacher, Mrs. Alvarez, she knew about the story, and she suggested I write about it. So I did because it really bothered me. And what happened was that I was doing community service. I was there and one of the little kids, I mean, not even in kindergarten, asked me to read something. It was the title, actually, I remember—I think—I remember it was the book—it—a fire eng—a fire comp—a fire engine—and the title—I still can't remember the title 'cause it's like blank. I guess it's like, shock or something, but I looked at the title, and they were like, "What's the book about?"—and I'm like—I couldn't read the title. And at that moment—just to—I don't know how to describe it. It's like—I was insulted? And I don't even know like the right vocabulary to describe it, but at that moment I was just—it was appalling to me to think that this kid asked me to read something that *he* could read—and I couldn't. And that—it was just like—"What am I going to be? Am I going to be a bum?" or, you know, it was like from that time forward I couldn't believe this. And there's been numerous examples when that's happened—when I just couldn't read a word. Another example was—and this also is—this is really bad; you're going to hate this. It's called Slave Day? And we don't do it anymore, and what—

P: Fraternity stuff?

N: No, no. It was for high school. It was to raise money. They would be a slave for someone for a day. It was in this chemistry class, and the teacher asked me to read, and I couldn't read a word.

P: She asked you to read something?

N: Out of the text, and I couldn't read a word. And it was a *stupid* word, but it took me ten minutes to decipher it. And she's the type of teacher that won't let you give up?

P: Um-hm.

N: So we sat there for ten minutes with my girlfriend sitting next to me and the whole class sitting behind me—'cause I sat right in the front row—trying to decipher this word. And I didn't get it until, until one of my friends goes, "Nick, you *know* this word," and I'm like, "What do you mean?" and he's like, "What's N.J.?" And I'm like, "Initial." And he says, "Just put *ly*." And it was *initially*. The word was *initially*. And I couldn't decipher it. I didn't know what it was. And it wasn't helping that it was in front of everyone, and I just got nervous and nervous and nervouser [*sic*].

P: Oh yeah. Yeah.

N: And that was—that was after I got labeled, but that was, I mean, it's the same example as before—a time when, as a junior in high school, I should be able to read.

P: Humiliating, yeah.

N: Yeah.

In the next section, he talks about his experiences at his former college, where he was admitted under a special LD program.

P: What about now that you're in college? Do you think that the label, overall, is good or bad? Does it make a difference?

N: If you're asking if I could get away with not being labeled, I probably could. Would I have come to college if I wasn't labeled? No.

P: Why not?

N: Because that step from high school to college is a tremendous step for any student, and for an LD student is a tremendous—it's like—it increases the gap greatly. I went to a school that had an official LD program, and they had specialists to work with you, an official testing process, someone to read tests to you.

P: What do the LD specialists do, when they work with you, that, say, a non-LD specialist could not do?

N: I don't know—I think they were more sensitive to the issue than some other people would be, but they, with me—I was different than a lot of students. I just needed assistance in writing. I don't need the total, overall guidance, and that's because I feel I hadn't had the guidance until my junior year, so therefore I didn't rely on it.

P: Right.

N: I had to rely on myself getting everything done. So therefore I just needed a minute—I guess—I just used a very small number of services, where other students would need like everything across the board. Like they would help them with emotionally, personally, you know, everything [*sic*].

P: So you were just mainly getting the writing instruction.

N: Right.

P: What did they do?

N: The sad part about it was it was nothing like what you've done here, where you made me sit down and read it over myself and try to learn why—what mistakes I'm making. They would just—I would hand them the paper and run. I really would just leave the office because I had this—I still do have this fear when people read my paper. I sit there and I get really nervous, and I'm uncomfortable. I feel like they're thinking to themselves, "Oh my God, this kid's made the same mistake twenty times!" And that's why, you know, I always left. It was bad—I mean, it was good that she was doing that for me, because she knew I was uncomfortable with it, but it's also bad in the sense that she was allowing me to continue to be—to not assist me to overcome my—to better myself, or whatever.

P: So what did she do with the paper?

N: She would just correct it, and I would come back like in, you know, a half hour or an hour and sit down with her and she'd say, "The idea is good, but you have a few mistakes here, and maybe increase, you know, be more specific here." Stuff like that. And she'd read the overall paper and give me feedback from it.

P: Would she actually fix the spelling errors?

N: Yeah, actually, she would, and that's what's—that's—actually, I had a spell checker on my computer, so I would fix the errors, but a lot of them, I'd have the wrong word, like um—

P: Yeah. And then it doesn't pick them up.

N: Yeah. And so—that's due to either laziness or just—I don't really know.

P: So did that special LD work help you with your academic life?

N: Yes, it did. Overall, I had like a 3.2 average. I got a 2.9 my first semester and a 3.38 my second semester, and I wouldn't have been able to got that without their assistance [sic].

Several professionals who advise LD university students share Nick's mixed feelings about LD support programs in secondary and postsecondary institutions and are adamant in their recommendations that LD students become "weaned from accommodations and guided toward self-sufficiency." Loring Brinkerhoff, Stan Shaw, and Joan McGuire base this advice on a study that found that only 38 percent of LD high school graduates had full-time jobs. Given what has happened in the high schools, they warn against advocating for all kinds of support that the student may not need and that may make the transition to professional life more difficult. They include a chart listing actions that foster dependence and ones that foster independence, the main idea being to "operationalize a mind-set" in which the counselor is not seen as helping the "passive" student, but is rather a "facilitator" in helping the student make decisions (1992, 425–26). While they recognize the need for select accommodations, they also support the least-restrictive environment movement.

P: What about using the word *difference* instead of *disabled*?

N: I've heard that, and I don't know. Yeah, it is a learning difference, but it also is a disability, so I don't know *what* it is. I would say that *difference* is politically correct? I guess that would be it.

P: So it's just a word?

N: Yeah. And that—I'm not into that. I'm like, I don't know—If people want to say I'm stupid, I don't care because for most of the—sometimes I would agree with them—but I let them say what they want.

P: What were you taking at that college? What about the textbooks? Were you still not reading the textbooks?

N: No. That's funny. Actually, I began to read them, and I was reading everything. What is weird is I did read everything, and so therefore—that's why I left [his former college]. Not because I read everything, but because I spent so much time on academics that I didn't do much else. And that's one of the reasons I left. So I was reading the material, but it would take me, you know, hours and hours on end.

The supreme irony here is that serious, hardworking students like Nick are still being told, verbally or nonverbally, that they're lazy, when some are spending every waking moment doing school work. They internalize what uninformed people say or imply about them. No matter how deeply buried, the low estimations teachers, parents, or peers have about these students' intelligence, even their morals, are revealed in sometimes offhand comments these students make about themselves.

Nick's story was fascinating as I spoke with him in person. Later, as I was transcribing the tape, I became more aware of quickly muttered comments he made, almost under his breath. Sometimes I had to play the tape on my stereo's highest volume to translate his remarks, but in many ways they are more revelatory than his more clearly articulated comments:

"she was allowing me to continue to be . . ."

"I didn't have the skills of the regular, normal students. . . ."

"not to better myself . . ."

". . . you learn to be ah—deceiving. . . ."

"If people want to say I'm stupid, I don't care because for most of the—sometimes I would agree with them. . . ."

"the wrong word . . . and that's due either to laziness or . . ."

In these words, Nick shows that he too, perhaps like some of the adults in his childhood, attributes his reading and writing difficulties to some kind of moral flaw. That young people are made to feel this way is outrageous. If we do nothing else in our various disciplines to alter educational philosophy and practice, if we agree on nothing else, we must change how society thinks of LD students, because students are absorbing these self-hating attitudes, in much the same way the self-deprecatory Brazilian peasants Freire describes began to think of themselves in the same negative way as did their oppressors (Freire [1970] 1988, 49).

And for LD students, *that* is the disability, and it is a learned one: the inner belief that one is somehow inferior to one's peers. Whatever initial difficulties someone like Nick might have with linguistic processing skills are compounded by the implication, or by the useless, potentially harmful advice, that if only he would try harder, concentrate more, spend more time—in short, if only he would be more normal—these problems would go away. When he follows this advice, spending far more time on schoolwork no doubt than are his self-righteous advisers, he sees only limited results and becomes even more alarmed with what he sees as his abnormality. Only the most determined, thick-skinned students continue to work so hard on written assignments. Many people feel it is not worth the aggravation and humiliation. They drop out.

It would not be that way, however, if educational institutions recognized different ways of knowing and if they took more advantage of computer technology. It would not be that way if students were allowed to *re-able* themselves by learning in ways that work best for them. In the next exchange, Nick talks about the role of computers in his life and the difference between handwritten and word-processed material.

P: What about written exams?

N: That's a—I just write them, and teachers give me a *B* too, on those, and I don't understand how because if I ever read my writing, like, just off the paper?—I don't know how they can count the information. I think they just go through and look for key words because I don't think it makes sense. I read it and it makes sense, but I know I write so much better on the computer 'cause that's the way I do it. I write it right on the computer and that quality—I think if you looked at my writing out of class and writing in-class test materials, there's like this huge gap. . . . But most teachers don't grade on your writing style. They grade on the information presented.

P: When you look at your writing, what would you say you usually do, or don't do?

N: Mistakes?

P: The mistakes, but also, what are the good qualities and what are the things you need to fix? I guess the mistakes, yes.

N: The things I always—Like I have a problem with past and present tense: *are*, *was*, *is*—stuff like that—*ed*'s. You know, should it be *needed* or *need*? I do that a lot. And spelling. I've gotten a lot better on writing, you know, complete sentences. I used to write incomplete, but not so much in college any more. The things I do well? I don't know. Um. Sometimes I think I have great intuitions. I come up with great things, but I don't know if it's an accident or if I can really write that way. [He showed me a letter to the editor he wrote that was published.] Like I think this is one of my best material that I've ever written [*sic*], and I don't know if that's because—I don't—. A lot of people that read it say, "Is this your writing? Did you write this?" And I'm like, "What do you mean?" They really question whether I wrote that or not.

Not only does Nick have to overcome many hurdles to get his writing into an academically acceptable form, but when he does write something he considers good, there are people who doubt his authorship (he didn't say whether they were teachers or students). Even he begins to doubt his own talent: "I don't know if it's an accident or if I really can write this way." I asked him more about the reception his writing usually receives.

P: Would you say that the instructors here, when grading the blue book [handwritten] exams, take off for the kinds of things you do—like the wrong words or the misspellings?

N: No, they don't, and I'm grateful for that. They usually don't take off for spelling mistakes, punctuation or structure mistakes, which is good, I think, because you just want the ideas. You want to know if the kid knows the material and can process it. So, no, they don't take off for that.

P: When did you start using the computer?

N: High school. My mom bought it for me Christmas my senior year.

P: Can you type? Touch type?

N: Yeah.

P: Where did you pick that up?

N: We were taught in school.

P: When did you start composing right on the computer?

N: Probably when I got the computer. Even before that, I've always done that. I remember my senior paper, I did it then. Before that, I never wrote anything, so ever since . . .

P: Is there any difference for you, when reading it over? Between writing in the blue books and writing on the computer?

N: Is there any difference? Yeah, there's a big difference—on the computer —'cause I make a lot of mistakes. Like I write the wrong word, or I don't know how to spell it, and it's easy on the computer. You just go backspace and go over it, or you just leave it, if it's a spelling mistake, and you just get it at the end with the spell check. Whereas when you're writing, if you make a mistake spelling it's like, scribble it out. And then most of the time I don't know how to spell it anyway, so I just leave it.

In many ways, Nick was more fortunate than many other LD students. He had a parent who realized what a computer could do for her son and who was able to provide one for him at home. He was also in a school system that enabled him to learn to type. Since so many other LD students have attested to the computer's role as a lifeline in their lives (see Chapter Five), providing them for such students should become a priority. Another priority might be a shift in emphasis from writing to speaking, or at least a sharing of emphasis, a point Nick makes below concerning the role of oral communication skills in what he calls "the real world."

P: This is probably a leading question—very unscientific—but do you think that reading and writing are the best measures of what you know?

N: No. You see, that's—this is the controversy I have about school, because when you get out in the "real world"—quote unquote the real world—we're in a fake world here—you're not given a written question you have to write down. It's more like, on the spot. You know, you're a salesman and the person says, "Well, why is this?" and you have to orally dictate, "Well, you know, it's because the economy is this way and this way." And you've got to know the things *orally*, and not writtenly [sic].

P: That's an excellent point.

N: Yeah. Just like in the criminal justice field. You've got to know the material orally. And it's hard to do oral tests. I mean, it's not feasible for teachers to be able to do oral tests, but I don't think it's the best—I guess written are the most efficient, but the most effective would be orally, I guess, because that's what you're going to be doing when you get a job and you have to communicate with other people. I've seen people that—people like my sister. Book smart. She's going to [Ivy League school]. She's applied early admission—just tremendous skills. Book smart. But IPC skills? [interpersonal communication skills] She can't get up and talk to people. She can't communicate. Like to a crowd or to someone she doesn't know. She gets real nervous and "Duhhhhh." And that's just her. That's her personality.

P: Here's another leading question. Do you think that schools should move away, a little bit, from the emphasis on the written? Do you think that college teachers should look at more alternate ways of conducting class or testing people?

N: [Pause] Yes and no. It would be interesting to see how people perform other ways, 'cause I think that's when you see how much information they do know. But writing is so important. It *is* important in our culture, and so I think college teachers *have* to teach and test that way, just to improve writing skills, but I do think they should move towards, maybe, not just testing but having one or two tests that are alternate.

P: Have any suggestions?

N: That's hard. But like I said earlier, it would be interesting to see how students perform orally on a test.

P: Well, it would sure give people like you—

N: An advantage.

P: Do you learn more from the professors who are better orally?

N: Yes, I do. I learn more when they speak energetically and they go crazy like [names his favorite professor] does. 'Cause that—I can't get excited by written material—like readings and stuff. I'm like, "Yeah, you know, whatever." For some of us to read it out loud and put feeling into it? Then I'd be like, "Oh, okay. Yeah."

P: So you must have hated English 135 [a course I taught, Introduction to Literature, which had a lot of reading].

N: I didn't *hate* it. I mean, I did the work, and it was a fun class when we got in discussions in class, but what I remember about the class overall is the discussions we had when everyone used to yell at me 'cause I used to say things.

P: [laughs]

N: But I used to say them just to get people *talking*. And that's why I have a problem in classes when—I don't understand—people don't ask questions. They don't talk. Like we have a Counseling and Interviewing class, and I noticed just the other day, yesterday, I was really tired, and if I didn't say anything, no one would say anything. It came up that I'm taking Group Dynamics next semester, and they're like, "You're gonna *love* that class." And yeah, I will, because I'll *talk*. But I don't understand why other people don't. I guess because they don't—that's not their skill.

P: They're not good at it.

N: Their skill is writing.

As I listened to Nick speak about his love of talking and how it would give him an advantage in school were it allowed to matter more, I realized that *learning disabled* would quickly become a misnomer for him if oral and written talents were weighed equally in academia. Presently, Nick is "disabled," but only because those who read and write easily might be called "advantaged," or "overly abled" in our society. As Nick rightly observes, writing is certainly important and must continue to be stressed. His situation, however, seems to suggest that were oral skills valued more, many bright students currently relegated to the metaphorical trash heap of our educational system would be *re-abled* in ways that would enrich the overall classroom culture. In our discussion of the pros and cons of labeling, Nick gives his views of the high school resource room. He seems to change his mind about labeling as he recalls its effects.

P: One of the controversies with LD is this whole business of being labeled.

N: The labeling theory.

P: Do you think that labeling from an early age is useful? Harmful? Do you have any thoughts about that?

N: Actually, I do. It's a necessity. There are some students that need to be labeled at an early age because they're just—their skills are just so deficient that it's impossible for them to function in a class without extra help. Do I feel that's fair? No. I've seen kids with more intelligence than I've have ever could have [sic] in my whole lifetime just get weeded out, just because they're in the resource room. If you're in the resource room when you're in the third grade, okay, when you go to junior high, you're in the resource room no matter what. You're not allowed to take Regents classes and then—it's just—it's just—. Like these kids—we're all together in elementary school, and we're all like, if you can picture it, we're walking down a path? All together. And then, one by one, they all just, like step off the path in different directions. And it's not in better directions, either. And I question whether that's right or not. I mean, not right or wrong, but whether that's fair to the students, because they have the ability, but by labeling them? They say, "Oh, all right, I'm a dummy. I'm gonna work construction the rest of my life." I mean, that was me. Up until that junior year when she told me I had the ability to go to college, I assumed I was going to go get a construction job and work construction the rest of my life. And that's not a bad job. It's not degrading. I mean, I could have made a lot of money working construction. But so many students have—they could do—they could achieve better goals than just giving up and taking that, but they don't because the schools says they can't early on. So then they just say, "Okay, I can't." And it's *terrible* because it's just taking their ability and saying, "You might have this ability, but we're not going to work to it because we just don't have the time or energy, so you might as well learn how to do this job and be happy with it. Be good at it." Fine, if that's what they want to do. But a lot of times, I would imagine that's not what they want to do. That they're just stuck with it.

The discussion about expectations continued. He referred again to his earlier story about his stepfather making a bet with him.

N: When people would say, "You're this way," I'd just to spite them, just to prove them wrong . . . And an example is that, when my stepfather bet me, he said, "No you couldn't do that," I'm like, "Okay. I'll do it." But once I proved it, it was like, "Whatever."

P: Not everybody would do what you did. Some people would say, "Yeah, you're right. I can't."

N: Yeah. And that's what I saw a lot of times. I used to sit in that room, and I'd get so frustrated at students because—

P: Which room?

N: The resource room. Because like, you know, you hang out in there and stuff, just sometimes. I'd go to my study halls there to get help, and I'd sit there and watch. I'd watch some students. They would—just to be *mad* and *stubborn*—they'd just sit there like this [He folded his arms in front of him] and not do the material.

P: Um-hm.

N: And it's like—I *know* they can do it. I've seen them do it before, when they're excited about something. You know, some of these kids—they—they can go into the garage, and like, know how to fix an engine—when it requires more skills than you could ever imagine!

P: Oh, I know.

N: I mean, you've got to know how to read. You've got to know how to calculate the numbers. And they could do it. And so I question whether it's the environment or—I don't know.

P: And also, the attitude has nothing to do with intelligence. It could have been caused by the emotional stress, or expectations, or something else—

N: Which could have been caused by the label.

P: Exactly.

N: And so, somehow they get in this circle, and then you don't know how to—that's how I see it—they're in a circle, and everything causes something, you know. They're being labeled does get them extra help, but it also causes them to feel this way.

Nick has discovered the paradox of LD labeling: it provides help in the form of readers, scribes, word processing, taped textbooks, and other necessary tools for many people, but at what cost? Who wants their peers to know they need "extra help" and must go to a special place to receive it? No matter what terms are used to describe learning disabilities or the room in which they are remediated, the targeted group will feel humiliated as long as they feel inferior to the mainstream. The solution, of course, cannot be an "either/or" answer. Total immersion in the mainstream, while not altering the mainstream, will not work because most classrooms from grade school through college are set up to accommodate linguistically talented people. Education is based on much reading and note-taking, and assessment is linked almost entirely with reading and writing ability. While "resource room" and other "extra help" places are more geared to the learning of LD students, they are, no matter how helpful and humanely staffed, by their very nature punitory because they make students feel inferior to the majority—that feeling being more disabling than anything. In the next section, Nick proposes ideas on making the mainstream more accessible to LD students.

P: Do you think that there are different kinds of intelligences?

N: People set these standards for writing styles—that this is right. This is the way they teach it. But why? Who said that was right? You know, someone came up with this idea that this is the way it should be, but now . . . You know, I think that people *do* think differently, and therefore, when they write, they *write* differently, so therefore people are *set* to learn a certain way, and some people just don't—they're just, you know, they would be intelligent if they were in an environment that was conducive to their learning habits. I mean, they would be, not everyone, but there are probably students who would be superior to the most intelligent people on this campus if they were in an environment conducive to their learning style. If people drilled me twenty-four hours a day, orally, I would be able to absorb a lot of information, but that's not the way it's done. You know, you've got to read it on your own. You've got to do it on your own.

P: Right.

N: So I do think there are learning differences. There are different intelligences.

Finally, when asked near the end of the interview to prioritize what should or should not be done, Nick talks about questioning the authority of experts—about those with Ph.D.'s not necessarily having all the answers.

P: Is there anything else you can think of? Absolute dos or absolute don'ts for college—

N: Students? For college professors?

P: For professors, or students, or anybody.

N: The necessity, the skill, is *understanding.* The biggest thing is, don't be close minded about the issue—because who says you're right? I mean, society says you're right, but society's been wrong before, and so how do we know that your way of saying "This is the way it's going to be" is the right way? So I think open-mindedness—being open-minded about allowing the person to come to you and say, "This is what I have difficulties with," and not immediately saying, "Well, what makes you different than other students? What gives *you* special privileges?" You know, I had—I have a teacher this semester I *despise.* And he says to me, he says, "You know what? I think I was learning disability [sic] when I was young because I couldn't do this. . . ." And I'm like, thinking, "Well, maybe he was," but, he kind of like was looking down and saying, "If *I* didn't have it, why should you?" And like, in the middle of class, he'll like—like I walked in late the other day, and the professor said, "Nick, you want to take that test at seven o'clock, you know, your normal time outside of class?"—in front of the *whole* class! And you know, I can handle that because, like, I know what he's doing, and I'm just like, "Whatever," but most students would crumble. They would die. They would be like, "Ahhhh," and start crying and be like all emotional.

P: Oh, yeah.

N: And he's done that several times. So I think understanding is a big thing, understanding that you're not—just because you have your Ph.D., you don't—you aren't necessarily right.

Nick's last statement here could double as a subtitle for this book: "Just because you have your Ph.D., you're not necessarily right." As we have seen, those who have studied the most about learning disabilities are those who disagree most vehemently with their equally knowledgeable colleagues. So much disagreement among experts seems to indicate that we should expand our search for answers. This one interview with Nick reveals several areas where we might begin.

First, it is obvious from the transcript that Nick's speech is vivid, detailed, and syntactically sophisticated—traits valued in any kind of communication, but not often measured orally, as Nick himself points out. To assess what students know almost exclusively through one medium—writing—privileges those who are talented in that area and is blatantly unfair to people like Nick, whose oral skills are far superior to those of many of his peers who today receive higher grades and status.

Second, reading and writing are, as Nick observes, vital to education and should continue to be stressed, but not to the exclusion of other opportunities for participation and assessment. People should not have to sneak off to a "special" (read "remedial") place in order to have access to textbooks on tape or the opportunity to take an exam orally. Such things should be designed into mainstream practice, not "to accommodate the disabled," but to value normal human beings whose natural talents respond more to oral texts than to written ones, who listen better than they read, who speak better than they write. The classroom climate would not be compromised by providing multi-modal learning; it would be enhanced for all involved. Nick's argument concerning requirements for "real world" success should be heeded: oral skills *are* necessary for almost every profession, and practice developing them is currently being compromised in mainstream classes in favor of reading and writing development. At the same time that "normal" (linguistically talented) students are allowed, like Nick's "book-smart" sister, to remain unreasonably frightened of speaking in front of a group and almost incapable of giving the most basic presentation, students like Nick are forced to endlessly and quite counterproductively edit a written report or paper that they could have presented orally.

What I am suggesting here is a broadening of imagination on the part of all teachers, on every level and in every field. We need to see reading as only one way in which people learn. For many English professors, including myself, curling up with a favorite novel and reading for hours on the back porch or at the beach is a luxurious activity, and one we cherish. We need to remember that for many of our students, deciphering meaning from pages and pages of sentences, words, and letters is not pleasurable, but often painful. Reading a chapter in a textbook may not be simply annoying, but torturous.

Although writing, even for writing instructors, may occasionally be unsatisfying or even frustrating, we often compose easily, filling several computer screens in twenty minutes or so, producing a text which, if not inspiring, has few technical flaws except for some hasty typographical errors. For many of us, writing is our creative outlet, our medium of choice. A blank page or computer screen is an invitation, an opportunity for artistic expression, and the resulting text something of which we are proud. For many of our students, however, the blank page or computer screen is not an invitation but a threat, and the finished text often a humiliating display of their written language difficulties.

While Nick is quite right to say that reading and writing are, and always will be, important in our society and should continue to be stressed, he is also right to say that the "real world" demands far better oral skills than some of our most academically successful students are today prepared to deliver. To even the odds for everyone, it makes sense to provide more opportunities in school and college for all students to learn and to be assessed using a variety of instruments. Textbooks and written exams, the workhorses of academia, should become more of a part, and not the almost exclusive whole, of school work. To maintain the status quo, with its overemphasis on the written word, is not only discriminatory, but an unrealistic representation of the world beyond graduation. In addition, it absolutely wastes the talents of those who might excel at speaking, drawing, or using technology, while denying "normal" students who may have a "disability" in those other areas the opportunity to "overcome" it.

Finally, it is time to stop being polite about slurs regarding people's skills. Just as stereotypical or derogatory racial and gender comments are no longer tolerated, remarks about people's intelligence based on their difficulties with reading and writing should not be acceptable. Since their main learning abilities may lie elsewhere, we should not judge them unless we are prepared to be similarly judged on our ease in the mathematical, artistic, or technological arenas.

The most helpful thing about resource rooms, Nick said, was the special education teacher's understanding of his situation. The most irritating aspect of the regular classes was some mainstream instructors' insensitive, or downright rude, insinuations about Nick's intellectual abilities. The insular nature of academic disciplines allows this kind of ignorance to flourish. What LD professionals know about these students' areas of expertise needs to be acknowledged and utilized by instructors across the disciplines. And if those mainstream instructors cannot or will not take the time to become informed about this, they should stop pontificating about that which they do not understand. Nick's anger at the professor who embarrassed him in front of an entire class is justified, as is his frustration with this same person who implied that Nick's disability was imagined, or something that could easily be overcome with a bit of self-discipline and moral fiber—traits of which this man no doubt imagined himself the model.

While Nick may be at a point in his life where he can now hear these comments in perspective, there are undoubtedly many younger or less confident students for whom such insults are devastating. Those in authority over young people must realize the power they have to influence students' confidence and self-esteem. A casual, careless remark made during class or even in the hallway on the way to get a cup of coffee can damage students' self-perception and motivation for the rest of their lives. It may also be time for others in authority, when overhearing such remarks, to grab the perpetrator by the collar (metaphorically speaking) and say (perhaps not in these exact words), "Listen, you ignoramus, stop spouting your arrogant, misinformed advice. If you don't know what you're talking about, keep your mouth shut! Students might actually believe what you say to them!" Teachers do influence what path these students take. In Nick's words, "We're all walking down a path. All together. And then, one by one, they all just, like, step off the path in different directions. And it's not in better directions, either."

Positive statements can be just as powerful, as was illustrated when Nick's chemistry teacher complimented his intelligence but advised him to seek help and then attend college. In just a few moments after class one day, one individual telling Nick he was smart may have counteracted the influence of an entire system telling him he was not. By analyzing his situation in a complimentary way, she convinced him to stay on an academic path, forging his own alternate literacy through his aptitude for speaking and listening.

As educators, we must stop insisting that all people educate themselves almost exclusively by the means that *we* find most convenient: reading and writing. Students like Nick, with his intuition, his listening and speaking skills, and his creativity, can help those of us locked into traditional ways of knowing and learning to imagine a different way to teach, to consider multi-modal classrooms and flexible assessments. In short, Nick's insights can help us invite his "reject room" colleagues back onto the path, to allow the "disabled," with their alternate intellectual capacities, to *re-able* their learning and development.

Monica

The second student I spoke with was Monica, an occupational therapy major who, like Nick, had managed a *C* average in high school, but unlike him, was not labeled as LD until she encountered substantial obstacles during her first year in college. Like Nick, she has reading problems that seem to stem partially from social pressure and partially from a difficulty with sounding out unfamiliar words. First of all, the more nervous she is when reading in public, the worse her reading becomes, and understandably so. But as with Nick, simple reading apprehension does not fully explain the extent of her difficulties. According to the testing that was eventually done on her during her first year in college, Monica's ability to decode new words remains at a third-grade level. While her vocabulary and oral word comprehension is appropriate to her age and grade, her overall reading ability is not quite at seventh-grade level, brought down by the weakness in decoding. Although she was tested in high school because she often confused word endings, her test performance at the time was high enough to keep her out of the LD category. In a paper she wrote for an occupational therapy course, Monica expresses anger that she was never diagnosed as LD in her elementary school years. The more she researched this topic, the more she saw her own history echoed in the typical problems LD children have. Not learning about LD until college, she said, confused and frustrated her.

In her writing samples, some of the errors she makes are the same kinds of errors most college students occasionally make: *to* for *too*; *were* for *wear*; *there* for *their*; *who's* for *whose*, and confusions over possessives (*Joseph younger brother*, instead of *Joseph's younger brother*). Like Nick, however, Monica makes many more of these, in my judgment, than do most college students. She also has many fused sentences, comma splices, and other punctuation errors of the type that many first-year students make. It is difficult to determine when the number of these kinds of errors crosses some threshold of normalcy. I do know, however, that she took a composition course from the faculty member at my institution most committed to having students eradicate such surface errors, so the fact that such mistakes stubbornly appear in her writing today is not due to ignorance. In fact, in describing her writing during the interview, she said she knew she was still making comma splices.

In addition to these common errors, however, Monica also makes errors less typical of other writers. In her research paper she wrote the phrase, *In Brad cause*, instead of *In Brad's case*. One of her sentences reads, "Brad has trouble writing *want* he wants to say." Later, she writes, "The same thing happens *went* he asked a question" (emphasis mine). The text from which these examples were taken was not a first draft, but a final, word-processed copy of a research paper handed in for a grade. They do not appear to be the result of simple carelessness, and they may be related to Monica's use of *slack*, when she probably means *flak*, in the following interview. From Monica's other writings come many spelling errors: *comennants* for *commandments*; *phrophet* for *prophet*; *scrad* for *sacred*; *vengens* for *vengeance*; and *teched* for either *teach* or *detected*. Many people, of course, make spelling errors, but these seem to reflect a difficulty envisioning the correct word. Therefore, she apparently makes do with phonetic spelling, except in the case of *phrophet*, where she realizes there is a *ph* in the word somewhere, but cannot produce the proper configuration of letters. In the interview, Monica says that her difficulties with written English are the result of her mind racing faster than her hands on the keys. That, too, may explain things, and I can attest to the speed at which she speaks. Since the purpose of this chapter is not to overanalyze bits of students' writing, but to hear their experiences, I mention these errors because they remind me so much of my former student Barbara's attempt to spell *specifically*. Early in the interview, I asked Monica about her academic history, and later about what she thought about labeling in general.

P: How did you come to be labeled?

M: When I was a freshman, I was an occupational therapy major, and I was taking all these classes like Intro to OT, Human Development, Anatomy and Physiology. Out of five classes, I got four deficiencies. I called home crying to my mother, "I studied. I really did study! I don't understand what happened." This, that, and the other thing. And my mother kept saying, "Well, if you'd stop socializing and study." And I'm like, "Mom, I do study." I kept telling her, "I study. It's not like I socialize. I study." And she kept telling me, you know, that I just fool around and I don't study. I got pissed at her. Well, I took Professor Twiss's reflex test. I took it five times. She allows you to take it until you pass. Five times my highest grade was a 52.

P: What's a reflex test?

M: In infancy, zero to four months, there's one reflex. Then four months to six months there's another reflex. She gaves you—she gives you the reflex, and then on the test, she kind of explains a little bit about it, and you have to give the reflex and the age it integrates, the age it comes into play. And I took that test five times and couldn't pass. So I went to [Professor] Twiss and I was crying, and I said, "I studied this. After five times you'd think I'd get better than a 52." And I'm crying. This is the end of my frustration, the end of my rope. She just said, "Well, let's go over it." So I calmed down and we went over it. And I knew everything. And she says, "Come in on Friday. You're taking it orally." I got a 92 on that exam.

P: You took it orally?

M: Orally. I got a 92. So that's when she encouraged me to go down to Academic Support and get tested.

P: What was the written test like?

M: It was fill in. It was a sentence, and you put in the words. I had to recall what the reflex is and what age it integrated, and I couldn't recall any of that. I kept mixing them up—putting one word—like, there's two words to the reflex. I put—I'd mix the words up. I couldn't do it.

P: But you could do it—

M: Orally. 'Cause she had a dummy out on the table, and she says, "What would this reflex be?" I'd show her exactly what it is. She'd say, "When does it integrate?" I told her exactly. And it was really—it was—I was shocked. I cried after that, too. [laughs] It was a very emotional freshman year.

P: Wow. So it was oral, but there was also the dummy there. Do you think that made any difference?

M: It was all hands on. It wasn't that. It was just that I couldn't interpret the text. The problem was interpreting the text. It was like that for all my classes. And I talked to [Professor] Walton 'cause I had failed the Bio lab practical, and I told him, I said, "If you just give it to me orally, I swear I will do a lot better." He goes, "If I do it for you, I have to do it for every single other person that passed—that failed." And I'm like, "I'm sorry, but I am being tested for an LD." He said, "Well, are you LD?" I said, "I don't know. I'm being tested for it." He said, "Well, what you get is what you get. I can't do anything about it." I ended up getting a straight *F* in the class.

P: Ew.

M: I know. [laughs] I can give you another example. When I took Bio 102, I took a night class with Garrahan. And I took the midterm, and he allowed me to take it in another classroom because I was considered LD. I take it by myself so I can talk to myself? And I went into the other room, and I just broke down and cried because I knew every single one of those, and I couldn't do it. It was matching. And I couldn't do it. And he comes in. Professor Garrahan comes in and looks at me, and he says, "Monica, are you okay?" And I just broke down crying, saying, "I *know* these. I studied. It's the same thing as 101! I'm gonna fail!" I'm hysterical. So he just looked at me and says, "What is oxitocin? Where does it come from?" And I told him.

P: What is what?

M: Oxitocin. It's a hormone. I told him exactly what it is. Then he said, "Look down at the paper. What do you think it is?" And I'm like, "*B*". He's like, "Okay." And then, "What does this one word do?" I told him. "Where does it come from?" I told him. "What do you think it would be?" I got the entire first page right.

P: Wow.

M: Just because he said, "What is it? Where does it come from? What do you think it does?" Then I'd look down at the paper. "What do you think it is?" And I got the entire first page right. I got a *C+*. I mean, it's not great, but it's good.

P: Yeah! But you couldn't do it on the paper?

M: No. And I don't understand why.

P: But you could recognize it after you said it out loud?

M: Um-hum. Which is why I try to push for my exams being [given] orally, or taken by themselves or on the computer.

Sometimes Monica's speech is so fast that she leaves out words. As I had done with Nick, I must have been automatically supplying the words in my head because her sentences seemed complete to me at the time. I was never confused about what events happened when. If her mind races ahead of her speech, which it seems to be doing above, then that supports her explanation below of why she omits words in her writing.

M: Part of [being] an LD student is frustration, and when you sit down and write a paper, and you have to actually write it out, and it takes longer. A lot of people like myself think faster than I write, so then I'd be writing down one thing and thinking another, so everything's all jumbled together. And then when you go back and read the paper in your mind out loud how you think you thought you wrote it, but actually you're not reading the words on the paper. And when you hand it in, it comes back with a horrible grade, and you can't understand why. One of the reasons I use a computer is because I think faster than I write. That's why I can type faster and get everything organized, and I can't spell, too. That's why—I would tell them, if someone's having a problem, to use a computer.

P: Can you explain more about how you read what you thought you wrote, but not what you *did* write?

M: Instead of *the*, I'll say *them*, or instead of *then*, I'll say *them*. If it's *right*, I'll say *left*. I can't read the words because one, I can't read out loud because I'm concentrating on the words on the paper because of the fact if you mess up, people laugh at you type thing. If you say *them*, they'll be yelling at you, "It's _then_!" I've never been good at reading out loud, so when I read the paper, I read it so quickly that I can't read the words right. It's not that I can't read. It's not that I don't know the words. It's just the fact that I get them mixed up. If it's *say*, I say *said*.

P: Why do you think you'll read a word that's not on the page?

M: I don't know. All I know is when I read—like say, a professor asks me to read in class, I don't want to say, "No. I'm not going to," 'cause then they'll say, like "Why?" And I don't want to say, "I can't read." So what I've done before in the past, is take a piece of paper and held it [*sic*] on top of the line below it, and then I can concentrate more on just that line. 'Cause I end up skipping lines and stuttering.

P: And that works for you?

M: People look at you funny, but at least it's better than missing words. I mean, I'm not classified as hyperactive, but I think I am. I can't sit down for long periods of time. I get frustrated, and the anxiety level increases. And then the professor, after you've read the whole thing will say, "Now what does that mean?" I'll have no clue what it means! I'm busy concentrating on what I'm reading, too busy making sure I get the words right, making sure that I pronounce them right. I don't know what it means! And then I'll get, "Well, you just read it." And it's like, "Yeah, I understand I just read it." And that's when I get really quiet and I just don't say anything. I'm not a quiet person, but sometimes in class, I do get quiet.

It's important, therefore, that instructors not leap to conclusions about a student's lack of participation in class. There may be a myriad of reasons why people dislike reading or speaking in class. While some of Monica's problems with reading and taking exams in class are influenced heavily by anxiety—no doubt the result of years of bad experiences in similar situations—anxiety alone does not account for the severity of her difficulties. In her next comment, Monica describes the frustration of having to deal with a person in authority who does not believe in the existence of learning disabilities.

M: And then you've got these professors who don't help you. Like I'm having trouble with [Professor] Olson right now because he doesn't believe in LD. He doesn't believe that people have LD's. He wanted me to take my test on a portable Macintosh in the class, in front of everyone, on the professor's desk. I told him I wouldn't do it. I said, "One, it's going to take me longer. This is an essay test. Two, there's going to be everyone looking at me, wondering why I have a computer. Three, everyone's going to be quiet, concentrating. I'm going to be typing on the keys." I said, "It's not fair to them. It's not fair to me, and I refuse to do it." He looked at me, and he said, "Well, that's the only way it's going to be." So I went down to Academic Support and I said, "I want to take this on a computer. He will not allow me to take it except in a class." So they fought for me. And they fought it to the point where I can take it at the same time in Academic Support. So the secretary had to stay later, just so I can take it 'cause he didn't want me to take it during the day.

P: Hmmm.

M: I mean, I think that's a little ridiculous.

What happened to Monica here has a similar precedent in case law. In 1989, a University of California, Berkeley math professor refused to allow a labeled LD student more time on an exam, claiming that learning disabilities did not exist. Although the university instructed the professor to provide the accommodation, he refused, whereupon the student sued. The university ultimately settled out of court, but the professor himself had to pay monetary damages sought by the student for having to make the case public (Brinkerhoff et al. 1992, 423).

P: Are there things that college professors could do, or not do, that would make your life a lot easier?

M: A lot of students are intimidated by professors. I've gotten, "I'm not going to deal with—I'm a Ph.D. I can take off as many points as I want. I'm a Ph.D. I've worked for this. I'm a Ph.D. I can do this how I felt it needs to be done." I was flabbergasted. I mean, what can you say after that comment? It's like, you know, they're not going to do anything. "I'm a Ph.D. I can do what I want. I can take off as many points as I want to take off." I was *so* angry at her.

We talked a bit then about her trouble with tests and with taking notes during class. When I suggested that she tape record lectures, she pointed out that many teachers speak too fast or too low, and that sometimes other talking or noise in the classroom makes it impossible to hear much of the lecture. At this point she showed me notes from one of her classes, as well as the same notes she said it took her three hours at home to "translate" into something of which she could make sense. All her hard work, however, did little good. She said, "I studied two weeks straight. Got a 65 on the exam. I was so angry."

In the next segment, as Monica relates more of her experiences, her anger continues to dominate. After a time, however, her tone modifies and she gives some clear, simple advice.

P: If you had a chance to speak for one half hour to writing teachers—all college professors—what would you say, in terms of dos and don'ts?

M: I'd start off by saying that an LD is not something we'd choose to have. We don't choose to have to feel frustrated. We don't choose to slack off on our work or not have work up to par. We work harder than a lot of regular students. We stay up late nights studying, and other people study twenty minutes before the exam. I'd tell them that people learn at different rates, different ways. I'd say, professors can make it a lot easier for LD students just by giving them the attention they need, either by computer, by oral exam, by tutoring. I'd explain the frustration—like the class clown. I mean, they might feel really uncomfortable in class, so they're frustrated, so they lash out, by either being very verbal with the professor or being—try to make jokes about things. Like if you asked them to read, they might say, "No, I'm not going to," or joke about things. Frustration level is great for them. A lot of people who feel frustrated don't want to come to class because they don't want to deal with trying to get the notes down and then taking the exam and not knowing any of the answers.

P: How could they test you on what you know? I mean, how would they do it differently?

M: This is only my experience, 'cause LD students are all different. A problem comes in when keywords aren't given, and if you don't have a keyword, you can't figure out the answer.

P: Can you explain that?

M: On an objective test, you can only go by those words on the test to find out the answer. Well, if you don't have one word in there to trigger a memory, to trigger something in your mind, then you can't find the answer. And by giving it orally, you can discuss more about the topic and get that keyword, and that's what triggers the memory, and then you can just—like that 102 exam that I took in Garrahan's [class]—[he] spoke to me orally, "What does it do? Where is it from? So what's the answer?"

P: So how did the keyword come up?

M: Because part of LD is word retrieval, and if you don't have that keyword, you can't find that word. So you have a problem of retrieving a word, retrieving information that you've learned, processing it, and turning it around—which is probably—that's why I have a lot of trouble in physics. I don't know if you remember Lawrence Santone [a student who has since graduated]. He helped me a lot. We sat in that physics room, and we did everything, every homework problem, every question in the book. We did it. I knew *all* of them. I took the exam. I ended up failing because of the fact that keywords aren't there, or he wants us to do it one way, and I'll do it another way, just the way that I've learned it.

P: You couldn't take that exam orally?

M: He wouldn't give it to me orally. He did not want to take the extra time to do it. I told him I'd come to his office hours. That's what he's there for. He said he was busy. He wouldn't do it. I mean, the keyword is what the most important thing is.

P: Can you give an example of a keyword?

M: I don't know. I can't think of one.

P: Well, you were talking earlier about Professor Garrahan, how he said, "What does it do? Where does it come from?" Do you remember what that triggered?

M: It just—it just like opened that folder in your mind. It just opened that folder and talked about the oxitocin, and once he said, you know, "What's the oxitocin?" I told him, "It's a hormone." He said, "So what does the hormone do?" So I told him, "It's the hormone for the mammary glands for milk." "Where does it come from?" [he asked]. And I'm like, "From the breasts," and he's like, "Okay, so where's the answer?" So then you look down, and you see the answer. I mean, he's not giving me the answer. He's just leading me in the right direction.

P: Right.

M: And if you go from that right to the next one, I'm still thinking about the oxitocin. I go to the next hormone, and I've got to sit back and I've got to think again, "What does this hormone do? Where does it come from? So what's the answer?" He went through the entire page like that. It wasn't like he was giving me the answer. He was just asking me questions. And that's what I have trouble doing: retrieving the information and switching it around and translating it to what the question is asking. But it's hard, you know. You get an objective test, and there's all these answers, like multiple choice. And the professor asks them orally and they just look at it, and they read it, and they read the answers, and I'm like, "Okay, I think I'd just rather take it myself, thank you." It's uncomfortable. It really is. I'd rather just sit there and discuss the information. Like Professor Hart's class. He gave me the test orally. It was on aquatics? He just sat in his office with the test in front of him. It was an essay test. He just looked at me and he says, "What do you think the qualifications of a pool should have?" So I told him, "The door should be wide enough that the wheelchair *and* the care-taker can walk through at the same time. There has to be either a chair lift or stairs getting in. There has to be a unisex dressing room for caretakers to change their clients" and this, that, and the other thing. He was like, "Fine," and went on to the others. If I had to sit there and write it, I'd be there forever.

P: How do you deal with reading textbooks?

M: I've had a lot of my books on tape. I listen to the tape and read along with it. The best way to learn is to get as many senses involved as possible. You hear it. You see it. Now after that, you do something with the information.

Of the three students I spoke with, Monica was the only one to have used taped textbooks, which she finds useful. This is consistent with what Christopher Lee says in his book, *Faking It,* about taped books being "a key to unlocking a world of words" (Lee and Jackson 1992, 53–54). In the next section, I asked Monica for her opinion on labeling. Like Nick, she has mixed feelings about it.

P: Do you think being labeled has helped you or hurt you?

M: I think it helped me in that I understand where my frustration is coming from. I understand it's not just me. That is, um, it's not me not being prepared. It's me not being able to process and translate information. It's given me a channel to go through to be successful in school.

P: What do you mean?

M: I can go to Academic Support. I can fight, with them, professors to get tests orally, professors' notes, all those things. I have someone to back me up and say, "No, she's not socializing all the time. She *is* doing work. She's just not being tested in the right way."

P: Have people said that to you? That you're not studying enough?

M: No one has said that to me. But I've gotten those computerized deficiency slips [that say] "Work is needed." And that's frustrating, too.

P: What do you think of labeling in general? Good? Bad?

M: I can go both ways on that. In elementary school if you're labeled LD, you go down to the resource room, and you get a lot of slack [she may have meant *flak*] from students laughing at you, teasing you. And I don't think that's right. I don't think labeling them is appropriate. I think LD students do need more help in the beginning because of learning gaps, but I think that mainstreaming is the best thing for them because they have the support of other students. They're just like other students, so they don't get the attitude that they're different—people laughing at them or anything like that.

P: But what if the mainstream requires lots of tests and written exams and taking notes and all the kinds of things you've been talking about?

M: I think they need to go through class just like everyone else do [*sic*], but you know, one period a day have a tutor who'd say, "What did you do today?" Discuss everything they'd done. Help them with their homework and also take tests during that period. So they skip class during a test. That's all students have to know. Then when you get older in high school . . . Kids are mean. They are cruel. I think that's where if you want to go to college, that's where preparation should take place. That's where you should learn how to study. That's where you should learn how to take notes, communicate with your professors in order to get your remediation. By then it doesn't really matter 'cause kids aren't as cruel in high school as they are in elementary school. They could be a little bit more mature to handle things. And then in college—um—I know a few kids who think they're special because they get teachers' notes and that's what causes teachers to get this stigma, and that's what causes them not to help with remediation for other students. So in college I think it [the label] would hurt the reputation of LD students. I mean, it explains frustration and why you are not as successful as others on exams. At the same time, it's not supposed to give them an attitude or give them [so that they claim?], "Well, I'm LD, you have to do this."

Monica, like Nick, has crystallized the ambiguity of the LD label. On the one hand, she says it partially explains her difficulties and enables her to more effectively fight for teaching and assessment practices that work for her. On the other hand, it singles her out, a painful effect, especially in elementary school, where "kids are cruel." She also recognizes that if some students use the LD label as an excuse for not doing work, it causes lasting damage among students and professors alike, trivializing requests for legitimate accommodations. As Monica continues, she describes the social ostracizing that occurred because of her failing grades in biology.

M: I was not asked to join study groups my freshman year because people thought, you know, "She's failing the class. Why bother asking her?" 'Cause they used to have Bio 101 study sessions, and my roommate would go to those, and one day I got so frustrated, and I said, "Why don't you ever ask me to go?" And there were a few people standing in the room, and they're like, "We didn't think you wanted to come." And I'm like, "Well, I'm a student too." And they're like, "Well, do you want to come?" And I'm like, "No. I don't really feel like coming." I mean, it's like, they're leaving me out.

P: And you could have probably helped them.

M: And they would have really helped me. That was a frustrating freshman year. I cried so much my freshman year.

P: That's a shame. Do you think that study groups would be a partial answer to LD students?

M: Yeah. Big time. 'Cause you're discussing the information, so you're reinforcing information. You can't just learn it; you have to do something with it. And even a good thing for a professor to do is before an exam, to say, "I'm holding a study session at this time. You're all welcome." It's not just for LD students. It could help everyone.

P: Do you think it would make any difference to change the name from *learning disability* to *learning difference*?

M: I don't think it would make a difference.

P: Why not?

M: *Learning difference/Learning disability.* It means the same thing. It really does. And both words are so close together people would mix them up anyway. That's a good example: *difference* and *disability*. I'd get those two words mixed up. [laughs] I would, definitely. Because you're thinking about one thing and you say another—because the words are so close together.

P: What about the idea of different learning *styles*? That's a term that's been bandied about, that some people learn better orally, that some people learn better if they see it. What do you think of that?

M: It's true, and I think we should change the name to learning *styles*.

P: If we're talking about different learning styles, where do you think your best talent lies? How would you capitalize on what you do best?

M: I do best in classes that involve discussion. It's fine if you lecture, as long as you dwell on important points. I do good on like study groups. Anything that's orally, I can do better on . . . [*sic*]. Professors who do oral discussions, essay tests—things like that would help me a lot.

At this point, Monica talked again about why she had so much difficulty with complicated essay questions or multiple-choice exams.

M: It's like fancy writing. They try to make it look real elegant [eloquent?]—like he's really intelligent. If you just give me a straight out question, I'll tell you what it is.

P: You could write it too?

M: Um-hum. I could write it—type it on the computer, I should say.

Monica said that her essay writing was fairly good, as long as she understood whatever question was being asked. Near the end of the two hours, I wanted to know what she thought was the most important thing for college professors to know or to do about LD students.

P: For purposes of emphasis, let's say you no longer have a half hour to talk to college teachers. You've got five minutes. You've got them in a room for five minutes, and you can say something to them, or give them advice—people who are interested in helping students with different learning styles. What's the most important thing for them to do or not do?

M: If I had five minutes, and I was up there in front of everyone, I'd start out by saying, "Is it your fault for having brown hair? Is it your fault for being tall, for being thin, for being short? Well, it's not the LD's fault for having an LD. But it is your responsibility to teach these students. It's your responsibility to get them through classes. Therefore, it's your responsibility to learn how they learn." I'd say stuff like—I'd go right to fairness. "Is it fair to test someone on what they don't know? Is it fair to word things in a way that people don't understand? Is it fair to humiliate them in front of class and do things they don't want to do?—like reading out loud and doing problems on the board? Is it fair to tell them they're not studying hard enough, when in all reality they are?" I'd say, "The people in your class who act up may just be frustrated and lashing out. It's up to you to teach the students. It's up to you to find out how they learn. All it takes is a five-minute conversation, to say, 'Is there anything wrong? If you have any questions, come talk to me. I'd be happy to discuss things with you.' It'll help if you say, 'Are you having trouble with class? Do you want to talk about the exam? You didn't do very well on it. Is there something I can do to help you?' It's your responsibility to help them through this, and by just giving them that little bit of attention, by giving them some indication that you care. I think it's the professor's responsibility to talk to them during office hours, to ask, 'Would you prefer to be tested in another way? Do you need any special remediation? Do you need to see a guidance counselor about being tested? I don't understand what an LD is.' It's okay. It's okay not to understand, just as long as you tell the LD student: 'I don't know what it is. I'd like to help you, but I don't know what to do.' That way you're telling the student, 'I'm ignorant. I don't know what to do, but I'm willing to help.' So as long as you keep an open line of communication. Then, after that, you've done your part. Then it's up to the student to come to you. It's up to the student to tell you what they need."

Monica's anger is more palpable than Nick's, but her request, although worded differently, is similar to his: that students and professors become more open-minded regarding accommodations, more tolerant of difference. The next interviewee eventually gives similar recommendations.

Janine

The third student I spoke with, Janine, had been living with an LD label for much longer than either Nick or Monica had. In first grade she was already in a special education class, but as she moved through the early grades, she took an increasing number of her subjects in a "regular" classroom. By sixth grade, she was back in the mainstream, but would leave class for extra help with her reading. In the first part of the interview, she talks about how she gave up getting help in the reading lab, a place for all students who needed help with reading, and began getting a different kind of help in the resource center, a place for LD students.

P: What was going on with your reading?

J: I can remember in junior high—the teacher—it didn't help that much? Like it was just not helping.

P: What?

J: The reading lab. It just didn't help for some reason. It got to the point where they realized that my learning disability was my phonics, and that's where I can't sound out words? I memorize all my words and everything like that. And the reading teacher in junior high tried to like teach me how to read, and it was just—her techniques wasn't [sic] working and everything.

P: So she was teaching you phonics?

J: Yeah. And it just wasn't working. And so that's when the resource center in my junior high stepped in and said, "We'll do reading with her. We'll do all the work with her," and stuff like that. And so, I think I was only in reading lab seventh and eighth grade, and I did more of the work in the resource center.

P: So the reading lab was not a resource room type place? It was for everybody who needed reading? And the resource center was more for special ed?

J: Yeah. You would come in and be like, "I need help with this." And you could do every subject in there with them, except for math.

P: How was your math?

J: It was good. It was really good.

P: So it was mainly the phonics, and reading?

J: Um-hum.

P: So what about today? How's your reading?

J: Much better. Like the resource center, they helped me more to learn how to work with my disability, and I learned how to work with it. Like they made me—like, I became a very organized person. Like when I got to junior high, I was taught right away to always use a dictionary. I was a *very* hard-working person, so I was very lucky that I got through it. And they just disciplined me to get organized and get structured and to know what I *have* to do, to know that I have to start studying a week before the test, and everything like that. And it was more like—they taught me how to use a computer. They taught me more how to work with my disability, instead of trying to teach me at that point.

Interestingly, Janine says how hard she had to work, and in the next breath attributes her success to being "lucky." It should be noted here that not "remediating" students but instead teaching them to work with their disability, as Janine's resource room teachers did, is another facet of the LD controversy. For example, the philosophy of Landmark College, a college exclusively for LD students, is critical of these "bypass" methods, arguing that teaching around the disability is essentially giving in to it (Meyer 1986, 30). Janine, however, found these "bypass" strategies very useful. Keith Whinnery, in an article in *Preventing School Failure*, writes that remediation of college students is often a waste of time. He points to research that suggests "basic skill acquisition levels off during high school . . ." (1992, 32). This argument, of course, is just one more aspect of the larger LD controversy, and the "right" policy may vary from student to student.

P: What about your reading in college? What about the textbooks? What's your major?

J: Occupational Therapy. One thing with my reading is, it's been getting much better. And since I'm very good about time and stuff like that, I know that for me to read something that a normal person could take like maybe an hour would take me probably two hours. And I know that—that I have to sit down and go do that. And every semester is different. When I first start the semester, I have to see what I have to do in every single class, and I have to start. So it's like a new beginning every semester. And like, some texts—like right now I have Abnormal Psych, which is very difficult for me because it's a lot of reading, and a lot of words that are difficult. So for me to take a sentence, I have to break it down, and figure out what the word is, look it up in the dictionary, figure it out in my head, and then remember it.

P: Wow.

J: Yeah. So it's *very* time-consuming. Very. And it's—like to me, it's very frustrating, but I've taught myself just—just to deal with it. So with other classes like, with my other reading, it's not—as long as I read it over and over and over again, and if I don't know what it is, I have to ask someone to say it, and then I'll remember it. I have to connect everything to remember it.

P: Do you use any taped texts? Would that help if you heard them?

J: No, I don't. I mean, I've tried using them and stuff like that, but to me it's just more—it's better for me to do on my own, I think.

P: If you don't know the word, it's not like you don't—you still would not know it if you heard it?

J: I *would* know it if I heard it. There's some—like, just the other day, one word I didn't know what it was, and I was like studying for three hours and I was just like—I went to my friend, and I asked her what it was. I mean, she said it, and I knew what it was.

P: What was it, do you remember?

J: No.

P: Was it a weird, Abnormal Psych word? Was it a regular word that might be in another course?

J: Yeah. It would have been in another course. But like the Psych words I'll look up, too. And like, another way they taught me how to read is— probably everybody learns this—is if you don't know the word, just keep reading the sentence? So I always do that, and then go back and figure out the word is.

P: But the taped texts don't help you?

J: It probably would. It probably definitely would, but Abnormal has been my most difficult class that I've taken here so far with the text because she uses it so much, you know, and it's so time-consuming. And I probably would have been better off if I did use the taped books, definitely. But I'm a very stubborn girl. [laughs] So I tried to do it on my own, and I just got to the point where I realized that I shouldn't have done it that way.

P: Why don't you want to use taped texts?

J: Well, I wouldn't mind or anything. I just didn't think of it.

Janine and Nick both described themselves as "stubborn," a trait Monica also has that might be described more positively as "determined." All three students are, however, self-deprecating to some extent. As I reviewed the three interviews, I could not help but wonder if these students with their relatively high grades and hopes for the future could subtly denigrate themselves, what about LD students elsewhere in less fortunate circumstances? What were *their* self-perceptions, if terms such as "lazy," "deceiving," "stubborn," and "stupid," were terms these three successful students used when referring to themselves? And what effect does this kind of self-concept have?

In the next section, I asked Janine to discuss her writing.

P: Tell me about your writing.

J: Well, I have a great story to tell. I never had a problem with teachers or with my writing or anything. But my junior year, I was doing a paper for my English teacher, and I was doing the same topic in another class, a social studies class. And I had all this research and everything, and I felt really strong about it, and everything like that. So I put all this time into it, wrote it over and over again, did it on the computer, and everything like that. And I handed it in. And she came down to the resource center a couple of days later and said that there was no way that somebody with an LD could write this paper. And she didn't think I wrote it. And she wanted to go through the board—the English board—and she wanted me to write it over. And I wouldn't write it over. She thought my mother wrote it for me. She thought the teachers wrote it for me. And I said, "No. There's no way I'm rewriting this paper." And so she ended up giving me a *B* on the paper and dropping the whole thing because I put up such a fit, and the resource center did and everything like that.

P: When she said there was no way someone with LD wrote that paper—why on earth would she say something like that?

J: One factor was—it was really, really good, and it really surprised her. And at the time, she was finding out that one of her kids had LD.

P: One of her own children?

J: Yes. And she did not want to face it. And she did not want to put her kid in to get help or anything like that. So, they didn't say that, but I think that had a factor with it too. [*sic*] And she just thought it was not possible that it could be my writing. She just thought it was too good and that somebody else *had* to help me do it.

P: When you say it was good, do you mean that it was technically perfect, or that it had a high level of sophistication, or both?

J: I think it was both because like the sentences were good. They were really good formed sentences [*sic*]. I used a thesaurus. I put *so* much time into it because I first wrote it for one class, and then I redid it for her. So like I put a lot of effort into it. I did it on the computer. I had the resource center—like one of my teachers read over it to like catch any mistakes or anything, so I think all around the spelling was good; everything was good about it.

P: How did you feel when she—

J: Awful. I've never felt so—'cause I've never—I guess I've never looked at my LD as being different or anything like that. And it just hit me really hard that she looked at me as being different, as not as equal. I've worked very, very hard to put as much effort into everything as everybody else—for people *not* to notice that I have an LD?—you know—and she just—it just *hit* me that I do have this disability and she thinks I'm different than everybody else. And that she would even *look* at me differently than someone else—really surprised me.

Years after this incident occurred, the pain of that teacher's insulting assumption about Janine is still raw. Like Nick's traumatic experience trying to read a preschool book title, this event in Janine's life marked a time she saw herself as different. I should point out that long after I had forgotten my original question, so caught up was I in her story, Janine related her example back to my inquiry about her writing that launched this particular memory. She did this frequently, as did Nick and Monica in their interviews, and the fact that they did this challenges the assertion that LD students often go off on tangents, never to return. For what it is worth, all three interviewees used detailed, well-developed examples to illustrate their points, and then always related them to the question at hand. Here Janine returns to discussing her writing in general.

J: But I can always remember my teacher in the resource center. She'd be like, "Janine, why don't you just do it on the computer?" But I would have to sit down and write the essay, then write it again, then type it, and then redo it and then redo it. And like, if I don't redo it and redo it and redo it, the errors are like, unbelievable. And I think I've never—like I think when kids learn where to put the commas—in high school, I cannot—I mean, I can remember being taught, but I don't remember remembering it. The teacher who helped me the most was when I came here, in English 100. I can't think of his name, but he helped me the most with my commas.

P: Was it Chris?

J: Yes! Tall? Skinny?

P: Yeah. [Chris was an adjunct instructor who has since left to take a full-time teaching position.]

J: Yeah. He helped me, and [Professor] Bonesteel helped me in English 101.

P: Well, that's good to know. How did Chris help you? What exactly did he do?

J: He did like techniques, like—I think it just stuck in my head more, the way he did it, and stuff like that. He had us sit there, and we had to do it over and over again. And I can remember the kids in the class saying, "*Why are we doing this?*" But it stuck in my head. See, the way for me to remember things, it has to stick out in my head. I have to—and also, by working with my boyfriend and my roommate on my English on like where to put the comma. They helped me more too. I just think like in high school, they didn't do that. They thought you learned it in junior high. They just assumed you knew it. Bonesteel did the same thing. She had more of a workbook type thing. And we had to sit in class and we had to put the commas [in], and she said it out loud. She made you do it out loud. She made you write it on the board. My biggest thing is, if I do it over and over and over again, then I'll learn it.

P: When you say it has to stick out in your head—?

J: Like when he would hand me papers back, or Bonesteel did, they wrote down exactly about the commas and stuff like that. And remembering where *but* goes or *however*. Just the other day, one of my friends—he's an English major—he said he was working with a junior high kid who had no idea where to put the commas. And he said the way he taught him was, he would say the sentence funny? He said, "Every time my voice changes, that's where the comma goes." . . . you know, where the sentence breaks? And so he read a couple of sentences to me out loud, and I could just *tell*, like I could *hear* where the comma was by the way he, by the way my friend read it to me.

P: Could you imitate the way he read it?

J: He would get higher—I don't have a good sentence. He would like change his tone of voice and stuff?

P: At the clause that needed—

J.: The comma.

P: Oh! Did he think of that himself?

J: Yup. He's incredible. [laughs]

P: So it's like a multisensory—

J: Yeah. And it's like really good to do because the more—if you read the sentence, you'll be able to—instead of saying, "Okay, you can tell here at the break because there's a verb and a noun in here; that's one sentence." You know, instead of doing it that way, because one of my hard thing [*sic*] is to tell the verb, the noun, and the adjective. That's really hard for me to do. I just don't know if I just didn't pick it up, or whatever, but it's really hard for me to do that. Like, when I read a sentence for some reason now, I can tell it's too short. Another thing is I worked a lot on my essays for English 101. I worked a lot with my boyfriend reading them over. He would read them, and then I would read them, and by reading it out loud to him, I could tell that it wasn't a full sentence. I could tell that something was wrong.

P: So reading it out loud helps?

J: Yes. With my writing, probably one of my biggest things is adding my endings, my *ed*'s and my *ing*'s. Sometimes it's very hard for me to catch.

I was fascinated with Janine's student-teacher friend who, while teaching comma use, changed his voice to help his junior high students differentiate between dependent and independent clauses. It made sense that this auditorially based technique might be more useful to some students than a word-based explanation involving more terms: nouns, verbs, etc. What made me less comfortable was Janine's insistence that she liked grammar and punctuation lessons. Although other students may have been tearing their hair out with boredom, Janine praised the workbook exercises done out loud and on the board.

J: I think the thing I remember about English 100 was the workbook. Even though everybody was like, "*Why* are we doing this?" and everything like that, but I think I learned a lot by doing it. 'Cause if I didn't understand it, I would ask him after class. I think exercises are the best way to learn anything.

It is possible that much of Janine's learning occurred after class with the individual attention I knew Chris always gave to his students. Later, Janine will say that one of the best things an instructor can do for an LD student is to be approachable so that students are not afraid to ask questions. We cannot, however, discount what Janine says about grammar exercises, as much as we might like to. Without doubt, contextualized learning and whole language practices benefit the majority of writers, including learning disabled ones. It may be, however, that explicit, repeated instruction helps some students or at least gives them more confidence regarding their proofreading abilities. While I cannot bring myself to endorse workbook drills as a way to help students who learn differently, I remember Frank Vellutino's general advice to me about learning disabilities in general: "Never say never." (1990)

In the next part of our discussion, I asked Janine about the kinds of errors she had made in a three-hour, impromptu essay our college used to require for graduation. (It now uses portfolios.) Those students labeled LD could use a computer for the test and take as much time as they needed. In her finished essay, Janine had frequent mix-ups with possessives and plurals, and in that way her error pattern resembled many other college students'. However, her text also displayed the kind of wrong-word pattern seen in both Nick's and Monica's writing. Here was Janine's topic sentence: "It is important to have class participation a significant component of 10 percent or more of the course grade in college classes for severely reason" [several reasons]. In defining class participation, she said it involved "the constructive decision [discussion] that students do informally during each class." Later, she wrote "it shows how much effect [effort] a student is putting into a class." In fact, she was quite consistent in her use of these wrong words, saying in her conclusion, "class participation is . . . a good way to get more classroom decision." She used *effect* for *effort* four times throughout the two-page essay. I asked her about those sentences.

P: What about some of the kinds of errors you made in here? [We look at the essay.] What happened?

J: Spell check. I thought that was the right word. I probably spelled the word wrong. I probably spelled *effort* the wrong way.

P: So you were going for *effort*?

J: Um-hum. And then spell check. I picked that one. It gave me choices, and I picked the wrong one.

P: And what about *decision* for *discussion*? Do you remember what you originally put into the computer? Were you attempting to spell *discussion*, and it misinterpreted it?

J: Um-hum. It put a listing of words, and I picked that word. And so I read over the essay again, and I didn't catch it. But if I read it again, I probably would have catched it [*sic*].

P: If somebody read that out loud to you, "but instead the constructive decision that students do informally . . .," would you pick that up?

J: Yes.

P: Okay. So it wasn't so much that your brain gave you the wrong word, it was that the spelling was off, and then when the spell check gave you a list of words, you picked the wrong one.

J: Yeah.

A few weeks after I had this discussion with Janine, a colleague of mine from another department showed me a paper he had received from one of his students. Almost every line had a wrong word error of the *effort/effect* type described above, making the text incomprehensible even to people used to deciphering all kinds of strangled syntax, including from the texts of new speakers of English, a group to which this student did not belong. Neither one of us had ever seen anything quite like this. Because the paper appeared to have been word processed, my only guess was that a too-generous spell checker had played a part in suggesting some of the words that appeared in that student's text. Perhaps, like Janine, this student tried to spell a particular word, was much further off base than the software creator predicted, the computerized dictionary displayed a crop of utterly unrelated words, and the hapless writer took the best (and wrong) guess. LD students are perfectly capable of inventing their own "bizarre" creations, most of which are phonetic enough to be understandable. They are sometimes betrayed, ironically, by what they may view as their electronic savior. If Janine, who is careful, bright, and highly motivated, is occasionally confused by spell checkers, other students may be also. Software, of course, will become more sophisticated in time, but students should be warned about being led down a computerized garden path of correctly spelled but absurd suggestions by a piece of equipment, designed by a person whose experiences with dictionaries might be quite different from theirs.[2]

In the next section, Janine discusses her experiences with reading, test-taking, and note-taking. Like Monica, she has much test anxiety, but she has learned how to deal with it. She echoes some of Monica's other concerns, especially regarding complicated multiple choice questions or essay questions with many complex modifying clauses.

P: When did you actually get the label?

J: It had to be elementary school. I'm not exactly sure what grade, but it was definitely elementary school.

P: Did they tell you anything about it?

J: I did not know exactly what my disability was. My mother knew, and she probably tried to explain it to me and everything, but I didn't know exactly what it was and couldn't explain it until probably seventh or eighth grade, junior high.

P: So how would you explain it?

J: I'd explain it as—my disability is with phonics, and that I memorize all my words. I'd explain that, that's why I have a problem with reading because if I hit a word I don't know, then it takes me longer to read, and the spelling, it takes me longer to do, and that's why I need more time on tests. And I've never taken a test in a classroom, except for math. I've never even tried. Like, I've taken small quizzes and stuff like that. So I've always had extended time, and it's always helped me, so I've never even tried to take it in a class because one, it would probably be a shock for me at first, and it would be very hard for me because I would look at everybody else, and I get very, very nervous, and everything like that. 'Cause my first time—'cause with occupational therapy, we take Bio and Extrems [Extremities], and everything like that. And like with Bio, you have like, lab practicals? And I took them all by myself, and I took them orally. Well, my Extrem teacher was like, "Janine, would you please just try it?" She's like, "You can have more time afterwards." And I was very, very nervous, and the first time I didn't do good because I was very nervous, but after that I did great. I got a *B* in the class. And with Neuro, I take them in with them, and I go back to the questions afterwards. And now, I just got to the point where I read the sentence. I can read the sentence three times in a minute and a half. And the more complex the sentence is, then I definitely have to go back to that question, but if it's a straightforward question, then I can do it right away. If they say, "What is this?" then I can do it. But if they say, "What does this have to do with this and this and this,"—and if I have to think—and if I have to figure out the sentence—because sometimes I have to figure out what the sentence is meaning, and then I have to figure out every single answer. And I have to think in my head, how I remember—all those answers. You know? So that's very time-consuming. But I know to myself now, to go back to those kinds of questions. Instead of getting frustrated, and getting nervous and upset and everything, I know I just have to go back to that question.

After having developed confidence from doing well on these exams, Janine has learned to take complex questions in stride, going back to them at the end. In her comments on note-taking, she critiques conventional classroom practice.

J: I think another technique that professors should do is—They think you know, that when you come to college you should be able to take notes. Every student should be able to take notes. If I read something out loud, you should just be able to take it. So I have to remember thinking that the whole time like, "Oh my God, I'm gonna have to take these notes. Nobody's going to write on the board. I'm dead." My first class is Bio, and he would lecture, and he wrote all the big words on the board, which I was so excited about because I would just write them all down and then go back and rewrite my notes. And that's what most of my professors do is write on the board, and I never had a note taker until I took Ortho and Neuro, and that's because she stood there for an hour and fifteen minutes and just lectures. And it's very dah, da dah, da dah, and it's very hard to write a sentence. And I'll get to a word I don't know, and I'll just sit there and try to figure it out, but she'll be onto another topic by the time I figure out what that word is, you know, so I just try my best to write what I think it is then just keep going. So it was just very hard for me to rewrite notes for her lectures and then rewrite my notes for the other classes. That's why I got a note taker. I think— .

P: You rewrite all your notes?

J: Yeah. All except for Ortho/Neuro, I get the notes for and I just read them over and study for them.

P: You get the notes?

J: I have a note taker and I get—they take the notes and I photocopy them.

P: Now the note taker—How does that happen?

J: She's in the class. She takes the class. So she takes the class, and then I just photocopy them afterwards. But I think that—she [the professor] doesn't *teach* the class; she just stands there and lectures. And I think a big thing is that, nobody—if she taught the class more, kids would remember it more, and it would be easier to remember. 'Cause I know one of my good friends is having a real hard time with the class, too, because the notes are just so much, and then you have to reread the notes and everything to study for the test. And like, in Dr. Peterson's class [another professor], I *learn* something, so I don't have to *re*learn myself when I get out of the class. But after her class, I have to *re*learn everything. You see what I mean?

P: Mmm.

J: Also, when LD students read something, they will struggle to read it, and then they have to go back and learn it, and other students can read it and learn it at the same time. That's why I have to go over things. That's why I have to rewrite my notes.

P: That must take you awhile.

J: Um-hmm.

For Janine, using the notes of a student who is also taking the class seems to work out fine. Some colleges have found, however, that students were somewhat unreliable as note takers, and that paid professional note takers were a better choice. (See Chapter One for further discussion of note takers.) In the next exchange, Janine talks more about testing. Like Monica, she excels at oral exams, but Janine still prefers written ones.

P: Do you think that writing, taking written tests, is the best measure of what you know? What about oral tests?

J: I think either/or. Like for some kids, oral tests are the best. Like when I took a lab practical for Bio, I can remember after taking the test, the oral test, she was like, "Janine, I think you're one of the brightest people I know. I know you know everything, and I know it's all in your head, and it's just a matter to get it out." Which is true. I know it. I just sometimes can't get it out the right way.

P: Orally or on paper?

J: On paper. I can't get it down on paper because my spelling, or something like that. Because like, for huge words, like for Neuro and all of my science classes and stuff like that, I have to memorize all the material, and let alone, and then if I have to write it, I have to memorize how to spell it too. And some of the words are just—you know how some people can get *close* to the words? [in attempting to spell them] I mean, for me it's just impossible to even get *close* to the words. Sometimes I can, and sometimes I can't. So that's like when I take my Neuro test, I have a TA in there, and I'll ask her how to spell a word when I don't know it.

Janine explained the arrangements for taking her Neurology tests. A teaching assistant would sit with her in the Academic Support office and help her both read difficult words off the exam and spell words she wished to write in her essay answers. Of course, the TA was not allowed to define words or supply answers in any way.

P: And then if you say, "I want to write—" you name the word, they can spell it?

J: Yeah. And they'll spell it. 'Cause if I were taking it on my own, I would just, like have to look it up. I'd take a dictionary out, and I'd find a way to do it. I would do it on my own. But when you're given a certain time period, you don't have the time to pick up the dictionary, pick up the text, and figure out what it is.

P: So this enables you to take it faster?

J: Yeah. Than if I did it by myself. And to do a better job on it, too. But to answer your question, like, I think writing essays is a good way to show you how to do it, as long as you're not by yourself. Like it might be really hard for somebody, like this girl Pam that's coming into the program who's LD. Her biggest problem is writing essays, and she cannot write. She can *not*. That's her LD, and it's awful, and I mean, she's just had *such* an awful time. She went to [names another college] for OT, and they did not work with her at all. So she left, and that's why she's coming here. But I mean, she has a computer that talks to her—

P: Yes! I've heard about those things!

J: Yes! It talks to her! It has a thesaurus on it. It has a spell check and everything. And she's like really nervous about the English and if people will be willing to help her and everything. And I told her yes and everything like that, but it's got to be her doing. Like, she's has to go to the teachers and everything. So every test I think is going to be different. Like multiple choice are good, and stuff like that, but essays definitely show if you know it. Like it's really easy to do multiple choice questions, but then again you might have somebody that's really hard to do it for [*sic*].

While Monica despises multiple choice questions, Janine finds them easy, recognizing that not everyone else does. Unlike Nick and Monica, Janine is convinced that the label saved her academic life. She does recognize, however, that junior high school students' judgment can be difficult to endure.

P: Do you think that the label, overall, was helpful?

J: Yes. If I ever had to confront somebody, and they fought their LD label or everything—to me—I feel that I am a very lucky person. And I feel like I'm lucky that I got caught. Because there's some people that haven't even found out, and they find out when they're in college. And your first reaction is, you fight it, and you deny it, and you can't handle it or anything. But I'm to the point where I know my limits. I know what I have to do, that I have to structure, and if I don't do it, then it's going to affect *me*. And it's not worth it.

P: A lot of people argue about the stigma—about going to the resource room. But you said you circumvented that. You managed to avoid—being different.

J: Just like—if somebody asked me now, if they asked me what it was, I would come out and tell them. But like in junior high and everything like that, it was very hard, because everybody went through these stages of finding out who you were, and finding out who was different and who fits where and who does what. So it was very hard. I mean, if I went back to junior high right now, I wouldn't be afraid of it at all because now I don't care what people think of me. But that was just a time when everybody cared what you thought about and everything like that. And I just reached a point in ninth grade where I just said, "I have this. I have to deal with this, and if people don't like it, then that's too bad. This is what I am, and this is how it has to be done," and everything like that. And I think if I didn't have that piece of paper that says I'm LD, then I would struggle even more. And I would blame myself more. If I didn't get extended time, if I didn't get what I needed, then it would affect me more. And I would put more on my shoulders, like it's all my fault. What am I doing wrong? Why can't I do this like everybody else? But I know when I see—even though every semester it's very hard. It takes my roommate a half an hour to do something, and it takes me like two hours to do it. But I just have to sit down, and I have to say, "Janine, you have to do this. You have no choice. Do you want to make it?" Every semester, I call my mom, at the beginning of the year, and I'm like, "Mom, I can't take this!" And she gives me that little speech: "Janine, you can do this; you know you can do this. Don't let them break you. You can handle this. You have proven—" So I think somebody with an LD, you always have to remind yourself about it and how you can make it and everything like that. I definitely think—I'm very happy. Like I went to a seminar yesterday, and the guy had an ADD [attention deficit disorder], and he described how he's on medication and people will look at it like, "You're dependent on this drug; you couldn't live—," and everything like that. And he—I can't think of the word how he said it, but like, "It's another way for me to function normally, to be able to function." So if I didn't know about my LD, I wouldn't be able to function.

It has been said that the LD label in effect blames students for what is really a flawed educational system. In many ways, that is true—remember that Janine referred to her labeling process as being "caught." Another way to view the label, however, as Janine explains, is that it helped motivate her to work around the system. Without it, she may have mistakenly attributed her linguistic difficulties to below-average intelligence.

P: Some people argue that LD doesn't exist—that it's just a matter of bad teaching, of motivating students. There are also a lot of arguments about how many people have this, has it been overdiagnosed, what causes it, and so on. Have you heard any of those arguments, and how would you answer them?

J: How I would answer is, like I said, my stepmother—she works with LD. She works in reading [in a middle school]. And I went to go visit her, and I went to school with her, and I sat in her classes. And what they're starting to do, and which I think is a very big thing, is that, instead of saying, these are the very high kids, and these are the normal kinds—you know how they used to have the high achievers and everything?

P: Oh yeah.

J: Now they have the three classrooms, the high achievers, the ones that are regular and everything, and the kids below; they have them all in one room. And everything they do is going to be slower. And I sat in the classroom with her, and just looking at them, I thought of different things they could do. And I think it's more like—with a kid with LD, you have to teach it to them differently. Elementary school and junior high is the most important time for a kid to learn something. And if they don't learn it then, then they're not going to be able to get it. And I was sitting there watching her teach science to these two kids? And I could just tell by the look on one kid's face, one of the girls, that she did not get it. And she did not connect. And my stepmother was about to move on, and I looked at her, and I shook her [my?] head, and she's like, "What?" And I'm like, "Ask her to write it on the board." And it was a problem or something, and my stepmother had already gone through it on the board. And one of the girls like stopped and struggled. And I said out loud, I'm like, "Picture her voice. Hear her voice in your head." And she got it. And she put in on the board.

P: No kidding!

J: Yeah. 'Cause that's what I do. If I remember something, and I remember exactly on the sheet, I can close my eyes and picture that sheet and remember it. That's how I remember it. And the other girl, the reason I said to stop is because, if she went on, she would have never got the rest —'cause the first—it had to do with photosyn—it had to do with plants. And she was talking about plants. And if she didn't get the first thing, and my stepmother went on, she would have been lost for the rest of it—the whole conversation because she was going to be thinking about that first thing that she did not get. And she'd be thinking about it the whole time, and she wouldn't be able to grasp the other concepts.

As mentioned before, Janine frequently supports her opinions with vivid personal examples, always relating them back to the discussion ("But to answer your question . . ."). Overall, her narrative voice is passionate, detailed, and clear. Occasionally, however, she reaches for a word that eludes her, so she settles for another. In a passage not transcribed here, Janine described how noisy computer labs can be. She said, ". . . I get very frustrated. I get very, like—disoriented—like, I pay attention to other things." It may be that she wanted *disoriented*, or it may be that she wanted *distracted*, but settled for the description rather than the term. In the above story of her stepmother's middle school science class, Janine begins to say the lesson is on "photosyn—" and then finishes, "—it had to do with plants."

As is the case with the sporadic verb tense slips ("I probably would have catched it"), these wrong-word or half-word occurrences are more noticeable because they have been transcribed. In speech the words were quickly swallowed and the sentence continued smoothly. These oral slips, however, may be somewhat related to the written slips in Janine's essay, which may be explained only partially by the confusing list of alternatives on the spell checker. If what Janine says is true, that sometimes she "isn't even close" to correct spelling, this factor, in conjunction with the occasionally misfired term she produces, may account for some of her word-level difficulties in reading and writing.

Near the end of the interview, I asked Janine to comment on learning in general.

P: What about other courses? For writing, reading, learning, in general.

J: The one class that I *love* right now is my Neuro class. Like when he mentions something, he'll go over and over it. Instead of just mentioning it once. 'Cause it's not going to stick in somebody's head if they just heard it once. And he explains it many different ways. The more ways you can explain it, the more the kid is going to make a connection. And he's very patient with me, and I'm not afraid to address a question to him at all. He does not intimidate me or anything. I'm very comfortable with him. He will always spend the extra time with me. Another big thing is that he will not schedule a test when we have other tests. He knows what classes we have, and he won't do that. And like we had a paper due? And he made it due way before finals started, so we wouldn't have to worry about it. He thinks about how we have other classes.

These three students' stories of when they did or did not learn are focused almost entirely on a transmission model of learning: much talk of lectures, of multiple-choice tests, and of obtaining "the information." This may be due to the nature of these students' majors, occupational therapy and physical therapy (Nick's former major), which cover in the introductory courses much memorization of muscle groups, technical vocabulary, and other material more conducive to "objective" testing. The theoretical positioning in these fields occurs later in the program, when students are required to critically examine what they read in professional journals and what they observe in clinical situations.

Another point Janine made in the comment above regarding her Neurology professor's awareness of his students' workload is worth considering. If we writing instructors consider the writing in our English or Textual Studies course to be the most vital work students will undertake in a particular semester and assume they will happily devote much thought and time to a topic of inquiry project for our class, we will be sadly misled. LD students spending an inordinate amount of time each week rereading textbooks from their other courses and rewriting chaotic lecture notes may not have much time remaining to explore ideas from our class, revise drafts, and respond thoughtfully to their peers' work—the time-consuming, intellectual tasks involved in many writing-intensive courses. In addition to all of this, LD students especially must carefully edit not only the writing they do for us but also that required in other classes. At the very least, we need to know that this is the reality of most LD students' lives. As we have seen, Janine was deeply grateful that one professor was considerate enough to stagger his major requirements with those of his colleagues.

P: Any other dos [for college professors]?

J: I think—be prepared to expect anything from someone. That they're going to have a kid that might not be able to handle this, and they should be able to handle every situation. They should be able to handle it if an LD student comes up to them—be able to handle it and be able to say, "I will work with you," instead of looking at it like, "This is just another problem for me." They should just be more supportive because we're just trying to get through this. . . . Like when a student comes up to them and tells them about their LD, if the teacher is very nice about it, that's going to make the student very comfortable in class. But if they're very awkward, then the kid's going to be very nervous, all the time, through the class. It's just going to affect the class.

P: Can you give me an example of being nice about it? I mean, is it any one thing they say? Is it their attitude?

J: Yeah. Like, I can remember addressing a teacher, and I told her about my LD, and she goes, "What is your problem?" And just right there, my stomach just dropped, and I had to take a deep breath and say, "All right, this is it."

P: Was it the way she said it?

J: Yes. It was her tone. It was the way she looked at me. And how it made it look like—just the word *problem*—I just think is an awful word. I don't think it's a problem. It's just something that's part of me. This is me. This is my package. This is something I have to do. This is not a problem. To me, it is not a problem.

P: What would be a better thing to say? Tone?

J: Um. Say, "All right, what can I do for you? How can I help you with this? Exactly what are the different things that you need?"

P: Anything else? If you had five or ten minutes to talk to a roomful of college teachers? What would you stress?

J: Like I said before, they should be willing to show the kid that they're willing to help them and willing to work with them and everything like that. And that they're *not* a problem and that they *are* here to help them and everything like that. And to be very open-minded with every situation because every situation is going to be different and to learn different techniques and to pick up little different things. And like me going to watch my stepmother teach a class, I thought of things that I remembered and taught *her* different things that she could do with the students. And I think a good thing to do is to go and sit and observe a class while another teacher is teaching it and look at the reactions of the kids, and you can tell what they're picking up and what they're not picking up and everything like that. And I also think that it's important—I think a teacher should be *required* to take a class about LD students because a lot of teachers don't know about it and—

P: College professors, too?

J: Um-hum. Definitely. Because the more they educate themselves about it, the better it's going to be. The more they find different techniques. And I think professors should talk to professors. I know, with me, I know professors have talked to other professors about me and found out what my abilities are, and I think if you're not clear what their LD is, to go talk to other professors and see how they were in the class and see what they can learn and pick up from and everything. I just think that they should put the effort into it.

Summary and Conclusion

What compounds this already complex issue is that there is no typical LD student. In spite of their similarity in age, race, class, and academic acumen, even these three did not always agree on what works best in helping LD students learn in a text-based environment. Monica relies heavily on taped texts, while Janine, although she said taped texts might be a good idea for her, has for now decided to continue her practice of setting aside large blocks of time to read and reread assigned chapters. Nick, on the other hand, primarily depends on listening intently in the classroom and uses texts selectively, reading only that which he feels is absolutely necessary. Monica finds multiple-choice tests horrific, while Janine views them as easy. Nick and Monica would like to take all of their exams orally, but Janine prefers written tests, even though she excels at oral ones.

Like many other experts on learning disabilities, these three students not only disagree about the usefulness of the LD label, but have somewhat conflicting views about it. Although they all mention the cruelty of elementary school children and those children's apparent inability to deal with any kind of difference, these three students, who have much experience with the label, have somewhat different views about its role in higher education. While Janine believes the label is absolutely essential in helping students secure the support they need to negotiate difficult college programs, Nick seems to change his mind about the label even as he describes its effects. As we saw in the transcript, he began by describing the label as a necessity, but then ultimately railed against its long-term effects, especially on students he saw languishing in his high school "reject room." Monica, who takes most advantage of the academic support services offered to LD students, and who views that office's professionals as absolutely essential advocates for the accommodations to which she is legally entitled, also sees the LD label as a potential tool of abuse by some students looking for privileged treatment, which in turn breeds resentment on the part of other students and skepticism on the part of instructors. To some extent, all three see the label as instrumental in helping them better understand why some types of learning are so difficult for them. They all see it also as a problem in itself. If there is a consensus here, it may be that the label, at least for now, is an evil necessary for obtaining access to ways of learning not yet available in the mainstream.

There are, however, similarities in these students' situations and many clear areas of agreement. All three have a metacognitive awareness of what they need to do as they revise their written work, at least regarding surface errors. They can identify what mistakes they typically make, and they each have developed successful strategies for minimizing them. They all have learned to allow much time to write and revise extensively, relying to some extent on trusted friends for proofreading. They all take advantage of computer technology, word processing, and whatever spelling or grammar checking capabilities are available, recommending it without hesitation for all LD students.

This issue of editing, however, and who should be doing the bulk of it, needs to be debated more broadly in higher education. While none of these students questions the necessity of surface correctness on final drafts, and each one plans for time-consuming editing sessions, there is an obvious question here regarding priorities. At what point does the writer's concentration on the minutia of verb endings and apostrophe use become a counterproductive use of time that might be better spent on more intellectually stimulating pursuits? Again, this question has no either/or answer. Of course, all students should be encouraged to learn how to locate and fix those surface errors they routinely make. As these students well know, poorly edited academic papers, business reports, or important correspondence documents will result in severe penalties for their authors. However, endless and frustrating editing sessions may quickly reach a point of diminishing returns if students associate this often fruitless exercise with "writing." Is it possible that LD students could be encouraged to feel less guilty about using editors, either computerized or human? This question should not be reduced to a debate about "lowering" the proverbial "standards." It is a complex and serious question about the best use of time that challenges faculty, students, and the public to reconsider priorities.

In addition to developing systematic revising processes and maximizing electronic editing tools, these students have other intersecting problems and solutions to them. Both Monica and Janine have a difficult time taking notes in class, especially if technical terms are not written on the board. They both spend many hours laboriously rewriting their notes, something that may surprise non-LD students and professors. Monica relies heavily on paid student note takers, while Janine uses them only for a class that is primarily lecture-based. In a lecture class where the professor explains concepts in several ways and stops frequently to answer questions, Janine can not only take notes successfully but says she learns much of the course material during the classroom session itself. Nick, too, depends on in-class learning, having succeeded in high school primarily through listening.

Both Monica and Janine were exasperated by exam questions they felt were unduly complicated. They preferred "focused" or straightforward essay questions, as opposed to those they viewed as being unnecessarily "elegant" (Monica's term) or "fancy." All three enthusiastically endorsed collaboration and oral discussion as the preferred mode of learning, with Monica calling study groups a "big time" answer to many LD students' problems with conventional teaching.

One of their biggest frustrations (a word all three students used, and one that peppered Monica's narrative) was the stated or implied judgment on the part of parents, teachers, or peers that these students were floundering in school because they were not working hard enough. What impressed me again and again as I heard the experiences of Nick, Monica, and Janine was the sheer number of hours they routinely invested in their schoolwork, only to have someone whose opinion they valued advise them that if they would only socialize less and study more, their grades would improve. Granted, these students are highly motivated, determined, and hard-working, and they may or may not be typical of all students, LD or otherwise, but I know I will try never again to deliver the familiar bromide about "working harder" to students about whose real work habits I know very little.

Other harmful exchanges ought to be avoided. Both Nick and Janine had painful recollections of being told that their best piece of writing could not possibly have been produced by them. The assumptions behind such remarks, that people with LD are incapable of writing well, are infinitely destructive. We heard Nick begin to doubt his own talent, to wonder if his good writing was somehow "an accident." For Janine, the moment when her teacher doubted her authorship became the moment Janine saw herself as different: "it just *hit* me that I do have this disability and she thinks I'm different than everybody else. And that she would even *look* at me differently than someone else—really surprised me." That teachers or students would make such casual appraisals is simply inexcusable, and if this is the result of labeling—that *difference* is doomed to mean *inferior*—then it may be time to eliminate the label, no matter what legal accommodations it permits.

When asked specifically for dos and don'ts regarding teaching methodology, when asked what they would advise if they had only five minutes to talk to a group of college professors, all three students emphasized the same thing, and it had little to do with classroom practice per se, or even with type of assignment. It had to do, rather, with professors' attitudes. What Nick resented most was the professor who singled him out in front of his classmates, drawing attention to the fact that Nick took exams outside of class time. This same professor implied that Nick's difficulty was either imagined or something which, had he the righteousness or self-discipline of the professor himself in his younger days, he could overcome. What infuriated Monica was the professor who refused to budge one iota from his established testing procedures, claiming that "it would not be fair to other students." While I heard, of course, only Monica's side to this incident, her obvious bitterness suggests that professors who will not change, perhaps for legitimate reasons, their evaluation tools, should at least do a more tactful job communicating to students their reasons why.

Another common belief held by these students, and articulated with varying degrees of tolerance, was that a Ph.D. should not be a blank check to do what one pleases. Monica's resentful imitation of her professor was painful to hear: "'I'm a Ph.D. I've worked for this. I'm a Ph.D. I can do this how I felt it needs to be done.' I mean, what can you say after that comment? I was *so* angry at her." And Nick, although a bit gentler in his criticism, is also wary of a terminal degree as a trophy of knowledge. "Understanding is a big thing," said Nick, "understanding that you're not—just because you have your Ph.D., you don't—you aren't necessarily right." He adds later, "Society's been wrong before."

As has been emphasized elsewhere in this book, respected professionals often disagree, and never with more ridicule and venom than when discussing learning disabilities. The consequences of these disagreements, however, have little effect on those disagreeing, compared to how they impact students, whether labeled or not. A professor who has recently read several articles about the quite real difficulties involved in diagnosing learning disabilities should nevertheless think twice before professorially declaring to a labeled LD student (as one professor did to Monica), that learning disabilities do not exist.

In addition to indicating what professors could *avoid* doing, these students had positive ideas about what professors could *do* to make LD students' academic lives easier. These recommendations do not involve complicated multisensory assignments or gimmicks designed for left-brained learners. Rather, they are simple things, attitudes really, that could be nourished. If there is one quality these students would like all their professors to possess, it is open-mindedness, a willingness to learn more about the students in their class, and thus learn more about teaching. Monica's advice to a hypothetical audience of college professors would be for them to simply ask students if they needed extra help or a different kind of teaching. While time is, of course, something most good instructors have precious little of to spare, they might consider using what time they *do* invest in student contact more thoughtfully. In the same time that they take advising students to study harder or revise more carefully, for instance, they might instead ask one or two of the questions Monica suggests: "Are you having trouble with class? Do you want to talk about the exam? Is there something I can do to help you?"

Finally, professors might do more of what none of these students mentioned directly but which obviously affected them more profoundly than they might consciously realize: recognize and praise what these students do well. Nick's decision to attend college was partially influenced by one high school teacher who took him aside and told him he had the ability to do so. That woman was one of the first people he mentioned in his interview. Monica wept with joy when she passed an oral exam her college occupational therapy professor insisted she take because, said this professor, she knew Monica would be able to succeed. After Janine took an oral exam, one of her professors told her that she [Janine] was one of the brightest people she knew. That comment, along with a periodic pep talk from her mother, undoubtedly gets Janine through many a difficult textbook chapter or grueling study session.

All three students are quite modest in their requests of professors. Although Monica and Janine stress that it is the professor's responsibility to learn more about students' learning preferences, all these students are really requesting is fewer negative remarks spawned from unenlightened assumptions. It is somewhat understandable that overworked professors attempting to teach, publish, hold office hours, and serve on committees might be wary of students who ask for different accommodations, for even more of their already nonexistent free time. However, much of the negative reception LD students often get may result from a knee-jerk reaction to change, or a defensiveness to a perceived criticism of the way these professors have always taught. It may stem from a panicky insecurity about their lack of knowledge concerning learning disabilities or an overeagerness to believe they do not exist—a convenience that would mean these teachers need not change anything.

For the most part, the fear of not knowing how to help an LD student in one's class is unnecessary. All three interviewees seem to

want their professors simply to relax and be just a bit more supportive, even honestly curious. Said Monica, professors need only give
LD students "some indication that you care." According to Janine,
professors "should be willing to show the kid that they're willing to
help them. If the teacher is very nice about it, that's going to make
the student very comfortable in class." Not one of these students
expects instructors to have a vast collection of multisensory strategies at their fingertips for use in every course with every LD student. "It's okay," said Monica, "not to understand what an LD is. So
long as you keep an open line of communication. Then, after that,
you've done your part. Then it's up to the student. . . ."

Nick, Monica, Janine, and no doubt many other LD college students, are accustomed to working doubly hard for their education.
They are acutely aware that the academic and professional worlds
are based on written language, and they are preparing themselves as
best they can to deal with that. As simple as this may sound, their
main request, as Nick said, is for "understanding," so that they can
continue to do what they need to do. As is obvious from all three
interviews, these young people have developed a sophisticated,
metacognitive awareness of their strengths and weaknesses. All
they want is a bit less aggravation in putting this knowledge about
themselves into practice.

There are, alas, no magical solutions to be gleaned from these
three interviews. While there may be some useful techniques or
unusual approaches that do help some students, the main change
that must occur is attitudinal. What needs to be challenged are the
harmful, negative assumptions about learning disabilities made by
misguided faculty, "normal" students, and perhaps most especially,
by LD students themselves. I asked the Director of Academic Support Services at Utica College, Steve Pattarini, what he would say
about LD students if he had five minutes to speak to the entire faculty. He said that "people must learn to believe that the manner in
which someone learns is not a reflection of that person's intelligence." If students and faculty truly believe that students can learn,
they will work together to figure out how (Pattarini 1994). If there is
an unconscious assumption, however, that these students cannot do
college-level work, they may be written off with lowered expectations, probably the most harmful, insidious form of prejudice.

All theoretical positions are, of course, molded by material circumstances, and in no academic controversy is that more true than
when regarding learning disabilities. The lenses through which we
all view different learning is heavily colored by our own education,
experience, and self-interest. If "learning disability" as a neurological difference does not exist as such, it puts LD professionals out of

business, or at the very least calls into question much of their academic preparation and professional research. On the other hand, if "learning disability" involves more than economic and sociological factors, then psycho-socialists have much homework to do if they wish to be more effective facilitators of learning for *all* their students.

Theoretical disputes about causes and cures are almost beside the point if students' written language difficulties mean that they will ultimately be judged as having inferior intellectual capabilities, and that is the reality of Nick's, Monica's, and Janine's experiences. Until there is a major re-conceptualization of intelligence, until linguistic-processing talents are not the exclusive measure of academic worth, those people with other strengths will continue to be discriminated against. As educators, we must become more skeptical of the theoretical assumptions that inform our classroom practice and assessment tools, especially perhaps if we believe in them so thoroughly because we know them to be valid for the way we ourselves learned. We must broaden our view of knowledge, teaching, and learning, being less quick to discard completely those theories and research methods engendered outside our field of expertise and which may have distasteful flaws. An either/or view of this controversy is inappropriate. We need to read more widely in unfamiliar academic territory, listen better to our colleagues and to our students, and research more thoroughly. Fear of being dismissed as "eclectic" should not prevent us from tolerating more patiently apparent theoretical contradictions, especially since no one theory today can account for the linguistic adventures of a small, but diverse group of students.

Notes

1. See also Kate Ronald's essay, "Personal and Public Authority in Discourse" in *Farther Along,* 25–39.

2. See Catherine Smith's (1991) essay on the perspectives of software creators, a topic that is further discussed in Chapter Five.

Chapter Five

Implications for
College Instructors

So far, this book has presented some of the conflicting theories and research of the learning disability field, and it has shown that most professional discourse in Composition Studies does not begin to explore this controversy. While various writing theorists focus on "basic writers," few recognize (or even mention) the significant number of students who might have a different way of processing linguistic symbols. What an exploration of the LD controversy will do for college writing instructors and their students is not yet entirely clear. Any pedagogical changes that might arise from a study of LD issues are perhaps less important than attitudinal changes on the part of students and especially on the part of instructors. How professors perceive students' difficulties with reading and writing influences how they attempt to address those difficulties. Instructors responding to student texts should be careful about using those written texts as a measure of that student's intelligence, educational background, or parents' reading habits. The idea of a learning difference is still hypothetical. However, a sensitivity to it as a possibility should alert college writing instructors to cues they might otherwise overlook or attribute to something not applicable. If nothing else, an awareness of the LD controversy will inform composition instructors about relevant laws and give them a direction for needed research.

In Chapter Three, we saw that the intense tutoring of one young child has suggested several things about learning. First, O-G methods, by themselves, could not motivate Joey. Second, whole language practices, based as they are on assumptions of a basic intuition for reading and writing, were extremely motivating but pedagogically inadequate for Joey, who does not easily intuit linguistic structures.

For him, an intense interest in the subject matter was vital, but not by itself enough. He also required explicit instruction and multisensory inroads, but the O-G lessons bored and frustrated him. Learning occurred when he was both deeply engaged in wanting to learn *and* when he had some kind of structured associative link with which he could connect the linguistic symbols he needed to use. Similarly, the three college students interviewed in Chapter Four had successful learning experiences when they were deeply engaged in reading and writing approaches made as multisensory as possible and tailored to their individual learning styles.

What does all this mean for writing instructors, and what should they do differently? Unfortunately, because this issue has not been adequately addressed by composition professionals, there are many gaps in the pedagogy that need to be filled. As Sherrel Lee Haight observes, even those professionals with doctorates specializing in learning disabilities are often frustrated by expectations that they perform "miracles" or find a definitive "cure" for learning disabilities. She points out that the many types of disabilities prevent any one treatment from being universally applicable. Her analogy regarding the treatment of cancer is interesting. Often a diagnosis of cancer will invite different treatments—surgery, chemotherapy, radiation, or nutritional therapy—from different physicians. Similarly, a diagnosis of learning disability might be treated with different recommendations by various experts in the same field (Haight 1980, 47–49). Those disclaimers offered, this chapter will lead the reader through a course of action to take if one suspects that there are LD students in a writing class.

Recognizing the Learning Disabled College Writer

What remaining processing difficulties will Joey have ten years from now? If he were to appear in a college writing course, what would his essays look like? First of all, it is clear that learning disabled children *do* show up as learning disabled adults attending college. As with everything else in the learning disability controversy, the statistics vary regarding how many college students today are LD. One study says that about 2 percent of college students are LD (Wilczenski and Gillespie-Silver 1992, 198), while others estimate that the number may be anywhere from 3 to 11 percent (Houck et al. 1992, 687). Paul LeClerc, former president of Hunter College, reported at a 1993 conference in Albany, New York, that the number of LD students at that school tripled from 1987–1993.

The numbers regarding how many of these students graduate also vary. One 1990 study indicated that only 6.5 percent of one group of LD students remained in college programs (Whinnery 1992, 32). However, in a study done by Vogel and Adelman, the graduation rate of LD students was slightly higher than that of non-LD students, although the former group typically took lighter loads and one more year to complete their studies (1992, 440). Some LD students will come to college already identified by their high school records and may spend several semesters in a basic or preparatory writing course or program. Therefore, professors who teach credit-bearing composition or writing-intensive courses might not encounter LD students until those students' second or third semester.

If instructors are not informed about LD students, the following cues might help alert them to students who may need different strategies for learning. These indicators, listed here without explanation, have been described in more detail in earlier chapters. (See also O'Hearn's [1989] and Richards' [1986] articles.) It should be kept in mind that these manifestations may be due partially to a combination of other factors such as carelessness, dialect interference, inexperience, and other social factors, so they should not, by themselves, be used by a writing teacher to diagnose learning disabilities. They are only cues to a possible condition that would need more careful investigation by LD specialists.

As Carolyn O'Hearn points out, although writing instructors are not LD experts qualified officially to test or treat such a student, they may be the first ones in a position to notice a severe problem with writing. Also, although having an LD label entitles students to many accommodations, it is not a classification too many people want following them around in their records for the rest of their professional lives. While some students gladly announce themselves as LD, others will go to any lengths to avoid that label, which is, of course, their right. Therefore, as O'Hearn points out, if we suspect that some of our students might be learning disabled, we are faced with a dilemma. If we ask them about their academic past, what classes they were in or what special problems with writing they may have had, we risk insulting them and losing their trust. On the other hand, if the college provides a tutoring program and accommodations for LD students, and we do not broach the subject with them, we may risk having them become discouraged and drop out of college when perhaps they could have been helped (O'Hearn 1989, 301). Here, then, are some of the possible idiosyncratic features of texts written by LD students, some typical error patterns, and some traits the students themselves might show.

Possible Indicators of Learning Difference

I. Textual Features

   A. Words

      1. omission of prepositions and articles

      2. omission of verbs and word endings

      3. dropped letters

      4. trouble with small words (*be, by, of, it, at*)

      5. trouble with abstract words (*were, where, that*)

      6. trouble with prefixes and suffixes

      7. odd use of apostrophe ("I have to put ga's in my car.")

      8. high number of spelling errors, some bizarre

      9. patternless, inconsistent spelling errors

      10. use of *"has"* for *"as"*

      11. use of *"dose"* for *"does"*

      12. misuse of pronouns

      13. odd malapropisms (*"sequoistered"* for *"cloistered"* for *"sequestered"*)

      14. words used are rarely more than three syllables long (C. Johnston 1984, 387). Note that other studies suggest the vocabulary of LD students may be just as diverse as that of non-LD students (Gajar 1989, 129).

      15. dysnomia (commonly known as the "tip-of-the-tongue" phenomenon, usually a feature of oral language, but sometimes evident in writing as blank spaces left for words that could not be recalled)

   B. Sentences

      1. unusually high number of punctuation errors, especially commas

      2. errors in parallel structure

      3. twisted idioms

      4. incoherent sentences or phrases (which, in a conference, the student may easily explain orally)

      5. may have comparable number of T-units (independent clauses), as "regular" papers, but these are not punctuated properly (Vogel 1982, 524; Gajar 1989, 125).

      6. trouble forming and punctuating complex sentences (Wiig and Fleischmann 1980, 45).

   C. Appearance of the paper

      1. if handwritten, an unusual mixture of capitals and lower-case letters

      2. if handwritten, all text written in block letters

      3. if handwritten, some backward or reversed-sequence letters

4. typed papers far more readable than handwritten (or printed ones)

5. all one paragraph

6. every sentence a different paragraph

II. Content

A. Papers rich in sensory detail

B. Narratives (once deciphered) both unconventional and creative

C. Essays shorter than other students' essays (due to time and effort involved in composing)

III. Students

A. May seem much more intelligent in person than what an initial glance at his or her written work might indicate

B. May be able to *talk* about a subject much more coherently than he or she can *write* about it

C. May be very perceptive of nonverbal cues such as other people's moods, as expressed in facial expression and tone of voice.

D. May notice obscure details in pictures or illustrations (Kahn 1980, 43)

E. May become totally absorbed in a story, essay, or poem that is read aloud

F. May do much better on work completed at home than on timed work done in the classroom (C. Johnston 1984, 387).

G. May compensate for difficulties by working very hard: rewriting everything, coming for extra help, seeking help in a writing or tutoring center, asking for "extra credit"

H. May compensate for difficulties by avoidance of writing situations: skipping classes and conferences, handing in assignments late or not at all, appearing bored by the assignment, finding excuses for not doing well

I. May claim to have always "hated" English

Let me emphasize that this list is a more of a collection of how various people, who do not all agree, have characterized the writing and the actions of people reputed to be LD. It should be used merely as a point of departure for the following discussion.

There have been many studies comparing the writing of LD students to that of their peers. While there are without question substantial problems judging such characteristics as quality, coherence, organization, and clarity, other features such as sentence complexity, spelling, vocabulary, and punctuation are more easily measurable. Vogel and Moran summarize a variety of studies, many of which have contradictory findings (1982, 211–13). In general, however, LD students' writing is not significantly different from that of non-LD students on a syntactic level (though a few studies indicate otherwise). In Vogel and Moran's study, many differences between LD and non-LD students' writing "diminish considerably" when errors in punctuation and capitalization are ignored (219).

They also summarize a study by Critchley in 1973 that showed dyslexic students using less sophisticated vocabulary than that used by non-LD groups. According to Vogel and Moran, Critchley "attributed this difference to a limitation in the dyslexics' word knowledge" (213). This assumption, however, should not be made hastily. Professors who assume their students know sophisticated vocabulary but cannot summon it up or spell it correctly (and therefore avoid it), will act differently toward their students than will those who automatically assume their students have a "limitation in word knowledge." Whether instructors have high or low expectations for their students is no small matter. If LD students use a less sophisticated vocabulary in experimental studies, researchers' speculations about the reasons why should be made very carefully. Other studies Vogel and Moran cite, however, indicate little difference in vocabulary level between LD and non-LD groups. The spelling differences are, as might be predicted, quite significant (212).

Research on writing is one area that cries out for collaboration between disciplines. Much of the research on LD students' writing has been done in the Educational Psychology field, which prepares its professionals for research but does not explore much Composition theory. Those in the field of Composition are more familiar with some of the pitfalls involved in attempting to assess writing, but they could benefit from their colleagues' background in experimental methods and statistical analysis. Whether or not LD students' writing differs in important ways from that of their non-LD peers is a question that has yet to be reliably answered. Future research projects addressing this question should be designed by professionals representing the perspectives of several fields. A mutual respect for each other's research methods, however, is essential, as Stephen M. North argues in *The Making of Knowledge in Composition*. He also points out the substantial, perhaps irreconcilable, differences in ideology that may render such collaboration difficult or impossible (1987, 346–47).

The many remaining questions regarding surface features notwithstanding, composition instructors may occasionally find a paper with so many of the indicators listed previously that they suspect the writer may have a learning difference. Whether or not an instructor should approach a student about pursuing testing and whether or not that student should decide to do so are complex questions with many practical, ethical, and possibly legal ramifications.

If it is obvious that a student could greatly benefit from untimed tests, scribes, tutors, access to computers, or other accommodations to which identified LD students are legally entitled, it makes sense for both student and instructor to do everything possible to secure the kind of practical assistance that could make the difference between academic failure and success. If, however, some instructors still harbor unfounded, negative assumptions regarding the intellectual abilities of learning disabled people, or if they associate the LD label with students they believe to be avoiding the "standards" that everyone else must meet, students must consider if changed teacher expectations due to the label would have a negative effect on their overall education. In one survey, faculty respondents indicated some doubt about LD students' graduation chances, as well as their ability to succeed in any major (Houck et al. 1992, 683). Given the sad but real possibility that the LD label could create limiting prejudgments of students, writing instructors also need to weigh both sides of this ethical dilemma.

In the final chapter of *Rhetorical Traditions and the Teaching of Writing*, Knoblauch and Brannon point to reader-response theory to help us better understand evaluation, and their observation is relevant here: "the extent to which readers' awareness either of the authority of the writer or of their own authority to be judges affects their perceptions of texts." Further, "in the absence of confidence in the authority of the writer, . . . readers will tend without hesitation to cite any idiosyncrasy of form or technique, idea or style, any authorial choice that challenges their personal preferences, as an 'error'" (1984, 161). In other words, the very fact that teachers, or any readers, have the authority to judge students' writing means that they will, indeed, judge it—and usually negatively. If they also are privy to knowledge that the writer is LD, they might inadvertently be less or more critical of that writer's text, based on their preconceived notions of LD people in general. Whether or not to invite students to identify and possibly stigmatize themselves in such a culture, in spite of the accommodations that would then become available, is a decision that should not be made lightly. As was seen in Chapter Four, the three students interviewed had mixed feelings about this, although they did seem more supportive of the label in higher education than in the earlier grades.

Critics of the learning disability field are accurate in their estimation that much of the terminology used to describe LD "clients" has negative connotations, and no group is more aware of this than LD students themselves. Written into existing legislation and therefore necessarily appearing in forms, institutional policy statements, and professional journals, terms such as *disabilities*, *limitations*, *disorders*, and *deficits*, when taken together indicate a troubling preoccupation with what is wrong (Johnston and Allington 1991). Like the resource room students Nick described in the previous chapter, there may be many labeled high school students who are "mad and stubborn" and programmed to feel that college is not an option.

Dependency is a related issue that students and professors need to consider when planning a course of action. While the three LD students I spoke with were labeled at different times in their lives, none of them took vocational courses or spent much time isolated in special education programs. Although each experienced frustrations in the mainstream, they were all spared the kind of dangerous dependency students can sometimes develop in the resource rooms of some non-progressive school districts. In an article called "Helping College Bound Clients with Learning Disabilities," which appeared in the *Journal of Rehabilitation*, the authors rightly advise counselors to consider many factors in assessing a student's chance of success in college (Satcher and Dooley-Dickey 1991, 48). Overall, the article seems to be in the students' best interests, but there also seems to be a disturbing assumption that the responsibility for "determining reasonable expectations" regarding a student's college career rests not primarily with the student, but with the vocational counselor.

While good, attentive advising is a valuable resource, it may be detrimental if advisors place unconscious restrictions on what students can and can not do. Also, since there is some evidence that traditional measures of academic promise "underpredict" the performance of college LD students (Wilczenski and Gillespie-Silver 1992, 201), even careful, sensitive career counselors may not be able to judge accurately whether or not students should attempt college. Students, of course, ultimately make the final decision, but they may be unduly influenced by the disabling terminology in which they may have been steeped during many years of "support," and they are to some extent at the mercy of those who write their recommendations. Satcher and Dooley-Dickey recognize that some students may not want to disclose their LD label. They therefore advise that "VR [Vocational Rehabilitation] counselors will want to include self-identification and request for support services as part of the client's IWRP [individualized written rehabilitation plan]" (1991, 49). While this disclosure is intended to help students, it may deny them the choice of whether or not they wish their new professors and peers to know their past academic history.

After carefully considering these issues, suppose a professor does decide to speak privately to a student whose struggles with written language do not seem to be caused by lack of effort, unenlightened high school teachers, or less-than-model family reading habits. Great care must be taken in how this subject is broached. It is illegal for classroom instructors to inform a student that she is learning disabled, and it is illegal to ask a student if she is learning disabled. Sally Townsend, a colleague of mine with a degree in LD, pointed this out, adding that we would never dream of trying to diagnose alcoholism or brain damage in our students or of asking them outright if they thought they might have these conditions (Townsend 1994). She suggested that instructors instead ask general questions designed to let the student know that help was available should they decide to seek it out. For example, Sally has asked questions such as, "I'm having lots of trouble reading your writing. Have other people ever said anything to you about this? Have you had similar experiences before this class?" (Townsend 1994).

At this point, the student knows the professor is open to ways of helping, and it is the student's decision to maintain the status quo or to pursue channels of help, which the professor can explain or help seek out, providing the student is interested. Sally emphasizes student responsibility in this matter. As all three students in the last chapter said in different ways, what matters most is whether students view these private chats as threatening or supportive. If a professor's tone is respectful, positive, and interested, students will have an easier time deciding what, if anything, they wish to do about any learning difficulties they may have.

If the conference described above results in a student's requesting information on LD or accommodations (or if a student comes to the college already identified as LD), professors and student should turn first to whatever resources their college already provides.

Resources

Whether LD students come to college already diagnosed, or whether they are diagnosed after demonstrating many of the above characteristics and being tested, they are of special concern to administrators since the passing of the 1973 Rehabilitation Act, especially Section 504. According to Susan A. Vogel, this law provided that colleges receiving any federal assistance must accommodate LD students, allowing them to "participate fully in all programs" (1985, 179–80). As this is usually interpreted, colleges are not required to test for LD (although many do), but they must provide services for students already labeled LD. (For a partial listing of tests, see Ostertag et al. 1982). Since the passing of the 1990 Americans with Disabilities

Act, issues regarding who will finance these services and accommodations have become more critical, and, as discussed in Chapter One, are currently and slowly in the process of being decided through case law.

What follows is a list of places on campus where help for LD students should be available. LD specialists and services are often located in offices and departments that might be called by different names on different campuses. There are often overlapping services (for example, tutoring available in both a writing and a math learning center). Interested composition instructors should read their own institution's student or faculty handbook, or the college catalog to see what services are available. Below are names of offices interested faculty members may look to for advice and help regarding students they suspect may be LD.

Academic Support Services

Office of Handicapped Services

Evaluation Center

Guidance or Advisement Office

Counseling Services

Library or Media Center

Reading Program

Learning Center

Writing Center and/or Math Center

Tutoring Services

Health Services

Academic Dean's Office

Student Services

The kind of help the student receives will vary, but support services may include testing, counseling, advisement, tutoring, scribes, or supplementary materials. Ideally, the LD specialist will communicate with the student's classroom instructors in order better to coordinate the work done in all settings.

Fairleigh Dickinson University, for example, began a program in 1988 that allows learning disabled students to be mainstreamed into regular college classes but provides a campuswide support system. This includes tutoring offered for every course taken during their first year. Regular faculty and staff receive training to be aware of the characteristics of and accommodations for learning disabled students. Time limits for testing may be extended, and a note taker or tape recorder may be provided. In addition, first-year students in the LD program take a course called "Metacognitive Strategies," which helps them become more aware of their particular learning process (Farleigh Dickinson University 1991). Other colleges may have more compartmentalized services of which individual faculty members are unaware, but determined composition instructors should be able to find someone on campus knowledgeable about learning disabilities. (For a further discussion of services offered see Cordoni 1982; Vogel 1982; and Ostertag et al. 1982.)

It may be that eventually the best way to handle alternative teaching or studying options will be to make them available for all students. Rochester Institute of Technology, for example, makes many resources in its Alternative Learning Department available not just to labeled LD students, but to everyone—faculty and students, labeled or not. While funding for the more individualized levels of support does depend to some extent on the official label, the department is open for all. Anyone can use available texts on learning differences, and there is a generous approach to sharing taped textbooks, lecture notes, and other materials. According to Jacqueline Lynch Czamanske, chair of the department, while non-LD students are "not coming down in droves," the idea of making "all education special" would help reduce the stigma connected with the LD label (1994).

Other options that might reduce unwanted attention to LD students and also improve higher education in general is to make information and materials that are usually restricted to LD students available in a more neutral site to everyone. Tape recordings of classes could be kept in the school library, behind the reference desk, to be used much like reserve materials. Any student could sign out the tape and headphones for several hours to listen to a missed class or one she would like to review. A professor's lecture notes might be available to the whole college community in much the same way. In addition, the "inside information" regarding instructors' teaching styles might be printed in the course schedules of classes. Courses might be coded as being primarily lecture-based, or as requiring much writing or oral discussion. While there may be some legitimate objections to making such information and materials public, the overall benefits in destigmatizing LD students and in opening collegewide dialogue about teaching and learning styles would probably outweigh any disadvantages.[1]

Composition specialists interested in additional information outside their field have vast resources. The ERIC files list many essays on learning disabilities, usually in publications such as the *Annals of Dyslexia*, the *Learning Disability Quarterly*, and the *Journal of Learning Disabilities*, as well as in journals dealing with reading, education, medicine, or psychology. There are also many articles in other publications not primarily focused on LD. Marc E. Helgeson and T. Hisama's (1982) article on using a "Multi-Modality Approach" to teach illiterate prison inmates appeared in the *Journal of Correctional Education*. In *Adult Literacy and Basic Education* was an article by Binnie L. Peterson entitled "One Approach to Teaching the Specific Language Disabled Adult Language Arts" (1981). Other articles on alternative teaching methods for the learning disabled appear in the following periodicals: *Brain and Language*; *Clinical Neuropsychology*; *Educational Psychologist*; *Journal of Educational Psychology*; *Journal of Classroom Interactions*; *Journal of Reading Behavior*; *Academic Therapy*; *Support for Learning*; *Reading Research and Instruction*; *Perception and Motor Skills*.

There are many dissertations on LD-related topics such as "dyslexia" and "multisensory," but these are usually for people obtaining doctoral degrees outside English or Composition Studies. Nancy Le Sanders Royal's 1987 dissertation studied the O-G-based method of multisensory teaching developed by Beth Slingerland, a remedial approach designed for LD students that is either strongly endorsed or vehemently condemned, depending on one's position in the LD controversy. Other dissertations studying the usefulness of O-G methods fulfilled requirements in the following fields: Special Education, Education (Curriculum and Instruction), and Clinical Psychology. These texts are but a sampling of the information on LD available across the disciplines. Countless documents and pamphlets are available from federal and state agencies, especially following the passage of the ADA, and the Internet is an ever-growing source of information and discussion opportunities. (One useful LD listserv, or electronic discussion group, is LD-List@east.pima.edu).

Alternative Approaches to Teaching and Assessment

Whether or not students are receiving outside help with their reading or writing, there are classroom techniques that not only accommodate LD students, but also broaden opportunities for everyone.

It should be pointed out again that some experts claim that by the time learning disabled students get to college, they really cannot be easily remediated—that if they have not overcome their disability by their eighteenth year, their best hope is that their teachers will help them find ways to work around their learning differences. From her research at McGill University, Maggie Bruck found that adult dyslexics' phonological awareness skills—that is, the ability readers need to distinguish syllables and phonetic sounds—never reach the skill level of normal readers (1992, 882). Nancy Pompian and Carl Thum, in their discussion of LD students at Dartmouth College, recommend "accommodation rather than remediation" (1988, 281), that is, helping LD students and college instructors adapt to each other rather than begin (once again) a remedial process that may be a disheartening waste of time for all concerned. As mentioned earlier, some may argue that this is a defeatist attitude —that by attributing students' problems to "learning disability," and relying on accommodations rather than renewed instruction, we may be putting limits on their progress.

As discussed in Chapter Four, the debate over whether or not to use "bypass" methods or more remediation is ongoing. While some teachers at Landmark College are on record as being against bypass methods (Meyer 1986, 30), Jackie Czamanske at Rochester Institute of Technology bases the philosophy of her Alternative Learning Department on the idea that "We do not remediate." She and her staff help students identify and take advantage of what they do well, and regularly discuss with students and professors across the disciplines Howard Gardner's theory of "multiple intelligences" (Czamanske 1994). Gardner believes that conventional intelligence tests unfairly privilege linguistic ability while they virtually ignore other intellectual capabilities which, were they identified, could be more fully developed and used (Gardner 1985, xi–xii). This emphasis on what talents their students *do* possess, the philosophy that drives RIT's Alternative Learning Department, is one that other institutions would do well to emulate.

In writing this chapter on "Implications for College Instructors," I am struck repeatedly with the enormity, perhaps even the impossibility, of the task. Whenever strategies, methods, or approaches are discussed, there is always the danger that they will be tried on and then discarded like so many platform shoes headed for a garage sale. I include ideas here more for what they may generate in readers than for the ideas themselves. What is important is not the "alternative learning strategies" but the larger concept of alternative learning. Rather than presenting a how-to on adapting to the status quo, I would like to describe this chapter much the way Jackie Czamanske summed up her program at RIT. She said her philosophy was about a "shift in values." Instead of concentrating on finding out if people are "learning disabled," she advises asking the question, "What do you do well?"(1994).

The suggestions I propose are here to spark questions about what happens in our classes, our courses, and our institutions, and how that might change if we really did conceive of learning in different ways, if we committed ourselves to finding out what our students did well and allowed them to teach us. What if we really did change our views of intelligence, and broadened our definition of "writing" to include much, much more than it currently does in academia? What if we took seriously Freire's concept of "co-intentional" education—that "Teachers and students (leadership and people), co-intent on reality, are both Subjects, not only in the task of unveiling that reality, and thereby coming to know it critically, but in the task of re-creating that knowledge" (Freire 1970, 56). How would college—or the world—change if we were to turn the teaching/learning model upside down? It is in the impractical spirit of challenging conventional ideas of teaching, learning, assessing, writing, and thinking that I approach this somewhat practical next section.

The strategies discussed below are not blanket recommendations. Some techniques will be appropriate for certain LD students but not others. MacLean Gander, English Department Chair at Landmark College, says there is no such thing as *the* way to teach students with language-processing differences. Their needs vary (Gander 1991). Instructors need to talk with and listen to their students individually, to take advantage of whatever metacognitive strategies students may already have. For example, they may already know whether they learn better by hearing words read aloud or by seeing them on paper, so they may have suggestions about how instructors can best help them. Instructors need to find out (diplomatically) what, if any, supplementary help these students are already receiving through a learning center or tutorial program. That way, the student's efforts can be reinforced rather than unnecessarily repeated. Finally, before any modifications in teaching or evaluating are made, the instructor and student must examine together the student's writing to determine strengths and weaknesses.

Teacher-Centered Instruction

Before beginning a discussion of what *to* do, I'd like to talk about what *not* to do. Some of the most time-honored institutional practices may be the worst possible way for LD students to approach learning. One person speaking from a lectern before a large group of students who are expected to write selected notes may present frustrating, often unnecessary hurdles to an LD student. Students able to absorb information orally might understand the actual lecture, but having to organize the information and quickly write readable notes is another story. For visually oriented students, the lecture might be almost useless. If LD students sit in the back of a large classroom or lecture hall (as many are wont to do), the instructor's facial expressions and eye contact, which might especially help LD students, will probably be lost. Being expected to read many chapters of material or long pieces of fiction at home and in isolation from other students may overwhelm LD students, whose reading level, by ordinary measures, may not be what their professors assume it is. Also, these students may need much more time to read what other students, or their professors, can read in much less time.

In general, LD students perform much more poorly on timed tests, especially the "objective," multiple-choice variety, than they do on work they either can take home, or at least have as much time as they need to complete. The added stress of completing work by a certain time adds to the difficulties they may have in reading and interpreting the test questions, and on keeping the *a*'s, *b*'s, and *c*'s straight on both test and answer sheets. Even an essay exam, if timed, may undermine everything they have been taught about taking their time and being careful to revise and proofread.

Many professors still require one long paper, due near the end of the semester. If an LD student's writing demonstrates the kind of severe surface and sentence problems discussed earlier, the professor might not become aware of it until much too late in the semester to do anything about it. In addition, LD students might require some guidance in completing the project in stages, rather than in one flawless package due on a given date. Also, if the long paper is unacceptable, little time is left for the student to revise it.

However, if institutional restrictions or practical considerations require that a course be taught by traditional methods, there are modifications that can be made even in this restrictive model. If a professor *must* lecture, the talk could have some kind of multisensory link. A clearly organized outline, either on a blackboard, an overhead projector, or a slide might accompany the lecture. Color-coded diagrams or charts, where possible, could supplement explanations of concepts, and a mix of bold and regular print on handouts is also useful. Landmark College uses "manipulatives," color-coded objects to teach abstract concepts (see Chapter Two).

Good teaching practices from methods courses should be resurrected: briefly reviewing old material, introducing new material in a way that relates to previous knowledge and to the students' lives, and a preview of what the basic structure of the lecture will be (Kahn 1980, 41). If a student asks permission to tape a class, the speaker might pay particular attention to the organization of lecture notes. Susan Vogel gives the practical suggestions that instructors speak more slowly and allow for students to occasionally provide copies of their lecture notes to each other (1982, 523). My colleague Sally Townsend suggests that LD students come up with a prearranged, nonverbal cue to inform the instructor they are struggling to keep up with the lecture or large-group discussion. This might be coughing, putting on or taking off a hat, or some other noticeable act. The point is to communicate without causing undue embarrassment. Providing some class time to discuss note-taking and summarizing might help all students see what is important and also might allow instructors to monitor how much review is needed. As I was walking across campus one day, I overheard one student say to another, "I have to have someone read my notes to me out loud before I can even *start* studying." I do not know the subject being discussed or if the speaker was LD, but this snatch of conversation reinforced for me the importance of the oral modality for some people.

If much outside reading is required, the instructor might require or encourage the formation of study groups, either in or out of class, so that students will begin to discuss what they are reading with each other. That way, students having trouble with the reading level may benefit from an oral discussion of the material. As we saw in Chapter Four, both Nick and Monica highly recommended study groups. Beverly Dexter points out that diagnosed LD students may be able to have their books tape-recorded through Recordings for the Blind, Inc. (1982, 346). While LD students are not visually handicapped, listening to a required novel or textbook chapter while walking or driving to school may help them to better manage their time if they are slow readers.

By expanding their knowledge base in whatever ways are available in an electronic age, LD students who do not read fast might partially compensate for years of negative "Matthew Effects"— Keith Stanovich's phrase for "the rich get richer and the poor get poorer" syndrome that applies to students and their reading habits. Those who read well and like to read *do* read widely and expand their prior knowledge, thus increasing the possibility that they will better understand progressively sophisticated materials on a wide range of topics. Those students for whom reading is a struggle, avoid it. This limits their knowledge base, further reducing the chances that they will understand subsequent texts they are asked to read. What this means for college writing instructors is that they too should consider alternative ways for their LD students to familiarize themselves with whatever readings might be required in the course curriculum. For example, instead of the entire class being required to read Elbow's *Writing With Power* on their own time, a small group could collaborate on an oral summary of it.

Short literary pieces particularly appropriate for oral reading could be read aloud in class by a teacher or a competent student. For example, Mark Twain's acerbic "The War Prayer," an excellent piece with which to provoke written response, can be read aloud in about five minutes. Not only is this method more dramatic than a home reading, where multiple distractions or reading difficulties can prevent students from reacting to the piece fully, but an oral reading is a community experience that can spark lively discussions. A writing-intensive Shakespeare class could take advantage of excellent film productions now available on videotape, such as Zeffirelli's films *Romeo and Juliet* and *Hamlet*, which can be used to supplement a student's struggle through seventeenth-century blank verse on her own.

If students must read large portions of material at home, their instructors might heed some sound advice from reading specialists: tell them what to expect from the readings, what topics will be discussed, and what sections are most important. Required texts should always be discussed or reviewed. Bernice Wong points out something reading teachers know but writing instructors may need to review: students need to be aware of *how* they read and what strategies help them best to comprehend or make meaning out of what they read (1988, 191). These "study skills" are often considered the domain of student support services rather than of classroom instructors. With an awareness of the LD student's typical problems and assets, teachers can construct assignments and evaluation tools in ways that are more compatible with their particular discipline and with different styles of learning. English professors who themselves enjoy reading need to be alert for possible multisensory options for those students who might not have the same facility with reading. Reading, of course, should still be encouraged, but not to the extent that it causes capable students to drop classes because of reading (or writing) assignments that are unnecessarily rigid.

Susan Vogel offers recommendations if multiple-choice exams cannot be avoided. First, LD students might be provided with a reader, so that they can *hear* the questions and possible choices. Second, they could be allowed to give their answers orally, so that they do not accidentally put down the wrong one. (Oral exams and readers are welcome options—and legal rights—for both Monica and Janine.) If students must write their answers, they should at least have the option to avoid the fill-in-the-dots answer sheet. The stems and answer choices should be free of complicated, overly modified sentence structure and double negatives. Finally, if possible, the untimed essay should be used in favor of the objective test (1982, 527).

Although written work is essential in evaluating students' progress in a writing course, other options are possible in other disciplines. For example, oral reports, diagrams, prepared video-tapes, or three-dimensional models are all ways in which LD students might better demonstrate their understanding of literature, science, math, etc. First drafts for LD students can take the form of a visual or graphic concept rather than something with words. Pat Fennelly at SUNY Albany has students sketch on the blackboard their reactions to a reading before they write about it (1990). Donna Richardson uses a "drawing-to-learn" method as a way into Wordsworth's poetry. By having students sketch, for example, the narrator's physical approach to Lucy's cabin in the poem "Strange Fits of Passion I Have Known," she allows students to do a kind of "visual paraphrasing" that might be an important first step in making meaning out of a text (1990, 141–45). While the option to do sketches was not designed specifically for LD students, it may very well be that this technique is an appropriate outlet for those who get a visual image of an idea prior to forming a linguistic one. I typically begin my Introduction to Literature classes with a few minutes of directed, informal writing. One day last semester I instead asked how we might sketch the plot development of Steinbeck's *Cannery Row*. Several people volunteered to put their five-minute diagrams on the whiteboard, and the discussion following their explanations was one of the most invigorating of the semester. Their visualizations taught me something about the novel, as did the process of sketching.

Carolyn Oliver, Director of Admissions at Landmark College, believes that although there are many kinds of learning disabilities, at least one-third of LD students are primarily oral learners. They need to speak often in class discussions, and they may need to compose orally. She recommends a teaching approach that emphasizes speech communication, and the writing classes at Landmark College have oral communication as a substantial component of their curriculum (1991). It should be noted, however, that the English classes at Landmark College (called "nation's costliest college" by *The Chronicle of Higher Education*) are typically composed of six to eight students. It is conceivable that virtually any approach to teaching would succeed in such conditions. By itself, this teacher-student ratio allows a luxury of individual attention and small-group contact most people cannot financially afford. The oral projects and closely monitored revision strategies possible in a group this size may not be practical in the classes of twenty to thirty that are typical at public four-year or community colleges.

Oliver also believes that some LD students may need to have structures of sentences, paragraphs, and essays made explicit. It is inappropriate, of course, to teach such patterns to students who can intuit them or discover new ones independently. However, some LD students may need concrete strategies for how to begin an essay or ways to get from one paragraph to another. MacLean Gander points out that even the much-maligned five paragraph theme (although he himself does not teach it) was a structure one LD student found extremely useful. After a tutor made that form explicit to him, the student produced what he considered his best piece of writing (Gander 1991). While explicit teaching of structures may be unnecessary, or even limiting, for most LD students, it may be crucial to the learning of *some* learning disabled people.

Student-Centered Instruction

As stated previously, the student-centered pedagogy being written about in many contemporary journals and being discussed at recent conferences might appear to be more widespread in actual practice than is actually the case. Everyone seems to know about freewriting, nongraded journals, peer response groups, one-to-one student-teacher conferences, multiple drafts, and so on. Often, however, "group work" consists of a class of twenty-five sitting in a circle with the teacher leading the discussion. The concept of "multiple drafts" degenerates into the instructor essentially editing the student's work and the student typing it over, and informal journals are sometimes graded for their grammatical correctness.

LD students must learn to question their own ideas, to view their writing from various perspectives, and to become their own editors. In this sense, they are no different from "normal" college students. However, LD students seem to have a greater need than other students do for an awareness of when and how they learn best, especially since the circumstances under which LD students learn are likely to be different from those of the majority, for whom most pedagogies are designed.

Response journals and reading logs, if used properly, help some LD students find their strong points and develop confidence and voice. Writing teachers sometimes abandon journals because they are often voluminous, error-ridden, or boring. However, experienced instructors' advice regarding selective or random reading of journals still applies, and there is no law saying teachers must read every word. The purpose of journals is to help writers develop fluency and explore ideas. Learning disabled students are especially in need of the positive feedback and encouragement that comments from professors or from other students can provide. The journal is useful for establishing a format through which other members of the writing community can respond substantively to creative ideas expressed by LD students in sketches, cartoons, or diagrams, forms that should be suggested and encouraged. Often, by seeing their ideas in another form, LD students can then write about them. Handwritten journals provide evidence of word problems students might be experiencing. Because students often write about their interests, alert readers can help them generate ideas for future writing projects. Usually unstructured and untimed, journals and reading logs might be some of the best outlets through which LD students can experiment with their written expression. Writing teachers should do everything in their power to make journal writing a positive experience for all students, but especially for LD students. Journals should not be graded on grammatical correctness.

For many of the same reasons, freewriting—focused or unfocused, uninterrupted writing—should also be encouraged. Those convinced they have nothing to say are free to write that opinion. As Peter Elbow explains it, the purpose is simply to get words down on paper without pausing to think about it (1973, 1–11). To be most effective, freewriting should be repeated over time so that it can be given a chance to do what it is supposed to do—encourage attention to ideas (not spelling and punctuation); develop fluency and voice; and convince inexperienced, tentative, or learning disabled writers that they *can* express themselves through words if, as the Nike slogan puts it, they "just do it." Providing a few minutes at the beginning, middle, or end of a class period in which students may do some informal, focused freewriting will demonstrate to them how much they can get down on paper in a short time. Nongraded freewriting is especially important for some LD students because it may give them success in a medium (writing) they may not have succeeded in previously. As Carolyn Oliver points out, however, freewriting may be less successful, even frustrating, for those LD students who do not yet have the automatization of basic word or sentence skills that most children have by seventh grade. Freewriting is often promoted as a way for students to overcome writing blocks, but for certain kinds of learning disabled students, even freewriting presents structural obstacles that must first be overcome by explicit teaching (1991).

Jackie Czamanske suggests a tape-recorded free flow of ideas as an alternative to freewriting or written journal entries. If the purpose of these strategies is to generate ideas and to make connections, some students may benefit more from this kind of articulation than from struggling with a notebook or even a word processor. Students should not be required to transcribe this tape; instructors could simply listen to portions the student might select, or the tape could be made only for the student's use (1994). This option to "free-talk" could be available to any student who might occasionally benefit from it, for instance when driving or walking, but the class community would need first to determine the purpose of this exercise.

For most LD students, it is especially important that small-group discussions and peer response be incorporated into the writing class. Of course, most students require some modeling and instruction on ways to respond to each other's work, and they should be encouraged to offer observations and questions rather than criticism and suggestions. Group work is especially helpful to LD students because it provides an opportunity to involve another sense (hearing) in their learning and writing process. It is multisensory because they can associate what is said with the person doing the talking. By listening to essays read aloud, they may be better able to understand the potential power of the written word. By reading their own texts aloud, they may read smoothly through many surface flaws, giving a more accurate presentation of their ideas. On the other hand, some students like Nick and Monica may loathe reading out loud in class and should not be forced to do so.

Revising through a multiple-draft process is especially important for LD students. No doubt used to having their spelling and grammar-related errors pounced upon, it might be a refreshing change to have their *ideas* responded to first. When reading an early draft by an LD student, instructors may have a special need for Peter Elbow's "believing game" (1973, 147–91). That is, teachers might need to make a special effort to *believe* there is an idea embedded in what might be a morass of poorly punctuated sentences and unusual spelling. By responding first to the student's opinions, validating creative descriptions or raising questions about convictions, instructors show that writing is important.

At the proofreading stage, the teacher/student conference is useful. It does little good for the instructor to spend time editing and fixing a student's errors. It is time-consuming for the teacher, discouraging for the student, and frustrating for both. Students need to develop editing skills if they are to succeed in the academic or business world. One method that seems to work well with LD students is to meet with them individually, providing both teacher and student with an uncorrected copy of the latest draft. Having students read each sentence out loud will help them detect many idiomatic or punctuation difficulties. Any remaining errors can be hinted at or directly pointed out by the instructor. If there is a spelling rule or grammar convention that is useful, both parties might pool their creativity to find a mnemonic device or multisensory trick to help the student remember it. Carolyn Oliver suggests that students point to and say aloud each word in their text. The multisensory aspect of this strategy (using hand, eye, and voice), will help keep the LD student focused. For high school and college instructors who wish to help LD writers improve their spelling, *Beyond the "SP" Label: Improving the Spelling of Learning Disabled and Basic Writers* by McAlexander, Dobie, and Gregg offers an extensive, systematic approach involving error analysis, useful rules, and memory aids. These one-to-one conferences are time-consuming but essential in establishing the human connection and the personal reaction LD students need for their writing. Conferences also help determine what kinds of surface errors the student is making and what approaches will best eliminate them. By taking notes on each meeting, students can begin to monitor their own progress and learn to check for themselves subsequent writing projects. Also, conferences often reveal a student's outside interests, suggesting engaging subject matter for future essays or papers.

Both student and teacher, however, need to determine how much time to invest in close editing. In fixing repeated errors, they may quickly reach a point of diminishing returns and decide to lean more heavily on a generous roommate to help out with proofreading. To what extent students should be encouraged to seek substantial editing assistance is something that needs to be addressed at cross-disciplinary meetings, workshops, or seminars. What some instructors may describe as "plagiarism" others may view as sensible, time-saving, legitimate collaboration. This is another controversial element that could have a "both/and" solution if students, faculty, and administrators conversed more frequently about such questions.

Computer Technology

That LD students should have more access to word processors and sophisticated editing software is one of the few noncontroversial conclusions most everyone makes. Much of what has been written in various disciplines about LD students has been speculation. However, many studies about word processing have been done that sufficiently demonstrate its special value to LD students. For more than three years, Terence Collins has worked with LD students at the University of Minnesota. He quotes one LD adult as calling word processing "liberation technology," and another as saying, "I can *see* my thoughts." In this study, LD students were enrolled in regular writing classes, but all students had access to computers. Collins reports that LD students, by using computers, were able greatly to reduce their fear of writing (1989, 4).

Numerous studies summarized by Marshall and Durst, in a *Research in the Teaching of English* Annotated Bibliography, deal with word processing and substantiate the findings of Collins and his colleagues. One study cited in the May, 1988, *RTE* was Carole McAllister and Richard Louth's "The Effect of Word Processing on the Revision of Basic Writers," presented at the 1987 CCCC in Atlanta. They concluded that word processing seemed to improve the students' revision practices (1987, 19–20). Also listed is Evelyn J. Posey's dissertation, "The Writer's Tool: A Study of Microcomputer Word Processing to Improve the Writing of Basic Writers." Although writing improvement could not be definitively measured, Posey found students became more motivated and took their work through more revisions (1986, 39).

Simply having access to a typewriter may be particularly valuable to learning disabled students. To illustrate this, I return briefly to my nephew Joey. The only word that he can write in cursive is his first name (see Figure 5–1).

As can be observed, his signature is not easily read or written. He makes a recognizable *J*, fakes his way through the *o* and *e*, which

Figure 5–1
Joey's signature.

must be somehow tangled in his mind, and finishes up with something looking vaguely like a *y*. One day I sat him in front of an electric typewriter and told him to find the letters in his name and type them. He promptly typed *Joey* and squealed with delight at seeing the letters appear (for once) correctly on the paper, at having the typewriter keys obey in a way that his hand would not. Similarly, LD college students required to write their work on a word processor might discover a control they are unable to achieve with handwriting.

As technology advances and Computer Assisted Instruction (CAI) becomes more sophisticated, composition instructors need to be alert for those programs which might especially benefit LD students. For example, some programs help students analyze their sentence structure by separating out individual sentences and spacing them one by one down the page. This aids in the late-stage editing process of checking for sentence fragments, exceedingly long phrases, or punctuation problems. The electronic separating of sentences is particularly helpful for LD students, who often simply need help isolating a sentence so that they can more easily consider its structure and meaning. As Joel Nydahl points out in a *College English* essay, one need not purchase an expensive CAI program to do sophisticated maneuvers with text (1990, 904). Any simple word-processing system can be used to separate sentences. One need only press the "return" key twice after every period or other end mark and the "sentences" will be isolated. If students have been neglecting to include such punctuation marks, that will of course be immediately obvious.

Taking advantage of the ability to add, delete, replace, and move sentences and paragraphs around in the text might also open new possibilities for LD students. Even if electronic word processing is not available, students could do a kind of mechanical word processing. If only the fronts of paper are written on, students can use scissors to cut and paste sections of their essays, experimenting with deletion and placement, and utilizing yet another sense—touch. Graphics programs and desktop publishing options might help LD students incorporate their nonlinguistic talents into papers and reports. The potential of hypertext and multimedia is only beginning to be investigated, and LD students might be the people best qualified to explore the almost spatial qualities of this new technology.

In a recent issue of the *Computing Teacher*, Michael J. Speziale and Lynne M. La France recount how a high school class of LD students used *HyperStudio*, a computerized multimedia program, to create a study guide for the Pennsylvania Driver's Manual. These teachers credit the nonlinear, collaborative, multisensory nature of the project for the successful results they report. "They [the LD students] amazed visitors who saw the quality of their work and who at one point wanted to know if they were gifted students." The student project leaders were reportedly "among the lowest readers in the class. They simply excelled in using the *HyperStudio* program and in the teaching/learning process being employed" (1992, 34).

Some word processors today have a feature that allows the user to program often-used words simply by pressing one assigned key. This could help a student like Barbara, who was taking a psychology course and needed to write several papers in which she needed to write "psychology" many times, a word whose spelling always eluded her. If she could program it once and then let the computer's memory work for her, it would save her much time and perhaps many futile attempts at memorization.

In a recent issue of *Change*, Norman Coombs and G. Phillip Cartwright describe the latest adaptive computer technologies and a way to find out about them in their article "Project EASI: Equal Access to Software and Information." For physically challenged people for example, there is "a sip-and-puff straw," through which they can use morse code to work with a computer. The authors also explain how they use the Internet for "distance learning" seminars (1994, 43–44).[2]

Writing for the *Times Educational Supplement*, Sally McKeown reports that "overlays" and "predictive word processing" software such as *PAL* and *MindReader* can "'learn' what the writer typically writes, and can produce a short word list on request, often after the first two letters are typed in." McKeown also reports on the findings of the National Council for Educational Technology, which looked at sixteen different spell checkers in various price ranges. For one misspelled word, some programs offered an overgenerous list of forty suggested alternatives, which of course can result in the kind of confusion LD students do not need (1992, S11),—and which contributed to Janine's choice of *decision* for *discussion* and *effect* for *effort*, as we saw in the last chapter. According to McKeown, some of the better programs provide ways of controlling the spell checker's lists. She also discusses the advantages of a "speech synthesizer," now available, which could help the student who wrote this sentence hear it: "Every day I can't how money days it is to Christmas." Finally, McKeown makes a point that is sad and sometimes all too true: it is often the students who need this technology the most who may not be placed in courses most likely to feature exposure to this sophisticated machinery (S11).

As instructors and therefore part of the institution, we need to use whatever influence we have to ensure that all LD students have regular access to computers, not simply for remedial exercises or typing purposes, but as often and for as long as they want in order to compose, revise, edit, and experiment. They should be encouraged to take advantage of the most sophisticated spell checkers, grammar programs, CAI packages, hypertext, multimedia, assistive technologies, and so on. While there already are many intersections between computer science and composition, there should be a more concerted collaboration among disciplines, with the needs of LD writers specifically in mind. In the same way that conceptions of teaching need to be rethought, so do conceptions of almost every aspect of the technology connected with it.

In "Reconceiving Hypertext," Catherine F. Smith critiques most past hypertext theory for focusing too narrowly on what are assumed to be universal thought patterns and concepts of reality. She uses the analogy of "gendered virtuality," as illustrated in Virginia Woolf's explanation in *Three Guineas* of how men and women in Britain in the 1930s would view academic buildings through different social and economic lenses (1991, 229.) In much the same way that men and women view the world differently, Smith argues, hypertext users might view virtual reality in ways quite different from that of the original designers of the program. This failure on the designers' part to anticipate different worldviews or thinking styles prompts Smith to ask provocative questions: "Have the designers of virtual realities encountered our differences? Do the systems those designers design know about difference?" (1991, 233). These questions, I think, are relevant in this discussion of learning differences and computer technology. Hypertext has tremendous potential for those whose thought processes may thrive in multisensory, associative, multimedia environments; however, if conventional, linguisto-centric minds have conceptualized its design, even hypertext may present for LD hypertext users some of the same intellectual frustrations they encounter every day in traditional classrooms and texts. Near the end of her essay, Smith proposes that a "new hypertextual cross-discipline" should research the intersections of composition and hypertext, and also consider some of the questions she raises about individual differences in perception, virtuality, and cognitive activity.

Peer Tutoring

In addition to the almost universal celebration of computers, another rare area of agreement in this controversial field is that LD students need confidence and self-esteem to help compensate for all the blows their egos have suffered as they progress through a school system that celebrates only good readers and writers. Edwin Cole, who has worked with dyslexics for over forty years, says, "An important part of therapy is to give the dyslexic child a morale boost" (1977, 56). Katrina De Hirsch summarizes Anna Freud's conviction that "in the theory of education the importance of the ego's determination to avoid pain has not been appreciated sufficiently" (1984, 96), and Vygotsky has emphasized how essential motivation and success are to learning.

By the time LD students get to college, many have figured out how to spare themselves the pain of failure at writing. They might avoid classes that require writing. They might feign laziness or boredom. They might blame late or incomplete assignments on the instructor, claiming that directions were not given or were unclear. If we are at this point unsure about using unconventional classroom practices, we nevertheless can be sure that confidence and morale-building activities will help LD students participate in reading and writing to their full potential.

In this vein, peer tutoring may be an untapped morale-boosting resource. One interesting outcome of peer tutoring, reported by several researchers, is its effect on the *tutors*. Thomas Scruggs and Lori Richter, in a review they did concerning the tutoring of LD students, reported that sometimes tutors gain more from the experience than do those being tutored. There is much anecdotal evidence demonstrating that tutoring improves the self-esteem of the tutor (1988, 285). In *Children as Teachers* (1976), V.L. Allen also discusses the advantages of having learning disabled students do the tutoring.

Another incident concerning my nephew has confirmed these findings for me. I said earlier that seven-year-old Joey had no problem typing his name on my electric typewriter. He also was particularly able at changing the ribbon cartridges, the kind of mechanical activity at which he seems to excel. When his four-year-old brother wanted a turn at the typewriter, I told Joey to show him how it worked. Joey, relishing the chance to demonstrate what he was actually good at, said proudly in an unusually clear sentence for him, "This how you do it, Beaner"—becoming, in a sense, a seven-year-old peer tutor.

More recently, Joey's confidence is increasing, and his speech is improving. I don't know if one is influenced by the other, or which came first. I would like to take partial credit for the language improvement and for the confidence because of the tutoring sessions I spend with him. However, I suspect that the change is due not solely to the success he is having with a typewriter, but to a phenomenal talent he has for playing Super Mario Brothers video game. Joey is much more proficient at this than his father, who (not for any lack of practice) has been unable to progress to the more advanced "worlds," in which Mario (and Joey) have adventures. Joey's loquacious younger brother, in rare awe of his brother, does a running commentary on Joey's progress: "Joey has to watch out for that turtle and those ducks 'cause they can shoot at him and he can get killed. But Joey will know what to do. He has to jump up just in time or he'll fall down that chimney, but Joey can do that." The same child who has so much trouble making an *S* or a *P* demonstrates an impressive fine motor coordination operating the Nintendo joy stick. The praise that Joey receives for his prowess at computer games, his new capability at swimming, and his recent conquering of a dizzyingly high slide at a local park—all these successes help him, I think, with his language skills. The morale-boosting activities that he's good at, the respect that he gets for his other accomplishments, and the resulting feeling that he is a successful part of a family or day-camp community—all these things may give him the confidence and the courage he needs to undertake something he knows does not come easily for him: writing. For college students, who have had, undoubtedly, many more years of failure at language skills than Joey has, confidence and morale are even more crucial.

As educators who know something about the importance of self-esteem in learning, we need to help LD students find what it is that they do well and help them to capitalize on it, whether or not it eventually helps them with their writing. When I was in elementary school, there was a classmate of mine who regularly and miserably failed our weekly spelling quizzes. His oral reading was embarrassing for us and for him, and his essays were hopelessly error-ridden. In science, however, he was the Einstein of St. Joseph's School. Every week he was allowed to go from class to class proudly showing his latest scientific demonstration of how the light bulb worked or how mud slides started. In working with his complicated three-dimensional models, he was always eloquent and clear. While we good spellers (who could barely use a slide rule) watched in admiration, David was allowed to forget for a moment his humiliation in writing and to star in his own scientific show, to repair his self-esteem by shining at that at which he was good. With all respect to our teachers, I do not think anyone back then consciously realized what David's homemade scientific experiments were accomplishing—maybe not even David. He was a peer tutor in the fullest sense, before it was a fashionable term. Today he is a successful engineer, no doubt spelling as badly as ever (and making much more money than his linguistically talented classmates who became English teachers).

Orality

While many students and instructors rely on written peer comments or computer technology to help students compose and revise,
they may want to take more advantage of oral commentary. One
study reported that when LD students were interviewed regarding
changes they might make in another person's draft, they "were able
to apply some substantive criteria when cast in the role of editor"
(Graham et al. 1991, 93). There could be several reasons for this. As
Knoblauch and Brannon point out in showing how reader-response
theory connects with composition practice, when readers are simply given the authority as editors to comment on a draft and judge
it, they will inevitably do so (1984, 161).

The oral nature of the interview may also account for these students' ability to quickly create editorial suggestions, which might
have taken them a long time to discuss on paper. Instructors of all
writers could take much more advantage of oral channels of insight.
In their book, *Instructional Strategies for Students with Special
Needs,* Dan Bachor and Carol Crealock suggest having a student
revise her draft after having heard it read to her (1986, 237). Now
that computers can "read" drafts to their users, any possible embarrassment from having a friend stumble over one's errors is eliminated. As a way to encourage more global revisions in, say, an argu-
mentative essay, Bachor and Crealock suggest having students pair
up and try orally to persuade their partners to take the opposing
view of an issue (240–41). In addition, class debates on a topic of
inquiry might help all students crystallize their thinking and force
them to consider other views. They can do this through reading different opinions, of course, but an oral discussion allows LD students to demonstrate an eloquence and insight that might not
immediately be evident in their written language.

Another option for oral work is protocol analysis, a method by
which tape recordings are made as students compose out loud (Brannon and Pradl 1984, 30). Although difficult to do, analyzing the tape
can reveal to both teacher and student the recursive, often unpredictable process of writing. Although this research method, well-
known in Composition circles, has not been utilized widely in LD
research, it should be explored as a way to help LD students develop
a metacognitive awareness of themselves as writers. Because they
can often say what they mean more successfully than they can write
it, analyzing a written *and* oral account of their composing process
might provide insights not obvious from just one mode.

To provide further insight into the writing and revising process,
the instructor could model it by completing the assignment along

with the students. Brannon and Pradl discuss the advantages of this strategy, among them finding out the difficulty level and usefulness of the assignment (34). If the instructor produces a rough draft, invites responses from the students, and then revises that draft with the input of student comments, all students are able to see the value of their own opinion as readers and to better understand the decisions writers must make. They also see firsthand the kinds of major revisions Elbow looks for in multiple drafts. The multisensory experience of seeing and contrasting the two drafts, as well as hearing the changes in them discussed in class, might particularly engage the LD student.

How an individual mind processes ideas is difficult to say. But it is possible that the synthesis of thought necessary for writers to make meaning need not come exclusively from work with pen and paper. For students talented in areas other than linguistic memory, a more visual, kinesthetic, three-dimensional, or yet-to-be-discovered process may be more appropriate. We might look briefly at the history of the writing across the curriculum (WAC) movement for some direction.

Writing Across the Curriculum

As many have pointed out (Russell 1991; Parker and Goodkin 1987; Martin 1976; Mahala 1991), the ancestor of WAC, the Language Across the Curriculum movement in Britain in the late 1960s, led by James Britton, had as its primary focus not student writing, but student learning. Note that it was called *language* across the curriculum. As David Russell observes, Britton and his colleagues believed, based on the work of Jerome S. Bruner, Jean Piaget, and Lev Vygotsky, that language and learning were inextricably connected. Therefore, written *and* oral discourse held the key to real thinking and learning beyond rote memory. No longer teaching only the children of the upper classes, the British reformers needed a way to invite the children of the working class into the academic world. Believing that students did not really "know" something until they could explain it in their own words, the early Language Across the Curriculum teachers employed various ways of encouraging students to use their own language: collaborative groups, class discussion, and informal writing. The movement caught on in the United States, argue Parker and Goodkin, after it was promoted as a solution to the "writing crisis," but many people embracing it were thinking of a fairly narrow definition of writing. Today, WAC still holds much promise, especially for LD students, because it emphasizes the connections between disciplines. But it can be effective only if it returns to its roots to include all forms of language and to encourage diverse voices, figuratively and literally.

Portfolios

The use of portfolios in teaching and assessing work shows much promise for all students and especially for LD students. Most portfolios are completed in stages, have periodic input from instructors or peers, include a variety of writing tasks, and provide writers with opportunities to showcase their best work. Time constraints are usually less rigid, and often the process of assembling the portfolio is as important as the products it contains. Portfolios designed primarily as teaching tools, sometimes called "formative portfolios" and used to examine the process of learning, are assembled differently than "summative portfolios," which are designed primarily to assess or examine the finished product. Most well-designed portfolios require a metacognitive statement, an analysis the writer makes about her progress as a writer and learner. All these factors make portfolios one of higher education's most revolutionary changes. They also seem particularly suited to the learning styles of a wide variety of students.[3]

Teachable Moments

In addition to providing LD students with the kinds of progressive writing practices described above, instructors should simply be alert for teaching opportunities that present themselves. The circumstances under which my nephew Joey learned—a combination of extreme interest in the subject matter and multisensory involvement—are no doubt fertile learning circumstances for older LD students as well. To take advantage of such situations, ripe for learning, instructors sometimes need only listen to their students.

One imaginative teacher of learning disabled high school students had tried several times in vain to help a boy divide into paragraphs his lengthy essay on how to change the oil in a car. The teacher asked the student to pretend to go through the procedure, miming the actual motions and explaining as he went along. The student positioned himself under a desk, pretending it was a car, and demonstrated how to change the oil. The teacher watched and listened. At one point, the teacher asked, "Why did you just now put down that tool and pick up that other one?" The student answered, "Because that part is done and it's time to do something else." Hearing himself answer that question, the student asked, "Would that be a good place for a new paragraph?" The same high school teacher once asked his students to include more sensory detail in their revised essays. One LD student, in describing stock car racing at Lebanon Valley, New York, wrote about the car engines revving so loudly that the roar vibrated the metal seats in the bleachers, which he could hear and feel. This student's vivid, sensory detail (although described with a halting, strangled syntax and spelling) surpassed the conventional descriptions churned out in Standard English by students in the accelerated class (Lindblom 1990). Being asked to include sensory detail gave this LD student an opportunity to demonstrate his ability to notice and describe what others might overlook.

Heuristics

Lee Odell has described a number of techniques that, although intended for students he calls "inexperienced," might be employed for learning disabled writers. Because Odell believes that thinking and writing are conscious and rational processes, he holds that they are teachable. Good writers, according to Odell, have a variety of "cognitive processes" at their disposal, useful in a host of different writing situations. These processes, which provide the basis for Odell's pedagogy, include focus, contrast, classification, change, physical context, and sequence (1977, 122). They are patterns of thinking reflected, according to Odell, more or less directly in writing.

Odell designs his teaching practice to help students develop these intellectual processes. Because they involve multiple senses, they might be ideal for LD students, whether or not Odell intended them as such. One of these techniques is to have students watch two-minute scenes from a television show, instructing them to take note of when the camera angle changes focus or perspective (1975, 50). Following a discussion of these various camera shots—long, medium, or close-up—or of shifts in detail or physical context, the students should have a more concrete awareness of detail and elaboration that they might then transfer to their writing.

A similar exercise involves the use of a magazine picture. By partially blocking out sections of the picture with pieces of construction paper, the student can see the effect of isolating a face, an eye, or another object. She can also see what happens when something is placed in the perspective of a larger background—for example a diver in isolation or a diver as a dot at the top of the cliffs of Acapulco. This mechanical manipulation of focus and detail should theoretically make the student aware of new possibilities for her writing (1977, 128). Odell and his researchers themselves had difficulties proving that any of these techniques "worked." Any attempt to measure writing development is, of course, complicated and always to a certain degree subjective. However, surmising what we do about LD students' sense of the concrete, their difficulties with linguistic symbols, and their generally positive response to multi-sensory pathways, it makes sense to explore unusual approaches such as these.

There are other strategies that some students may find helpful, depending, of course, on what they are being asked to do. Candace Bos recommends the use of "think sheets" to help students brainstorm ideas. Unlike conventional brainstorming exercises, this one invites students to "represent visually" some of their ideas (1988, 109). Jacqueline Lynch Czamanske and Carla Katz in the Alternative Learning Department at Rochester Institute of Technology have students use "mind mapping," a graphic sketch of their ideas, instead of standard freewriting, which depends heavily on how rapidly students can write or type.

Scaffolding can also be useful, if instructors who use it are theoretically aware of its benefits and limitations. Bachor and Crealock use "sentence shells" to help students generate ideas: "I believe _____ is the correct position to take because _____ " (1986, 240). In my research classes, I have used a more elaborate sheet (see Figure 5–2), designed to invite students to begin thinking about multiple sides of a controversial issue, in preparation for a longer investigative report that includes both primary and secondary research. In this project, they must ultimately take a position and support it.

Students in my class are given this self-response sheet after they have interviewed several people with opposing viewpoints and completed other primary research such as a survey or questionnaire. I came up with an earlier version of this sheet one frustrating day several years ago when I could not get students to stop listing dictionary definitions and purposeless facts. In a sudden fit of exasperation, I scribbled it on a piece of tablet paper and told a student to fill it out. The next day, after struggling overnight with that form, this student said his project finally had some direction. He told me that he had never thought about framing ideas that way before. On the one hand, I was pleased that he finally had some insight into this project, but I also mentally imagined Knoblauch and Brannon's objection to "practicing with mechanical 'invention heuristics' in order to find something to say" (1984, 5).

Inside my head, I argued with them. It is true that in using this fill-in-the-blanks sheet, there is a danger that students will think all arguments must be set up this way, and all they need do is plug ideas into an artificial frame and thinking and meaning making will

Figure 5–2
Scaffolding for a persuasive essay.

SELF-RESPONSE SHEET

In my investigative report, I am researching the controversy regarding

_____. Some   people   believe

_____   for   several

reasons.   First,   _____

_____.   Also,

_____.   On   the   other   hand,

some   people   feel   that   _____

_____.

They have several reasons for feeling this way:

_____;

_____;

_____.   After   carefully

considering all points of view in this controversy, I believe that

_____.   I   have   several   reasons   for   taking

this   position: _____;

_____.

---

be done for them. I try to challenge that assumption by discussing
in class this admittedly simplistic form and the limits of its use.
And I do believe it has a use. Patricia Bizzell credits Mina Shaughnessy for pointing out in *Errors and Expectations* that advanced
writers use much more often than do basic writers sentence structures that contain relational idioms. Bizzell observes, "Perhaps the
very forms of sentences using relational words can be used as an
heuristic to initiate students into the kind of reasoning acceptable
in academic discourse" (1978, 355). One might also argue that this
scaffolding supports and extends a Vygotskian "zone of proximal
development" for new academic writers, LD or otherwise, guiding

them toward the academic conventions of assertions and support and stretching their willingness to consider other perspectives (Vgotsky 1986, 187).

There is a possibility, however, that heuristics can truncate thought as well as stimulate it, and that their simple format can be a liability as well as a strength. It is for these reasons that such "recipes" should be used only after grounding them carefully in one's own philosophy of teaching. After much thought, I have decided to use these scaffolds because I do not think their advantages and disadvantages are mutually exclusive or theoretically contradictory. Furthermore, even if such exercises *are* problematic, I think students are capable of participating in theoretical debates regarding the use of heuristics; in fact, all pedagogy should be contextualized, discussed, and debated in the classroom. One point that RIT's Jackie Czamanske made is that students are not included often enough in the discussions of education's long-term purposes and goals (1994). All students should be participants in a class articulation of how a course, an assignment, or a writing project fits not only into their academic programs and their professional plans, but also into their daily lives. Even the humble think sheet can be contextualized in this way. And it should be.

Mnemonics

One area of research that may have indirect applications for writing instructors is mnemonics—the use of associative links to aid memory. In Chapter Three, we saw how Joey learned to recall "motorcycle" through an associative, kinesthetic, and auditory link, the kind of deliberate memory trick Vygotsky describes as uniquely human behavior (1978, 51). This use of concrete memory aids could be used more effectively even in higher education.

Several researchers have had success with using mnemonics, or "keyword strategies," to help adolescents remember fact-based information and terminology. In research that appeared in the *Journal of Educational Psychology*, Pressley and Dennis-Rounds worked with students in helping them memorize cities and the products for which those cities were known. Students were first trained in mnemonic strategies. That is, to trigger the memory that the city of Lock Haven is known for paper products, researchers pointed out the concrete term *lock* and asked students to picture "an interactive image between a lock and a paper" and as an example they were shown a sketch of a lock on a newspaper (1980, 577). Students were encouraged to create their own interactive images for the cities and products they were then asked to memorize. Students trained in this strategy were able to remember the city/product pairings better than those in the control group, and the scores of those with the most instruction in keyword strategies were higher than the scores of those with the least instruction (578–81). Other researchers report success using mnemonics to teach vocabulary (Pressley, Levin, and Delaney 1982, 84) and spacial and associative learning (Scruggs et al. 1992, 160). In addition, researchers have reported success using mnemonics not only with LD students but with non-LD students and academically talented students as well.

Although there are many reports available on similar research, this keyword method has some obvious limitations, one of which is pointed out by Pressley, Levin, and Delaney in the *Review of Educational Research* (1982, 84). It really can be used only if the words to be linked sound somewhat alike or have a concrete term embedded in one of them (i.e., *lock* in Lockhaven). The researchers designing experiments on keyword strategies, of course, use words that can be readily associated, and the data from these numerous studies must always be read with that in mind.

Other critics rightly point out that mnemonic keyword strategies, even if they are successful, are applicable only to low-level memory tasks, and not to the higher-order thinking processes crucial to college work, such as critical reading and writing projects. What mnemonics may do for students, however, is to make easier whatever memorization tasks are still necessary in college courses. It may therefore indirectly aid in higher-order thinking by freeing time for more intellectual tasks. Writing instructors have in their classes students like Nick, Monica, and Janine, who may have spent large portions of the previous evening trying unsuccessfully to memorize the required technical vocabulary of their health science courses, leaving their drafts for writing class untouched. If mnemonic strategies can help make LD students' recall of multisyllabic words more efficient, that in turn may render the initial stage of the writing process faster and less frustrating. If mnemonics can help them use their study time more efficiently and succeed more often on the memorization exams encountered in other classes, it will boost their confidence and self-esteem—useful outcomes for college writing students.

We teachers cannot proceed as if ours is the only course or the most important one our students take. We need a more complete, holistic understanding of what our students' lives are like, not to be academic voyeurs, but to make sure we are not unnecessarily belaboring certain areas or working at cross purposes. To use an analogy: today, many people visit a variety of medical specialists to receive their various checkups or treatments. In a span of several years, an individual may visit an allergist, an internist, a podiatrist, a dermatologist, a cardiologist, and a chiropractor. Each specialist serves a purpose and may plan a course of action or write a prescription. If they are unaware of each other or have no clue what other medications the individual patient might be taking, their own diagnoses and treatments may do more harm than good. Wouldn't it be great if just once all those specialists sat down together, with the patient, and as a team constructed a unified strategy? In order for such a meeting to succeed, the participants would have to show mutual respect for each other, including the patient. What I am suggesting in the LD controversy is that all educators—students, researchers, theorists, instructors, administrators—at least be willing to sit down, metaphorically, at a *round* table, and with mutual respect for each others' expertise, talk about different ways of knowing, learning, researching, and writing.

Strategy Instruction and Self-Efficacy

Related to mnemonics is other research in which students use self-monitoring strategies both to generate and revise texts. At the University of Maryland, in the department of Educational Psychology, researchers have done much work with LD adolescents and composition skills. Using "contentless production signals," which are simply requests for students to write more, researchers analyze the texts produced by both experimental and control groups. Steve Graham's research indicates that LD students who received such "production signaling" did indeed extend the length of their texts, although not all of the expanded text was "functional." Graham defines "functional" text as that which provides "reasons or elaborations," and "nonfunctional" text as that which is repetitious or "unrelated" (1990, 782–87). In spite of some mixed individual reactions among the twenty-four fourth- and sixth-grade students who were prompted to "write (say) some more about this," Graham reported an increase in the quantity of student text and a slight increase in quality (787).

Expanding Meichenbaum's work from the 1970s, and influenced by Vygotsky, Steve Graham and Karen Harris have done a lot of work with LD adolescents in trying "to increase diversity of vocabulary and the quality of their [students'] written stories" (1987, 69). Their basic training method involves researchers (or selected participating teachers) explaining to students the "story grammar" elements outlined by Stein and Glenn such as "main character, locale, time, starter event, goal, action, ending, and reaction" (Graham and Harris 1989, 355). Students in the different groups are given different levels of training; those in the group getting the most instruction are taught to use a five-step mnemonic pattern to help them learn these grammar elements and are trained to ask questions of themselves as they write and revise their work. The questions include: "Who is the main character? Who else is in the story? When does the story take place? Where does the story take place? What does the main character want to do? What happens when he or she tries to do it? How does the story end? How does the main character feel?" (Sawyer, Graham and Harris 1992, 345).

Other studies include instructions such as, "write down story-part ideas for each part; write your story; use good parts and make sense." Students in the most highly trained group also received training to use "self-instructions or self-statements" such as "Take my time, good ideas will come to me"; "Let my mind be free"; and other statements the students conceive of themselves (Sawyer, Graham, and Harris 1992, 345). This is called "self-regulated strategy development," and researchers claim that the LD students who underwent such training had better structured, higher quality compositions, according to holistic scoring. (Graham and Harris 1987; Graham and Harris 1989, 357–60; Sawyer, Graham and Harris 1992). These researchers point out that this "procedural facilitation," also called "modeling" and "scaffolding," is a strategy "that will ultimately be run autonomously" (Graham et al. 1991, 104). If we accept for a moment that students' writing does improve or at least change as a result of these strategies, instruction in their use may encourage students to look again at their texts in much the same way critical readers might.

There are, of course, several problems with the assumptions informing this methodology, one of which is the arbitrary linking of adherence to conventional "story elements" with "quality." Certainly, whether or not one composition should be judged to be of higher quality than another, based partially on whether or not it has more than one character ("who else is in the story?"), is at the very least debatable. In addition, the instructions to "write your story; use good parts and make sense" do not seem particularly helpful. Had these researchers been better informed by reading a broader band of similar previous research, they may have better anticipated objections to their assumptions and provided more sophisticated explanations of their assessment procedures and pitfalls. They would have been aware of the relative failure of many large-scale, well-funded assessment attempts to establish once and for all what constitutes growth in writing and why it occurs. For example, in 1984, Knoblauch and Brannon warned against what they call "the myth of measurable improvement" (165), and Edward White has frequently and eloquently discussed problems inherent in assessment (see especially his book, *Developing Successful College Writing Programs* [1989, 99]). Paul Diederich's 1974 text, *Measuring Growth in English,* illustrated how evaluators often hold wildly varying assessments of students' texts, and only after much discussion and negotiation can graders arrive at anything approaching consensus.

Graham's recent research is arguably similar to the kind of cognitive process research and prewriting instruction done by Lee Odell in 1974 and explained in his *RTE* report, "Measuring the Effect of Instruction in Pre-writing." Both Odell and Graham investigate the effects of explicitly taught heuristics, and both attempt to measure the results of that instruction on student texts. Stephen North, in his section on "The Experimentalists" in *The Making of Knowledge in Composition,* writes a thorough review of Odell's piece and the control problems inherent in this kind of research (1987, 141–96). I agree with North's analysis, and space prohibits a complete discussion of Odell's or Graham's research here. However, when contrasting Graham's research of the late 1980s with Odell's research of the early 1970s, it is clear that they encountered similar problems but handled them differently in their respective research reports. In reporting the ratings of his students' post-instruction essays, Odell cites mixed results in determining their quality, although he does not use that term. The judges he used to rate the pre- and post-instruction writings "frequently disagreed" with each other "about the presence or absence of conceptual gaps in the essays they were scoring" (1974, 238). Odell, however, spends time and space in his Results section acknowledging this disagreement and asking important questions about why it happened. While Graham and his colleagues briefly mention that "many product characteristics, such as quality, have proven difficult to define, much less measure" (Graham et al. 1991, 90), and call for future research into judgments of quality (109), their research reports proceed with this important issue largely unproblematized, using *quality* and *improvement* uncritically, as if all readers have the same definition of those terms.

Dictation

The kind of research discussed above is quite widespread in the field of Educational Psychology, and researchers using these strategies consistently report that students trained in strategy instruction show changes not only in the quality of their texts, but also in more measurable elements such as increased length of composition, more diverse verbs, adverbs, and adjectives (Graham and Harris 1987, 69).

Graham and his colleagues have also done much work with LD students and dictation. They compared text produced in various modes: handwriting, word processing, "normal" dictation (speaking into a tape recorder), and "slow" dictation, a method used by Marlene Scardamalia and her colleagues in the early 1980s, in which an examiner, functioning as a scribe, transcribes the student's speech at a rate determined by the speed at which the student has written a previous essay. The researchers report that students generally produce longer essays during the "slow" dictation mode, but results were so mixed or qualified that it is difficult to get a clear idea whether this method is more or less helpful for LD students. For example, Graham reports that essays generated during "slow" dictation often contained more of what the researchers call "nonfunctional text," which they define as "repetitious" or "unrelated" segments (1990, 782). These terms are also unproblematized, with no acknowledgment that what may be deemed repetitious by some readers might be judged as emphasis by others. What some judges may view as "unrelated" segments might be viewed as an analogy or related example by others. Finally, what may be "nonfunctional elements" to the reader, may have been quite useful to the writer, perhaps helping her in her process of discovering or modifying ideas mentioned later in the "functional" segment.

The rather loose employment of the term "functional" is the kind of word use that keeps this and similar research off the reading lists in Composition doctoral programs, and I am not suggesting here that we should read Graham et al.'s conclusions without a strong dose of healthy skepticism. However, if we disregard this work completely, we may also be disregarding what may indeed be one of the most empowering writing options for many LD students: dictation. If Graham and his colleagues can help us better understand which kinds of dictation might be more helpful to students, if he can help us ask better questions about this mode of composing—whether he asks them himself or causes us to ask them—his research, no matter how flawed from our perspective, is worth reading with an open mind.

Graham and his colleagues, because they do extensive work with LD students, may be more sensitive than are mainstream composition researchers to the mechanical difficulties these students face when asked to put pen to paper or fingers to computer keyboard. In research not usually seen in mainstream composition journals, Graham et al. report that "when the mechanical demands of writing were removed, or when prompted to write more, these [LD] students were able to generate a considerable amount of new content" (1991, 94). It is, of course, much easier to measure quantity than quality. Candace S. Bos, who has provided an overview of similar studies of LD and "normal" writers, says that LD writers "were five times more likely than the non-LD matched subjects to terminate the text prematurely" (1988, 128). If tape recorders and/or scribes are helping LD students compose more, that in itself is no small thing. If it is true that various forms of oral dictation provide a usable, viable option for LD students, then writing instructors need to look further into this area, especially if we allow our concepts of writing to expand beyond the niceties of surface correctness and are flexible enough to permit, even encourage, other forms of composing. For example, author Ruthie Bolton dictated into a tape recorder the text of her well-received autobiography *Gal: A True Life*.[4] A more inclusive conceptualization of writing, one that includes dictation, is the kind of re-formatting of thinking that could alter mainstream pedagogy, opening possibilities not just for the benefit of labeled LD students, but for society in general.

Re-Thinking Theory and Practice

The research of Graham et al. with LD students and writing instruction is something college composition instructors should be aware of. Since it is at least arguable that some students might benefit from explicit instructions in pre-writing strategies, work in this area is important. These researchers' occasionally unreflective use of terminology invites readers outside their immediate methodological circle to dismiss their work—with North's explanation of "Diesing's law" applicable here: "Methodological sympathies cut across the boundaries of field, whereas methodological differences— disagreements over how knowledge is made, what knowledge can be—can create insurmountable barriers" (1987, 365). While Graham acknowledges Marlene Scardamalia, Carl Bereiter, and their colleagues from the early 1980s as research ancestors with connections to the composition field, Graham does not include in his bibliography the work of Lee Odell or that of *his* predecessors in cognitive process research from the 1960s—Young, Becker, and Pike. It is significant that much of Graham et al.'s work appears in *Learning Disability Quarterly* and in the *Journal of Educational Psychology*, while Odell's appears in *Research in the Teaching of English*.

These journals represent different fields but are reporting on arguably similar investigations: how and if students' texts can improve after writers are given explicit heuristics. While the reports in *RTE* look more like the reports in the *Journal of Educational Psychology* than they do the essays in *CCC* or *College English*, I would guess that not many individuals have on their coffee tables *both RTE* and the *Journal of Educational Psychology*, much less those two plus *College English* and the *Learning Disability Quarterly*. And even if composition instructors, while waiting in their therapist's or dentist's office, should happen upon one of Graham's reports, it is likely that they would quickly dismiss his research at the first unproblematized use of "quality" or "improvement." Well aware of the subjective nature of reader response and the complicated nature of "quality," composition instructors who read research reports employing that term in an apparently naive way will not lend much credibility to the research. And that's a shame. While it is necessary to be critical readers and to be appropriately skeptical of research that makes unreflective assumptions, it may not be in all our students' best interests to play what Elbow calls "the doubting game" with every article not methodologically or philosophically in tune with our own interests (1973, 147–91).

Compositionists need to investigate research in other disciplines. They also might want to conduct their own studies in these areas, or better yet, to collaborate with their colleagues down the hall or across the campus on designing research projects together. As difficult as it might be, we need to nurture more of a "both/and" approach to qualitative and quantitative research. I say this, well aware of the deep philosophical and ideological differences between camps that North discusses in his book, especially in his critique of Scardamalia and Bereiter's 1983 essay, "Levels of Inquiry in Writing Research," when they call for similar collaboration (North 1987, 353–57). North's argument, that ideological differences are not easily dispensed with, is a compelling one, and one about which some of us probably remain too naively optimistic.

In the last few pages of his book, North also argues, if not for collaboration between and among these different groups, at least for more respect for differing "modes of inquiry." He writes that "All methods, and all kinds of knowledge, would have to be created equal" (370–71). These clinical experiments on heuristics, dictation, learning disabilities, and writing are being conducted now in Educational Psychology, not Composition, a trend North predicted in his discussion of the future of a Composition field increasingly segmented by discourse, methodology, and politics. While there may be valid professional reasons for researchers to remain intellectually committed only to their own narrow specialty, one result is that other groups' research, however flawed, which might productively alter concepts of "writing" both for us and for our students, is not merely being discounted in Composition circles; it is not even being read.

There are ideological differences involved in this controversy that may indeed prove to be insurmountable, especially if we focus solely on the dichotomies. Ann E. Berthoff argues that what she calls "killer dichotomies," are "hazardous to both our theory and practice as writing teachers" (1990, 13). In the collection in which the Berthoff essay appears, editors Kate Ronald and Hephzibah Roskelly also warn against the danger of "either/or-ness" and of even creating categories at all. It can divide the discipline, they say, and make competition and exclusion inevitable. They call for a movement toward what they call "thirdness" (1990, 7). And James Zebroski, using the 1916 battle of Verdun as the epitome of modernist binary opposition, says that "post-modernism . . . accepts plurality and mixture . . ." and so should Composition (1990, 175).

There is a danger in dichotomizing "the controversy," with its two basic sides, as is done for much of this book. How one interacts with an LD student is dependent on how one perceives that person: different or disabled; normal or not normal; hardworking or lazy; smart or not-so-smart. Ease with written language occurs on a continuum unquestionably influenced by educational opportunities and other social factors. But it is *also* more of an innate talent for some than it is for others. People with frustrating difficulties with language may have a different neurological framework *and* they may be from an oppressed economic group *and* they may be speaking English as a second language *and* they may have emotional problems *and* they may be below average in intelligence. Some of those factors, however, automatically and legally place them in categories outside the definition of LD. To recognize categories is not to invent them. If some educators tend to think in dichotomies such as "smart" and "not-so-smart," and if they are consciously or unconsciously placing LD students in the latter group—and it is clear even from the three stories we heard in the last chapter about the way those students were treated that some people do think this way—then it is important to recognize these false dichotomies so that they may be challenged. LD students are not "slow." Granted, the IQ test and other measures of ability are problematic, and different schools may have a sliding cutoff regarding who gets labeled and who does not. However, it is obvious that many educated people do not even understand the legal definition of LD, much less the more complex issues surrounding it. The less we know about something, the more we may be tempted to find easy answers or more readily believe what one expert tells us. However, college writing instructors can no longer stand on the edges of an issue that so deeply affects some of their students.

Rather than cast theoretically based aspersions at our colleagues in Educational Psychology and other fields, it would be more productive to pool our collective knowledge about writing theory, self-reflectiveness, research methodology, assessment, and measurement —to "replace competition with cooperation," as Kenneth A. Kavale puts it (1988, 17). We may differ philosophically with regard to the "story grammar" taught in the educational psychology experiments. However, there is no reason why this research, with its promise and its flaws, could not be discussed in graduate composition courses and in college writing classes, where teaching styles and research methodologies should be contextualized anyway. So what if we never measure "quality" or "improvement" to everyone's satisfaction? If LD students can write more, dread it less, stretch their vocabulary, add evidence and elaborate more on examples by a combination of heuristics, mnemonics, dictation, and other options, and generally develop more confidence and voice, isn't that worth pursuing?

To study with at least a moment of belief the work of our colleagues in Educational Psychology and other fields, and to discuss the implications, if any, for Composition Studies is not to deny that writing and learning are, were, and always will be shaped as well by socioeconomic and political forces. To put research into boxes and to read only what fits neatly in "our box" is to adhere to the traditional binaries that more connected ways of learning are supposed to challenge. We must be aware of the methodological conflicts Steve North so clearly points out, and we must approach all research critically.

We can also read it with a bit of cautionary belief. What if "slow dictation" really does encourage LD students to "write" more than they might otherwise do in a more conventional setting, a setting *we* might prefer? What if experiments with heuristics and self-instructional strategies, in spite of their glaring methodological gaps, can get us to rethink our own theory and practice? Charles Bazerman argues that such inter- and intradisciplinary conflicts, for example a field's discourse practices (and by extension its view of how knowledge is made) should be part of college curricula and that students should take an active part in such debates (1992, 61–68). The occasions for such potentially stimulating opportunities, however, are nonexistent if professionals in various disciplines remain so blindingly skeptical or ignorant of their colleagues' work that they cannot see connections to, intersections with , or even confirmations of their own work. If they read only a narrow band of research that is most philosophically similar to their own, they may be eliminating the kind of dialogic opportunities Freire argues are essential to the constant rethinking necessary for truly critical teaching.

Notes

1. I am indebted to my student Allicia for making the suggestions outlined in this paragraph.

2. See also Carmela Castorina's article on Project EASI in the same issue of *Change* (March/April 1994). For a humorous view of voice-activated computers see Linda Winer's "It Ain't Me, Babe," in *New York Newsday*, July 29, 1994.

3. Information on portfolios is abundant, but here are some excellent selections:

Belanoff, Pat, and Marcia Dickson, eds. 1991. *Portfolios: Process and Product.* Portsmouth, NH: Boynton/Cook–Heinemann.

Bishop, Wendy. 1990. "Designing a Writing Portfolio Evaluation System." *The English Record* 40: 21–25.

Elbow, Peter, and Pat Belanoff. 1986. "SUNY Stonybook Portfolio-Based Evaluation Program." in *New Methods in College Writing Programs,* ed. Paul Connolly and Teresa Vilardi. New York: MLA, 95–105.

Greenburg, Karen, and G. Slaughter. Nov. 1988. *NOTES from the National Testing Network in Writing* 8: ERIC ED 301-888.

Roemer, Marjorie, Lucille M. Schultz, and Russel K. Durst. 1991. "Portfolios and the Process of Change." *College Composition and Communication* 42: 455–69.

Tierney, Robert J., Mark A. Carter, and Laura E. Desai. 1991 *Portfolio Assessment in the Reading-Writing Classroom.* Norwood, MA: Christopher Gordon Publishers, Inc.

Yancey, Kathleen Blake, ed. 1992. *Portfolios in the Writing Classroom.* Urbana, IL: NCTE.

4. See R.Z. Sheppards' article, "When Southern Gothic Is Real Life," in *Time,* June 27, 1994, 77.

Conclusion

This book has been about gaps in Composition pedagogy and about the lack of awareness even the best-trained writing instructors often have concerning learning disabilities and the controversy surrounding them. With all the confusions and contradictions that exist in the field, learning disability practice may not have answers, but it suggests questions about writing and learning that instructors today need to ask.

Those who most closely study the human mind are also most acutely aware that we understand very little about how it works. We can, however, argue the following points. First, many talented people have almost inexplicable difficulties processing written language, resulting in unsuccessful experiences in an education system that is based almost exclusively on books and writing. Second, regardless of the original cause of their difficulty, students treated as inferior beings often will simply fulfill low expectations. Negative reactions from school authorities, parents, and peers wreak havoc with students' self-esteem, exacerbating any difficulties they may already have. Third, the potentially substantial contributions from supposedly learning disabled people toward more lively, instructive, interactive classrooms may be lost because of unfounded fears they will "slow down" regular classes. Ironically, these classes may already be stagnated from over-dependence on same-thinking, linguistic-based minds. We need, therefore, to remain open to a broad range of theoretical and practical possibilities that may result in the educational reform that everyone today seems to want but no one can determine how to achieve.

As has been reiterated throughout this text, the main difference between disagreeing camps in the LD controversy is *why* some students have trouble with written language. Neuroscientists at one end of the continuum are convinced that a neurological difference accounts for the problem; sociologists at the other end believe language difficulties are societally caused. Extreme views that unquestionably eliminate either view are, however, premature, considering what we know (or, rather, what we do not know) about how people learn to speak, read, and write. If available research proves anything, it is that reasons are complex, and answers are not simple. Regardless of the proliferation of research on composing that occu pies the Composition and Rhetoric field, and the reading experiments and brain research of the LD field, we simply do not yet know enough about learning to exclude each other's work.

The LD controversy is important to Composition Studies for two reasons. First, the debate concerning top-down or bottom-up teaching strategies does not end with whether to teach phonics or interesting stories first. It continues through secondary school and college in the discussion about how to design not only composition courses, but also writing-intensive courses across the curriculum. Second, the LD controversy is important because of the heterogeneous perspective it offers on ways of knowing. The "universality of experience" argument has been attacked recently because it denies certain groups their unique experiential reality and allows their voices to be lost. Similarly, the belief that everyone learns the same way may be more a blissful hope than a reality—and an avoidance of a complicated issue.

The different experiences of women and ethnic groups have long been ignored in academia, and their voices are just now beginning to be heard. Before learning disabled people can be heard, they must be recognized—not as *dis*abled but as *abled* in ways they and we must discover. It is partially the overemphasis on linguistics-based knowledge that has resulted in these students being labeled LD in the first place; if we open the curriculum to a wider spectrum of ways of knowing, these students can become re-abled. Norman Geschwind called learning disability "the pathology of superiority," implying that some dyslexics have a perspective so different from the majority that they are misunderstood and cast aside as inferior (Rawson 1988, 13). Although what we know about people's minds is at this point far too limited to make such a claim, it is interesting to consider the ironic possibility that we might be harming our best young minds by forcing them to conform to a way of thinking far more limited or two dimensional than what they do naturally.

How can students with learning differences be recognized without being ostracized? How can they participate in mainstream courses in ways that allow their talents in other areas to bolster their learning, as well as that of others? Composition Studies needs to explore what the LD field can tell it about alternate, multisensory learning. The LD field needs what Composition Studies can tell it about environments most nourishing to people's development as writers. As discussed earlier, Stephen North points out that even within the same field, one kind of research vies with another for respectability. Empirical research may be valued over case study, and classroom practitioners' observations may not be as influential as the reports of those doing funded empirical research. With the present dearth of knowledge about writing development—the reams of reports notwithstanding—we need to privilege more than one kind of research. Many special education teachers and others who work with LD students do not hold doctoral degrees. Many well-published Ph.D.'s do not work directly with first-year college students who exhibit the language difficulties this book has addressed. We need at least to consider the personal knowledge and testimony of students, parents, and teachers who must deal every day with learning differences about which most college professors and academic writers know very little.

I have attended meetings at which people ridicule and dismiss whole language, and where invented spelling is viewed as the ultimate educational horror. I have been at conferences attended by New York State language arts teachers at which a keynote speaker's disparaging reference to DISTAR, an Orton-based, reading/writing method, was met with concurring, sympathetic laughter and shaking heads from the audience. Ironically, this confidence about how writing should or should not be taught comes in a poststructuralist time when certainty is being rightly exposed for its tendency to blind those who have it, preventing them from envisioning other perspectives. As writing instructors, we must of course make informed decisions about what we will do in our classrooms. We must form convictions about how students best learn to write, and then we must act on those convictions. However, the theory that informs practice stays healthier when it remains somewhat in flux and when we periodically and critically examine what we are doing; we are better theorists if we are, as Paulo Freire puts it, "less certain of 'certainties.'"[1]

As instructors, we need to believe that people think in many ways. We need to break out of binary categories regarding right and wrong ways of learning, and to challenge ourselves and our students to change classroom culture from over-reliance on single-modality teaching. Questions about writing need to be recast, with ideas regarding what it means to compose solicited from people with a variety of learning styles. Composition specialists, who are for the most part people who like to write, may have a hard time tolerating or even imagining unconventional ways of writing, much as they might want to include and respond fairly to all students. Incorporating multisensory options into regular coursework and assessment will expand educational opportunities for everyone and reveal talents that many students, LD or otherwise, may not have known they had.

We also need to rethink how students use the limited hours available for reading, studying, writing, and other intellectual work. Editing and proofreading issues need to be examined and discussed publicly with students, educators, and people from the business and professional communities. Can we agree that clean, well-edited text is *both* vitally important *and* achievable in a variety of ways? Can we appreciate good writers that may need more support than others do from editors or from state-of-the-art computerized aids? Can we recognize different processes of writing?

As researchers, we need to work more daringly with colleagues not just from other disciplines, but also from different research traditions and to cooperate in the full sense of the word—both speaking with and listening to each other, and producing better knowledge. While all research should be subjected to a healthy examination of its procedures and conclusions, it should not automatically and cynically be dismissed in favor of more familiar approaches. Negativism can kill creativity. Research projects that may be plodding around the same territory for years may break into a run with the help of new perspectives. Both Composition Studies and the LD field are now in need of this kind of synergy.

This book is not a claim to know. It is an invitation to explore, to include, to not exclude. It is a call for a rethinking of writing and learning, for a positive yet critical examination of all research methods, and for an open-mindedness regarding intelligence. It is also a challenge to broaden and enrich the learning of all students and teachers by recognizing all the ways of knowing that will allow learning disabled people to become re-abled.

Notes

1. Quoted by Ann E. Berthoff in the Foreword to Freire and Macedo's *Literacy: Reading the Word And the World.* South Hadley, MA: Bergin and Garvey Publishers, 1987, xii.

Works Cited

Allen, V. L. 1976. *Children as Teachers.* New York: Academic Press.

Anderson, Gordon S. 1984. *A Whole Language Approach to Reading.* Landhame, MD: UP of America.

Bachor, Dan G., and Carol Crealock. 1986. *Instructional Strategies for Students with Special Needs.* Scarborough, Ontario: Prentice-Hall Canada.

Bartholomae, David. 1979. "Teaching Basic Writing: An Alternative to Basic Skills." *Journal of Basic Writing* 2: 85–109.

———. 1980. "The Study of Error." *College Composition and Communication* 31: 253–69.

Bazerman, Charles. 1988. *Shaping Written Knowledge: The Genre and Activity of the Experimental Article in Science.* Madison, WI: Univ. of Wisconsin Press.

———. 1992. "From Cultural Criticism to Disciplinary Participation: Living with Powerful Words." In *Writing, Teaching, and Learning in the Disciplines.* Ed. Anne Herrington and Charles Moran, 61–68. New York: MLA.

Bazerman, Charles, and James Paradis, eds. 1991. *Textual Dynamics of the Professions: Historical and Contemporary Studies of Writing in the Professional Communities.* Madison, WI: Univ. of Wisconsin Press.

Bennison, Anne E. 1987. "Before the Learning Disabled There Were Feeble-Minded Children." In *Learning Disability: Dissenting Essays.* Ed. Barry M. Franklin, 13–28. London: Falmer Press.

Benton, Arthur L., and David Pearl, eds. 1978. *Dyslexia: An Appraisal of Current Knowledge.* New York: Oxford UP.

Berthoff, Ann E. 1981. *The Making of Meaning: Metaphors, Models, and Maxims for Writing Teachers.* Portsmouth, NH: Boynton/Cook.

———. 1990. "Killer Dichotomies: Reading In/Reading Out." In *Farther Along: Transforming Dichotomies in Rhetoric and Composition.* Ed. Kate Ronald and Hephzibah Roskelly, 12–24. Portsmouth, NH: Boynton/Cook–Heinemann.

Bertin, Phyllis, and Eileen Perlman. 1980. *Preventing Academic Failure: A Multisensory Curriculum for Teaching Reading, Writing and Spelling in the Elementary Classroom.* Scarsdale, NY: Monroe Associates.

Bizzell, Patricia L. 1978. "The Ethos of Academic Discourse." *College Composition and Communication* 29: 351–55.

————. 1986. "What Happens When Basic Writers Come to College?" *College Composition and Communication* 37: 294–301.

Black, F. William. 1973. "Reversal and Rotation Errors by Normal and Retarded Readers." *Perceptual and Motor Skills* 36: 395–98.

Blalock, Jane W. 1982. "Persistent Auditory Language Deficits in Adults with Learning Disabilities." *Journal of Learning Disabilities* 15: 604–09.

Blake, Robert W., ed. 1990. *Whole Language: Explorations and Applications.* Brockport, NY: New York State English Council.

Blakeslee, Sandra. August 16, 1994a. "New Clue to Cause of Dyslexia Seen in Mishearing of Fast Sounds." *New York Times.*

————. 1994b. "Odd Disorder of Brain May Offer New Clues To Basis of Language." *New York Times.*

Boehlert, Robert. 1993. "Making Higher Educational Institutions Supportive of College Students with Disabilities: The Legal Perspective." Panel presentation at conference, Higher Education for Persons with Disabilities: Challenges and Opportunities, sponsored by University of the State of New York and New York State Education Department, Albany, New York.

Bos, Candace S. 1988. "Academic Interventions for Learning Disabilities." In *Learning Disabilities: State of the Art and Practice.* Ed. Kenneth Kavale, 98–122. Boston: Little, Brown.

Brannon, Lil, and Gordon Pradl. 1984. "The Socialization of Writing Teachers." *Journal of Basic Writing* 3: 28–37.

Brinckerhoff, Loring C., Stan F. Shaw, and Joan M. McGuire. 1992. "Promoting Access, Accommodations, and Independence for College Students with Learning Disabilities." *Journal of Learning Disabilities* 25.7: 417–29.

Britton, James. 1982. *Prospect and Retrospect: Selected Essays of James Britton.* Ed. Gordon M. Pradl. Portsmouth, NH: Boynton/Cook.

Britton, James, Tony Burgess, Nancy Martin, Alex McLeod and Harold Rosen. 1975. *The Development of Writing Abilities.* 11–18. London: Macmillan Education.

Bruck, Maggie. 1992. "Persistence of Dyslexics' Phonological Awareness Deficits." *Developmental Psychology* 28.5: 874–86.

Calkins, Lucy McCormick. 1986. *The Art of Teaching Writing.* Portsmouth, NH: Heinemann.

Carrier, James G. 1986. *Learning Disability: Social Class and the Construction of Inequality in American Education.* New York: Greenwood Press.

Castorina, Carmela. 1994. "Project EASI: Spreading the Word About Adaptive Technologies." *Change: The Magazine of Higher Learning* 26.2: 45–47.

Chall, Jeanne S., Vicki A. Jacobs, and Luke E. Baldwin. 1990. *The Reading Crisis: Why Poor Children Fall Behind*. Cambridge, MA: Harvard UP.

Clark, Diana Brewster. 1988. *Dyslexia: Theory and Practice of Remedial Instruction*. Parkton, MA: York Press.

Clay, Marie M. 1972. *Reading: The Patterning of Complex Behavior*. Auckland, New Zealand: Heinemann.

———. 1979. *The Early Detection of Reading Difficulties*. Auckland, New Zealand: Heinemann.

———. "Learning to Be Learning Disabled." 1987. *New Zealand Journal of Educational Studies* 22: 155–73.

Cole, Edwin. 1977. "Afterward: Reflections After 40 Years of Treating Children with Specific Reading Disability." In *Developmental Dyslexia*. Ed. Drake D. Duane and Paula Dozier Rome, 53–56. New York: Insight Publications.

Cole, Peter G. 1993. "A Critical Analysis of Siegel's Case for Revision of the Learning Disability Construct." *International Journal of Disability, Development and Education* 40.1: 5–21.

Coles, Gerald. 1987. *The Learning Mystique: A Critical Look at "Learning Disabilities."* New York: Fawcett Columbine.

———. 1991. Letter to the Editor. *Journal of the American Medical Association* 265: 725–26.

Collins, Terence. 1989. "University of Minnesota Research Confirming the Impact of Computers on the Writing of Learning Disabled Students." *Composition Chronicle* 2: 4.

Coombs, Norman, and G. Phillip Cartwright. 1994. "Project EASI: Equal Access to Software and Information." *Change: The Magazine of Higher Learning* 26.2: 43–44.

Cordoni, Barbara K. 1982. "A Directory of College LD Services." *Journal of Learning Disabilities* 15: 529–34.

Cowley, Geoffrey. 1992. "The Misreading of Dyslexia." *Newsweek* (Feb 3): 57.

Critchley, MacDonald. 1973. "Some Problems of the Ex-Dyslexic." *Bulletin of the Orton Society* 23: 7–14.

Czamanske, Jacqueline Lynch. Interview with author. Rochester Institute of Technology, Rochester, New York, April 11, 1994.

Damasio, Antonio R., and Hanna Damasio. 1992. "Brain and Language." *Scientific American* (Sept.): 89–95.

De Hirsch, Katrina. 1984. *Language and the Developing Child*. Baltimore: Orton Dyslexia Society.

Denckla, Martha Bridge. 1978. "Critical Review of Electrocephalographic and Neurophysiologogical Studies in Dyslexia." In *Dyslexia: An Appraisal of Current Knowledge*. Ed. Arthur L. Benton, and David Pearl, 241–49. New York: Oxford UP.

Dexter, Beverly L. 1982. "Helping Learning Disabled College Students Prepare for College." *Journal of Learning Disabilities* 15: 344–46.

Diederich, Paul. 1974. *Measuring Growth in English.* Urbana, IL: NCTE.

Dillon, Sam. April 7, 1994. "Special Education Absorbs School Resources: A Class Apart, Special Education in New York City." *New York Times.*

Dowdy, Carol A. 1992. "Identification of Characteristics of Specific Learning Disabilities as a Critical Component in the Vocational Rehabilitation Process." *Journal of Rehabilitation* (July/Aug./Sept.): 51–54.

Duane, Drake D., and Paula Dozier Rome. 1977. *Developmental Dyslexia.* New York: Insight Publications.

Durst, Russel K., and James D. Marshall. 1988. "Annotated Bibliography of Research in the Teaching of English." *Research in the Teaching of English* 22: 434–52.

Einerson, Allen, and Adelaide Bingham. 1991. "Again the Issue is Literacy: How Students with Learning Disabilities Perceive Writing." Presentation at Conference on College Composition and Communication, Boston, MA.

Eisenberg, Leon. 1978. "Definitions of Dyslexia: Their Consequences for Research and Policy." In *Dyslexia: An Appraisal of Current Knowledge.* Ed. Arthur L. Benton and David Pearl, 30–42. New York: Oxford UP.

Elbow, Peter. 1973. *Writing Without Teachers.* New York: Oxford UP.

Emig, Janet. 1971. *The Composing Processes of Twelfth Graders.* Urbana, IL: NCTE.

————. 1978. "Hand, Eye, Brain: Some 'Basics' in the Writing Process." In *Research on Composing: Points of Departure.* Ed. Charles R. Cooper and Lee Odell, 59–71. Urbana, IL: NCTE. (Rpt. in *The Web of Meaning: Essays on Writing, Teaching, Learning and Thinking.* 1983. Ed. Dixie Goswami and Maureen Butler. Portsmouth, NH: Boynton/Cook, 110–21.)

Fairleigh Dickinson University. 1991. *Passport: For the Journey of a Lifetime.* Rutherford, NH: Fairleigh Dickinson University.

Farnham-Diggory, Sylvia. 1978. *Learning Disabilities: A Psychological Perspective.* Cambridge, MA: Harvard UP.

Fennelly, Pat. Interview with author. State University of New York at Albany, Albany, New York, Jan. 5, 1990.

Franklin, Barry M., ed. 1987a. *Learning Disability: Dissenting Essays.* London: Falmer Press.

————. 1987b. "From Brain Injury to Learning Disability." Ed. Barry M. Franklin, 29–46. In *Learning Disability: Dissenting Essays.* London: Falmer Press.

Freire, Paulo. [1970] 1988. *Pedagogy of the Oppressed.* New York: Continuum.

Freire, Paulo, and Donald Macedo. 1987. *Literacy: Reading the Word & the World.* South Hadley, MA: Bergin & Garvey.

Galaburda, Albert M. 1983. "Developmental Dyslexia: Current Anatomical Research." *Annals of Dyslexia* 33: 41–53.

———. 1989. "Learning Disability: Biological, Societal, or Both? A Response to Gerald Coles."*Journal of Learning Disabilities* 22.5: 278–82.

Gajar, Anna H. 1989. "A Computer Analysis of Written Language Variables and a Comparison of Compositions Written by University Students with and without Learning Disabilities. *Journal of Learning Disabilities* 22: 125–30.

Gander, MacLean. Interview with author. Landmark College, Putney, Vermont, July 10, 1991.

Gardner, Howard. [1983] 1985. *Frames of Mind: The Theory of Multiple Intelligences.* New York: Basic Books.

Gills, Paula. 1991. "Serving the Needs of Linguistically Handicapped Students in the Writing Center: A Challenge for the '90's." Presentation at Conference on College Composition and Communication, Boston, MA.

Graham, Steve. 1990. "The Role of Production Factors in Learning Disabled Students' Compositions." *Journal of Educational Psychology* 82.4: 781–91.

Graham, Steve, and Karen R. Harris. 1987. "Improving Composition Skills of Inefficient Learners with Self-Instructional Strategy Training." *Topics in Language Disorders* 7.4: 66–77.

———. 1989. "Components Analysis of Cognitive Strategy Instruction: Effects on Learning Disabled Students' Compositions and Self-Efficacy." *Journal of Educational Psychology* 81: 353–61.

Graham, Steve, Karen R. Harris, Charles A. MacArthur, and Shirley Schwartz. 1991. "Writing and Writing Instruction for Students With Learning Disabilities: Review of a Research Program." *Learning Disabilities Quarterly* 14: 89–114.

Graves, Richard L., and Harry M. Solomon. 1980. "New Graduate Courses in Rhetoric and Composition: A National Survey." *Freshman English News* (Spring): 1–13.

Gregg, Noel. 1983. "College Learning Disabled Writers: Error Patterns and Instructional Alternatives." *Journal of Learning Disabilities* 16: 334–38.

Greenhouse, Linda. Nov. 19, 1993. "Court Rules For Parents In Training of Disabled." *New York Times.*

Guyer, Barbara Priddy, and David Sabatino. 1989. "The Effectiveness of a Multisensory Alphabetic Phonetic Approach with College Students Who Are Learning Disabled." *Journal of Learning Disabilities* 22: 430–34.

Haight, Sherrel Lee. 1980. "Learning Disabilities: The Battered Discipline." *Journal of Learning Disabilities* 13: 47–50.

Hallahan, Daniel P., James M. Kauffman, and John W. Lloyd. 1985. *Introduction to Learning Disabilities*. Englewood Cliffs, NJ: Prentice-Hall.

Hasselback, Richard. 1993. "Making Higher Educational Institutions Supportive of College Students with Disabilities: The Legal Perspective." Panel presentation at conference, Higher Education for Persons with Disabilities: Challenges and Opportunities, sponsored by University of the State of New York and New York State Education Department, Nov. 30, Albany, NY.

Helgeson, Marc E., and T. Hisama. 1982. "Teaching Basic Reading Skills to Incarcerated Non-Readers: The Brickwall Analogy and a Multi-Modality Approach." *Journal of Correctional Education* 33.4: 25–28.

Houck, Cherry K., Susan B. Asselin, Gretchen C. Troutman, and Jane M. Arrington. 1992. "Students with Learning Disabilities in the University Environment: A Study of Faculty and Student Perceptions." *Journal of Learning Disabilities* 25.10: 678–84.

Houston, Linda S. 1994. "Learning Differences: Accommodations in English Classrooms." Presentation at Conference on College Composition and Communication, Nashville, TN.

Hughes, John R. 1978. "Electroencephalographic and Neurophysiological Studies in Dyslexia." In *Dyslexia: An Appraisal of Current Knowledge*. Ed. Arthur L. Benton and David Pearl, 205–40. New York: Oxford UP.

Hunter, Paul. 1990. "Learning Disabilities: New Doubts, New Inquiries." *College English* 52: 92–97.

Huston, Anne Marshall. 1992. "New Study on Dyslexia: Questionable Conclusions." *Chronicle of Higher Education* (March): B7

Ives, Nancy R. 1993. "Learning Disabled Students in the Composition Classroom." Paper delivered at CCCC, San Diego, CA.

Jaschik, Scott. 1994. "Colleges and the Disabled." *Chronicle of Higher Education* (April 20): A38–9.

Johnston, Christopher L. 1984. "The Learning Disabled Adolescent and Young Adult: An Overview and Critique of Current Practices." *Journal of Learning Disabilities* 17: 386–91.

Johnston, Peter H. 1985. "Understanding Reading Disability: A Case Study Approach." *Harvard Educational Review* 55: 153–77.

Johnston, Peter, and Richard Allington. 1991. "Remediation." In *Handbook of Reading Research*. Vol. 2. Ed. Rebecca Barr, Michael L. Kamil, Peter Mosenthal, and P. David Pearson, 984–1012. New York: Longmans.

Kahn, Michael S. 1980. "Learning Problems of the Secondary and Junior College Learning Disabled Student: Suggested Remedies." *Journal of Learning Disabilities* 13: 40–45.

Kaufman, Helen S., and Phyllis L. Biren. 1976–77. "Persistent Reversers: Poor Readers, Writers, Spellers"? *Academic Thereapy* 12: 209–17.

Kavale, Kenneth A. 1988. "Status of the Field: Trends and Issues in Learning Disabilities." In *Learning Disabilities: State of the Art and Practice.* Ed. Kenneth A. Kavale, 1–21, Boston: College Hill Press.

Kavale, Kenneth, and Steven Forness. 1985. *The Science of Learning Disabilities.* San Diego: College Hill Press.

Kavale, Kenneth A., and James H. Reese. 1992. "The Character of Learning Disabilities: An Iowa Profile." *Learning Disability Quarterly* 15 (Spring): 74–94.

Kehl, Shelley. 1993. "Making Higher Educational Institutions Supportive of College Students with Disabilities: The Legal Perspective." Panel presentation at conference, Higher Education for Persons with Disabilities: Challenges and Opportunities, sponsored by University of the State of New York and New York State Education Department, Nov. 30, Albany, NY.

Knoblauch, C. H., and Lil Brannon. 1984. *Rhetorical Traditions and the Teaching of Writing.* Portsmouth, NH: Boynton/Cook.

Laurence, Patricia. 1975. "Error's Endless Train: Why Students Don't Perceive Errors." *Journal of Basic Writing* 1: 23–42.

Lavers, Norman. 1981. "Strephosymbolia: A Possible Strategy for Dealing With It." *College English* 43: 711–15.

Lazarus, Belinda D. 1989. "Serving LD Students in Postsecondary Settings." *Journal of Developmental Education* 12: 2–6.

LeClerc, Paul. 1993. "The View of College Presidents: Supporting Post-Secondary Educational Opportunities for College Students with Learning Disabilities." Panel presentation at conference, Higher Education for Persons with Disabilities: Challenges and Opportunities, sponsored by University of the State of New York and New York State Education Department, Nov. 30, Albany, NY.

Lee, Christopher, and Rosemary Jackson. 1992. *Faking It: A Look into the Mind of a Creative Learner.* Portsmouth, NH: Boynton/Cook–Heinemann.

Lehmkuhle, Stephen. April 13, 1993. "Reading Problems Tied to a Defect of Timing in Visual Pathways." *New York Times.*

Liberman, Isabelle Y. 1983. "A Language-Oriented View of Reading and Its Disabilities." In *Progress in Learning Disabilities.* Vol. 5. Ed. Helmer R. Myklebust, 81–100. New York: Grune and Stratton.

Liberman, Isabelle Y., Donald Shankweiler, F. William Fischer, and Bonnie Carter. 1974. "Explicit Syllable and Phoneme Segmentation in the Young Child." *Journal of Experimental Child Psychology* 18: 201–12.

Lindblom, Kenneth. Interview with author. East Greenbush, NY, March 22, 1990.

Longo, Judith. 1988. "The Learning Disabled: Challenge to Postsecondary Institutions." *Journal of Developmental Education* 11: 10–14.

LoPresti, Gene Frank. 1978. "Four Basic Skills Students: A Naturalistic

Study of Reading/Writing Models They Bring to College." *DAI* 48: 585A. Indiana University of Pennsylvania.

Loxterman, Alan S. 1978. "College Composition and the Invisible Handicap." ERIC ED 168 016.

Lunsford, Andrea. 1979. "Cognitive Development and the Basic Writer." *College English* 41: 38–46.

———. 1980. "The Content of Basic Writers' Essays." *College Composition and Communication* 31: 278–90.

Lyman, Donald E. 1986. *Making the Words Stand Still*. Boston: Houghton Mifflin.

Macrorie, Ken. 1984. *Searching Writing*. Portsmouth, NH: Boynton/Cook.

Mahala, Daniel. 1991. "Writing Utopias: Writing Across the Curriculum and the Promise of Reform." *College English* 53.7: 773–89.

Mangrum, Charles T. II, and Stephen S. Strichart. 1988. *College and the Learning Disabled Student: Program Development, Implementation, and Selection*. Philadelphia, PA: Green and Stratton.

Mann, Virginia A. 1989. "*The Learning Mystique*: A Fair Appraisal, A Fruitful New Direction?" *Journal of Learning Disabilities* 22.5: 283–86.

Marshall, James D., and Russel K. Durst. May 1988. "Annotated Bibliography of Research in the Teaching of English." *Research in the Teaching of English* 22: 213–27.

Martin, Nancy. 1976. "Language Across the Curriculum: A Paradox and Its Potential for Change." *Educational Review* (June): 206–19.

Mastropieri, Margo A., Thomas E. Scruggs, and Joel R. Levin. 1985. "Mnemonic Strategy Instruction with Learning Disabled Adolescents." *Journal of Learning Disabilities* 18.2 (Feb.): 94–99.

McAlexander, Patricia J. 1991. "A Comment on 'Learning Disabilities: New Doubts, New Inquiries.'" *College English* 53: 224–26.

McAlexander, Patricia J., Ann B. Dobie, and Noel Gregg. 1992. *Beyond the "SP" Label: Improving the Spelling of Learning Disabled and Basic Writers*. Urbana, IL: NCTE.

McAlexander, Patricia J., and Noel Gregg. 1989. "The Roles of English Teachers and LD Specialists in Identifying Learning Disabled Writers: Two Case Studies." *Journal of Basic Writing* 8.2: 72–86.

McAllister, Carole, and Richard Louth. 1987. "The Effect of Word Processing on the Revision of Basic Writers." ERIC ED 281 232.

McCarthy, Rosaleen, and Elizabeth K. Warrington. 1990."The Dissolution of Semantics." *Nature* 343 (Feb. 15): 599.

McKeown, Sally. 1992. "Literacy and a Superfluous Stoat." *Times Educational Supplement* 3963 (June 12): S11.

Meyer, Thomas J. 1986. "At America's Costliest College, Learning to Read Is a Major Accomplishment." *The Chronicle of Higher Education* 31.18 (Jan. 15): 1, 30–31.

Morris-Friehe, Mary, and Janice Leuenberger. 1992. "Direct and Indirect Measures of Writing for Non-learning Disabled and Learning Disabled College Students." *Reading and Writing: An Interdisciplinary Journal* 4: 281–96.

Mullin, Anne E. 1994. "Of All Places: Students with Learning Disabilities in the Writing Center." Presentation at CCCC, Nashville, TN.

Mullin, Anne. 1995. "Toys ARE Us: Manipulatives in the Writing Center." Presentation at CCCC, Washington, D. C. National Institute of Mental Health. 1993. *Learning Disabilities.* NIH Publication No. 93–3611.

Nelis, Karen. June 15, 1993. "Mainstreaming Goes Slow, Advocate Argues." [Albany] *Times Union* (Albany, NY).

North, Stephen M. 1987. *The Making of Knowledge in Composition: Portrait of an Emerging Field.* Portsmouth, NH: Boynton/Cook.

Nydahl, Joel. 1990. "Teaching Word Processors to be CAI Programs." *College English* 52: 904–15.

Odell, Lee. 1974. "Measuring the Effect of Instruction in Prewriting." *Research in the Teaching of English* 8: 228–40.

———. 1975. "You Mean Write It Over In Ink?" *English Journal* 64: 438–53.

———. 1977. "Measuring Changes in Intellectual Processes as One Dimension of Growth in Writing." In *Evaluating Writing: Describing, Measuring, Judging.* Eds. Charles Cooper and Lee Odell. 107–32. NCTE.

O'Hearn, Carolyn. 1989. "Recognizing the Learning Disabled College Writer." *College English* 51: 294–304.

Oliver, Carolyn. 1991. Interview with author. Landmark College, Putney, Vermont, July 10, 1991.

Orton, June. 1966. "The Orton-Gillingham Approach." In *The Disabled Reader: Education of the Dyslexic Child.* Ed. John Money, 199–139. Baltimore: Johns Hopkins Press.

Ostertag, Bruce A., Ronald E. Baker, Robert F. Howard, and Laurel Best. 1982. "Learning Disabled Programs in California Community Colleges." *Journal of Learning Disabilities* 15.9: 535–38.

Parker, Frank. 1985. "Dyslexia: An Overview." *Journal of Basic Writing* 4: 58–67.

Parker, Robert B., and Vera Goodkin. 1987. *The Consequences of Writing: Enhancing Learning in the Disciplines.* Portsmouth, NH: Boynton/Cook.

Pattarini, Steve. Interview with author. Utica College of Syracuse University, Utica, New York, May 26, 1994.

Patten, Bernard M. 1978. "Memory and Mental Images in Verbal Deficit Modification." *Bulletin of the Orton Society* 28: 217–24.

Patterson, Kathleen A. 1994. "Teaching Disability Studies in the Freshman Composition Classroom." Presentation at Conference on Composition and Communication, Nashville, TN.

Pennington, Bruce F., Jeffrey W. Gilger, David Pauls, Sandra A. Smith, Shelley D. Smith, and John C. DeFries. 1991. "Evidence for Major Gene Transmission of Developmental Dyslexia." *Journal of the American Medical Association* 226.11: 1527–34.

Peterson, Binnie L. 1981. "One Approach to Teaching the Specific Language Disabled Adult Language Arts." *Adult Literacy and Basic Education* 5.4: 251–55.

Polanyi, Michael. 1958. *Personal Knowledge: Towards a Post-Critical Philosophy.* Chicago: Chicago UP.

Pompian, Nancy W., and Carl P. Thum. 1988. "Dyslexic/Learning Disabled Students at Dartmouth College." *Annals of Dyslexia* 38: 276–84.

Posey, Evelyn Joyce. 1986. "The Writer's Tool: A Study of Microcomputer Word Processing to Improve the Writing of Basic Writers." *DAI* 48: 39A. New Mexico State University.

Pressley, Michael, and Janice Dennis-Rounds. 1980. "Transfer of a Mnemonic Keyword Strategy at Two Age Levels." *Journal of Educational Psychology* 72.4: 575–82.

Pressley, Michael, Joel R. Levin, and Harold D. Delaney. 1982. "The Mnemonic Keyword Method." *Review of Educational Research* 52 (Spring): 61–91.

Radetsky, Peter. 1994. "Silence, Signs, and Wonder." *Discover* 15.8 (Aug.): 60–68.

Rawson, Margaret Byrd. 1988. *The Many Faces of Dyslexia.* Baltimore: Orton Dyslexia Society.

Raymond, Katherine. 1993. "Making Higher Educational Institutions Supportive of College Students with Disabilities: The Legal Perspective." Panel presentation at conference, Higher Education for Persons with Disabilities: Challenges and Opportunities, sponsored by University of the State of New York and New York State Education Department, Nov. 30, Albany, NY.

Rennie, John. 1991. "Dyslexia: A Problem of Timing." *Scientific American* (Nov.): 26.

———. 1992. "Defining Dyslexia." *Scientific American* (July): 31–32.

Richards, Amy. 1985. "College Composition: Recognizing the Learning Disabled Writer." *Journal of Basic Writing* 4: 65–79.

Richardson, Donna. 1990. "Descriptive Sketches: Drawing to Learn in Subjects Generally and in Wordsworth's Poetry in Particular." *College Teaching* 38: 141–45.

Richardson, Lynda. April 6, 1994. "Minority Students Languish in Special Education System: A Class Apart Special Education in New York City." *New York Times.*

Rojewski, Jay W. 1992. "Key Components of Model Transition Services for Students with Learning Disabilities." *Learning Disability Quarterly* 15 (Spring): 135–50.

Rome, Paula Dozier, and Jean Smith Osman. 1977. "Remediation: Procedures for Helping the Dyslexia." In *Developmental Dyslexia*. Ed. Drake D. Duane and Paula Dozier Rome, 30–44. New York: Insight Publications.

Ronald, Kate, and Hephzibah Roskelly, eds. 1990. *Farther Along: Transforming Dichotomies in Rhetoric and Composition*. Portsmouth, NH: Boynton/Cook–Heinemann.

Rose, Alan M. 1986. "Specific Learning Disabilities, Federal Law, and Departments of English." *ADE Bulletin* 84: 26–29.

Rose, Mike. 1983. "Remedial Writing Courses: A Critique and A Proposal." *College English* 45: 109–28.

———. 1988. "Narrowing the Mind and Page: Remedial Writers and Cognitive Reductionism." *College Composition and Communication* 39: 267–302.

Rothstein, Laura F. 1986. "Section 504 of the Rehabilitation Act: Emerging Issues for Colleges and Universities." *Journal of College and University Law* 13.3: 229–265.

Royal, Nancy Le Sanders. 1987. "The Long-Term consequences of Specific Language Disabilities: The Secondary School Years (Dyslexia)." *DAI* 48: 02A. Univ. of San Diego.

Rubin, Hyla, and Isabelle Y. Liberman. 1983. "Exploring the Oral and Written Language Errors Made by Language Disabled Children." *Annals of Dyslexia* : 111–20.

Rumsey, Judith M. 1992. "The Biology of Developmental Dyslexia." *Journal of the American Medical Association* 266.7 (Aug. 19): 912–15.

Russell, David R. 1991. *Writing in the Academic Disciplines, 1870–1990: A Curricular History*. Carbondale and Edwardsville: Southern Illinois UP.

Rutter, Michael. 1978. "Prevalence and Types of Dyslexia." In *Dyslexia: An Appraisal of Current Knowledge*. Ed. Arthur L. Benton and David Pearl, 9–28. New York: Oxford UP.

Satcher, Jamie F., and Kathy Dooley-Dickey. 1991. "Helping College Bound Clients with Learning Disabilities." *Journal of Rehabilitation* (July/Aug./Sept.): 47–50.

Sawyer, R. J., Steve Graham, and Karen R. Harris. 1992. "Direct Teaching, Strategy Instruction, and Strategy Instruction With Explicit Self-Regulation: Effects on the Composition Skills and Self-Efficacy of Students With Learning Disabilities." *Journal of Educational Psychology* 84: 340–52.

Scruggs, Thomas E., and Lori Richter. 1988. "Tutoring LD Students: A Critical Review." *Learning Disability Quarterly* 11: 274–86.

Scruggs, Thomas E., Margo A. Mastropieri, Frederick J. Brigham, and G. Sharon Sullivan. 1992. "Effects of Mnemonic Reconstructions on the Spatial Learning of Adolescents with Learning Disabilities." *Learning Disabilities Quarterly* 15: 154–62.

Senate Report (Labor and Public Welfare Committee) No. 94-168. 1975. "Education for All Handicapped Children Act of 1975." Public Law 94-142. *U.S. Code Congressional and Administrative News* 1: 44th Congress, First Session.

Shaughnessy, Mina P. 1977. *Errors and Expectations: A Guide for the Teacher of Basic Writing.* New York: Oxford UP.

Shaywitz, Sally E., Jack M. Fletcher, and Michael D. Escobar. 1991. *Journal of the American Medical Association* 265 (Feb. 13): 726.

Shaywitz, Sally E., Bennett A. Shaywitz, Jack M. Fletcher, and Michael D. Escobar. 1990. "Prevalence of Reading Disability in Boys and Girls: Results of the Connecticut Longitudinal Study." *Journal of the American Medical Association* 264.8(August 22/29): 996–1003.

Sheppard, R.Z. 1994. "When Southern Gothic Is Real Life." *Time* (June 27): 77.

Shor, Ira. 1980. *Critical Teaching and Everyday Life.* Boston: South End Press.

Siegel, Linda S. 1992. "An Evaluation of the Discrepancy Definition of Dyslexia." *Journal of Learning Disabilities* 25.10 (Dec.): 618–29.

Slingerland, Beth H. 1982. *Specific Language–Not Learning–Disability Children.* Cambridge, MA: Educators Publishing Service.

Smith, Catherine F. "Reconceiving Hypertext." 1991. In *Evolving Perspectives on Computers and Composition Studies: Questions for the 1990s.* Ed. Gail E. Hawisher and Cynthia L. Selfe, 224–52. Urbana, IL: NCTE.

Speziale, Michael J., and Lynne M. La France. 1992. "Multimedia and Students with Learning Disabilities: The Road to Success." *The Computing Teacher* 20 (Nov.): 31–34.

Stanovich, Keith E. 1989a. "Has the Learning Disabilities Field Lost Its Intelligence?" *Journal of Learning Disabilities* 22.8 (Oct.): 487–492.

———. "Learning Disabilities in Broader Context." 1989b. *Journal of Learning Disabilities* 22.5(May): 287–97.

Tannenbaum, Gloria. 1989. Lecture given at the New York Branch of the Orton Dyslexia Society, Inc., Capital District Regional Group, Nov. 14, in Colonie, NY.

Townsend, Sally. Interview with author. Sauquoit, New York, June 7, 1994

U. S. Equal Employment Opportunity Commission/ U. S. Department of Justice Civil Rights Division. September, 1992. *The Americans with Disabilities Act: Questions and Answers.* EEOC.BK–15.

University of the State of New York, The State Education Department. 1991. *Access, Equity, Opportunity: Affirmative Action Plan.* 6th ed. Albany, NY.

Vail, Priscilla. 1987. *Smart Kids With School Problems: Things to Know and Ways to Help.* New York: E. P. Dutton.

Vaughn, Sue Fisher. 1994. "The Impact of the Americans with Disabilities

Act of 1990 (ADA) on the Writing Class." Presentation at Conference on College Composition and Communication, Nashville, TN.

Vellutino, Frank R. 1987. "Dyslexia." *Scientific American* (March): 34–41.

———. 1979. *Dyslexia: Theory and Practice.* Cambridge, MA: MIT.

———. Interview with author. State University of New York at Albany, Albany, New York, Jan. 3, 1990.

Vellutino, Frank R., and Donna M. Scanlon. 1987. "Phonological Coding, Phonological Awareness, and Reading Ability: Evidence from a Longitudinal and Experimental Study." *Merill-Palmer Quarterly* 33: 321–62.

———. 1991. "The Preeminence of Phonologically Based Skills in Learning to Read." In *Phonological Processes in Literacy: A Tribute to Isabelle Y. Liberman.* Ed. Susan Brady and Donald Shankweiler, 237–52. Hillsdale, NJ: L. Erlbaum Associates.

Vogel, Susan A., and Pamela B. Adelman. 1992. "The Success of College Students with Learning Disabilities: Factors Related to Educational Attainment." *Journal of Learning Disabilities* 25.7 (Sept.): 430–41.

Vogel, Susan A., and Mary Ross Moran. 1982. "Written Language Disorders in Learning Disabled College Students: A Preliminary Report." In *Coming of Age: Volume 3: The Best of ACLD.* Ed. William M. Cruickshank and Janet W. Lerner, 211–25. Syracuse, NY: SUP.

Vogel, Susan A. 1982. "On Developing LD College Programs." *Journal of Learning Disabilities* 15: 518–28.

———. 1985. "Learning Disabled College Students: Identification, Assessment and Outcome." In *Understanding Learning Disabilities: Interdisciplinary and Multidisciplinary Views.* Ed. Drake D. Duane and Che Kan Leong. New York: Plenum Press.

Vygotsky, Lev Semenovich. 1978. *Mind in Society: The Development of Higher Order Psychological Processes.* Cambridge, MA and London: Harvard UP.

———. 1986. *Thought and Language.* Cambridge, MA: MIT.

Walker, Jeffrey. 1990. "Of Brains and Rhetorics." *College English* 52: 301–22.

Whinnery, Keith W. 1992. "College Preparation for Students with Learning Disabilities: A Curriculum Approach." *Preventing School Failure* 37.1 (Fall): 31–4.

White, Edward M. 1989. *Developing Successful College Writing Programs.* San Francisco: Jossey-Bass.

Wiig, Elisabeth H., and Noemi Fleischmann. 1980. "Prepositional Phrases, Pronominalization, Reflexivization, and Relativization in the Language of Learning Disabled College Students." *Journal of Learning Disabilities* 13: 45–50.

Wilczenski, Felicia L., and Patricia Gillespie-Silver. 1992. "Challenging the Norm: Academic Performance of University Students with Learning Disabilities." *Journal of College Student Development* 33 (May): 197–202.

Winerip, Michael. A. April 8, 1994. "A Disabilities Program That 'Got Out of Hand': A Class Apart Special Education in New York City." *New York Times*.

Wong, Bernice Y. L. 1987. "How Do the Results of Metacognitive Research Impact on the LD Individual?" *Learning Disability Quarterly* 10: 189–95.

Zebroski, James Thomas. 1990. "Rewriting Composition as a Postmodern Discipline: Transforming the Research/Teaching Dichotomy." In *Farther Along: Transforming Dichotomies in Rhetoric and Composition*. Ed. Kate Ronald and Hephzibah Roskelly, 168–82. Portsmouth, NH: Boynton/Cook–Heinemann.